Palgrave Studies in Economic History

Series Editor
Kent Deng
London School of Economics
London, UK

Palgrave Studies in Economic History is designed to illuminate and enrich our understanding of economies and economic phenomena of the past. The series covers a vast range of topics including financial history, labour history, development economics, commercialisation, urbanisation, industrialisation, modernisation, globalisation, and changes in world economic orders.

More information about this series at
http://www.palgrave.com/gp/series/14632

Luciano Maffi

Private Bankers in the Italian 19th Century

The Parodi of Genoa in the National and International Context

palgrave
macmillan

Luciano Maffi
Bocconi University
Milan, Milano, Italy

ISSN 2662-6497 ISSN 2662-6500 (electronic)
Palgrave Studies in Economic History
ISBN 978-3-030-63360-8 ISBN 978-3-030-63361-5 (eBook)
https://doi.org/10.1007/978-3-030-63361-5

Cover illustration: Yogi Black/Alamy Stock Photo

This Palgrave Macmillan imprint is published by the registered company Springer Nature Switzerland AG
The registered company address is: Gewerbestrasse 11, 6330 Cham, Switzerland

Acknowledgments

This book is the outcome of a research project conducted mainly in the three years I spent between 2017 and 2020 as a research fellow at the Department of Economics of the University of Genoa pursuing the topic of "Banking and finance in Genoa in the 19th and 20th centuries". Starting from the premise that the Genoese financial elite played a prominent role in the economic development of Italy, and observing that the existing literature on economic history, while sketching out an accurate reference framework of this period, has been limited by the type of information available and thus yet to shed light on certain critical links, I recognized the need—together with the other members of the team—to develop the analysis of these issues in innovative terms, in particular, examining in greater depth the relational strategies of family groups and how they fed into the national and international economic dynamics of the period. We were also stimulated by the fact that certain archives had recently been reorganized—particularly that of the Banca Parodi at the Archivio Doria Economic History Study and Documentation Center of the Department of Economics—, making it possible to embark on an in-depth study with the goal of filling in these gaps.

I am thus indebted to a great number of people. My long list of acknowledgements must begin with Maria Stella Rollandi and Andrea Zanini, who not only provided the initial input for my focus on this topic, but also acted as guides throughout the research process. Without them, the project would probably not have been possible. I cannot thank them enough for their support and encouragement. And I would like to extend this to all the other members of the economic and financial history research team of the University of Genoa Department of Economics, first and foremost Marco Doria, with whom I had the opportunity to discuss both specific aspects of nineteenth-century Genoese finance and economics and aspects of the long-term international historiographic debate on credit and finance systems; Luisa Piccinno, who provided precious advice on nineteenth-century Genoese history, particularly business history; and Marina Romani, who offered numerous stimuli, especially on private bankers in northern Italy in the nineteenth century and their network of Jewish bankers on the national and international level. Marina is the liaison in Genoa for the National Research Project titled "The Long History of Anti-Semitism: Jews in Europe and the Mediterranean (tenth–twenty-first century). Socio-Economic Practices and Cultural Processes of Coexistence through Discrimination and Integration, Persecution and Conversion" (2015NA5XLZ—SH6). I am very grateful to her for having involved me in a number of research initiatives of pertinence to this project. They offered me an excellent opportunity to refine the focus of my research for this book, which is thus also a part of the above National Research Project. Thanks to her support it was possible to organize an important historical conference in Genoa titled "Borghesie nazionali, borghesie cosmopolite: banca privata, finanza, reti (Italia, secoli XVIII–XX)" [National bourgeoisie, cosmopolitan bourgeoisie: private banks, finance, networks (Italy, eighteenth–twentieth century)], which fostered a great deal of constructive debate on the role and development of private banking. I would also like to thank Gaetano Sabatini, Giuseppe De Luca, Daniela Felisini, Germano Maifreda, Massimo Fornasari, Pietro Cafaro, and Giampaolo Conte for their many suggestions and willingness to discuss these topics with me.

I examined the relations among private bankers in papers I presented in 2018 and 2019 at the 32nd and 33rd International Conventions of AISG (Italian Association for the Study of Judaism) in Ravenna. The papers were titled "Banche private in Italia nel XIX secolo. Il network ebraico dei Parodi di Genova" [Private Banks in Italy in the nineteenth century: the Jewish network of the Parodis of Genoa], which I coauthored with Marina, and "L'attività economico-finanziaria e le relazioni degli Avigdor di Nizza nel XIX secolo" [The financial activities and relations of the Avigdors of Nice in the nineteenth century]. The discussions in Ravenna helped me hone my understanding of the enduring factors underpinning the Genoese experience, factors that constituted the bases for developments in the twentieth century. I would like to thank Mauro Perani for his outstanding competence in organizing these symposia and to all the scholars who discussed my papers.

Part of the material used for this book was obtained from the archives of the Rothschild banks in London and Paris. The Rothschild Archive granted me an archive research bursary, which allowed me to travel and sojourn internationally and to access materials in London and the Archives Nationales du Monde du Travail in Roubaix. My heartfelt thanks thus go to the members of the Bursary & Education Committee of the Rothschild Archive Trust and to the director of the Archive, Melanie Aspey and her staff, who supported and aided me in my research.

My debt of gratitude extends to the economic history research group of the Università Cattolica del Sacro Cuore led by Mario Taccolini: Giovanni Gregorini, Riccardo Semeraro, Maria Paola Pasini, and Gianraimondo Farina, from whom I received precious suggestions, scientific support, and unflagging encouragement. And a special nod to Professor Taccolini, who has been an invaluable scientific and human reference point for me for so many years.

I am also indebted to Guido Alfani of Università Bocconi, who coordinates the European project titled "ERC Consolidator Research Grant for the project SMITE-Social Mobility and Inequality across Italy and Europe, 1300–1800" and on whose team I am currently working. My warmest thanks to him and all the members of his team.

This study also benefited greatly from the discussions and comments of certain colleagues over the years. A partial list includes Gian Luca Podestà, Mario Rizzo, Luca Mocarelli, Paolo Tedeschi, Jean-Pierre Williot, Manuel Vaquero Piñeiro, Emanuele Camillo Colombo, Andrea Maria Locatelli, Ivan Paris, Dennis Marco Montagna, and Marianna Astore, who all merit my most sincere gratitude. I would also to thank the Parodi family.

Naturally, none of these persons should be held responsible for any of my opinions, errors, or erroneous interpretations.

Lastly, on a more personal note, I must thank my parents, who have always given me their full support in my work as a historian. And Sara Cavanna, Alberto Anelli, Graziano Bertelegni, Francesco Debiaggi, Gea

Finocchiaro Aprile, Robert Burns, and Matteo Pirola: I thank you for the great benefit of your enduring affection and patience.

Codevilla
August 2020

Luciano Maffi

Contents

Abbreviations

ADG	Archivio Doria di Genova (Dipartimento di Economia di Genova)
ANMT	Archives Nationales du Monde du Travail
ASCD	Archivio Storico della Camera dei Deputati
ASGe	Archivio di Stato di Genova
ASR	Archivio di Stato di Roma
BR	Banque Rothschild
FP	Fondo Parodi
RAL	Rothschild Archive London

List of Figures

List of Tables

CHAPTER 1

The Bankers

1.1 *Bancherii* and Merchant Banking. Types of Credit and Finance in Medieval Italy

The preeminence of Italian credit and financial operators originated in the Middle Ages with inventions and innovations that laid the groundwork for the progressive development of the figure and role of the banker—and, more generally, the bank—on the international level. With the establishment of appropriate standards, instruments, and techniques for meeting both demand for credit and the necessities of credit suppliers, these innovations have gone, in part, to inspire and mold practices that are still in use today.[1]

While money-lending was in its infancy in early-Medieval Europe and remained so into the period of the Crusades, the expansion of trade

[1] Felloni (2008, 93–149). There is a great deal of literature on this subject that is unified in attributing a preeminent role to Italian financial operators. These range from the classic works of Fernand Braudel, Jacques Le Goff, Carlo M. Cipolla, Jacques Heers, Roberto S. Lopez e Raymond De Roover: Braudel (1973), Le Goff (1956), Cipolla (1956, 1976), Heers (1961), Lopez (1956), Lopez et al. (1982), and De Roover (1948, 1953), to the more recent works by Neal (2015), Ferguson (2008), Abulafia (1997, 17–34), Taviani (2018, 427–447), Hunt and Murray (1999), Kindleberger (1984), and Epstein (2000). There are also many Italian historians who have addressed this topic: Fornasari (2017), De Simone (2011), Palermo (2008), Vannini Marx (1985), and Marzo Magno (2013).

L. Maffi, *Private Bankers in the Italian 19th Century*, Palgrave Studies in Economic History, https://doi.org/10.1007/978-3-030-63361-5_1

and contact with the Arab and Byzantine economic cultures triggered a process of evolution. During the late Middle Ages (eleventh–fourteenth century), changes in economic life, dictated by an expanding market supported by innovative technical instruments (such as double-entry bookkeeping), favored the appearance of certain types of credit that placed the Italian peninsula at the forefront of European finances.

These innovations fell into two categories: contracts for pecuniary interest and credit securities. As regards the former, creditor and debtor began using the services of a notary public, who would draw up such a contract in the presence of witnesses in order to prevent any discrepancies of interpretation or other problems intrinsic to two-party agreements. Giuseppe Felloni observes that pecuniary contracts were by far the most pervasive credit vehicle in that period. There were, however, significant variations among them: they differed by nature, amount, and duration, as well as by the interest rate and method of repayment.[2] Generally speaking, three types of contract dominated: *contratti di censo* (credit in exchange for municipal revenue), mortgages, and exchange loans. Other financial arrangements, such as bank deposits, cash advances, and assignment of receivables, existed at the time but were less common.

Other instruments gradually joined pecuniary contracts for certain economic and financial operations and were refined over the centuries. These credit securities—bills of exchange, bills of lading, insurance policies, and public debt securities—would eventually enter into widespread use. But their development, requiring legislative innovations, was relatively slow before they were widely adopted in the modern age for commercial operations, sea transport, and State finances.

In its discussion of bankers and their practices, this book provides a detailed examination of credit supply in Italy. Creditors within this context may be divided into two categories. On the one hand, we have companies whose business involves profiting from loans, lending their own money or third-party money held on deposit. These are most similar to modern-day banks and bankers. On the other, a creditor could be any party that draws on its own resources to offer credit, with or without interest. This category includes a diverse array of investors ranging from private individuals lending their relatively modest savings to wealthy people reaping significant profits from credit operations.

[2] Felloni (2008, 102).

Generally speaking, there was a broad range of credit practices in Medieval Italy exercised by various different parties, each with their own characteristics. It is not always possible to make a clear distinction between capitalists who invest their own money and bankers dealing exclusively in brokering credit. Religious institutions, confraternities, and charitable institutions (*ospedali*, originally providing lodging for crusaders) also often extended credit, having accumulated large sums through donations, returns, and member dowries. However, we will not find the origins of the modern banker in this type of credit operations: they trace their lineage instead back to the moneychangers and merchant bankers.

Italy was particularly distinguished by a process of development of trade—the maritime republics were engaged in flourishing trade with the Far East—that boosted demand for capital, the accumulation of savings, and new financial practices. Genoa, of course, was a very prominent maritime republic and it is here that we have documented the appearance of new professional figures in the twelfth century known as *campsores* or *cambiatores* or *bancherii*. The latter term derives from the fact that these men worked behind a *bancus*, i.e., a desk or table set up in the local market square.[3]

The *bancherii* represent a professional category that cannot easily be categorized under a single activity. They performed a variety of monetary operations typical of a bustling marketplace like Genoa in the Middle Ages: they were moneychangers, bankers, and merchants dealing in trade by land or sea.

Some of these professionals became specialized, becoming owners of a *bancus de scripta* ("*de scripta*" because they recorded financial transactions in ledgers). Their activities are documented in Genoa, Venice, Siena, and Rome and are akin to those performed by today's banks: they exchanged currency, negotiated bills of exchange, accepted deposits, performed clearing services on behalf of clients, and provided small loans to small-scale merchants, artisans, and the State while also being involved to some extent in trade.

It was in the late Middle Ages, when Italians enjoyed primacy in Europe in trade and finance, that the figure of the merchant banker appeared. The so-called Lombard merchants were from Genoa, Asti, Alba, Piacenza, Milan, Venice, Bologna, Florence, Lucca, and Siena. They

[3] Felloni (2008, 133).

operated mainly with their own capital and frequented international fairs, their sphere of operations extending to France, England, Germany, and Flanders. Some of them specialized in money trading.[4] This sort of activity not only required access to considerable capital, but also a new form of organization, which the merchant banker, originating as a solitary professional, achieved by drawing family members or external persons into his affairs. This allowed him to deal in considerable sums while managing the attendant risks.

A new type of company took form in late-thirteenth-century Tuscany known as the "*compagnia di negozio*", established by notarial deed and endowed with legal status and distinct assets (share capital). A number of such "*compagnie*" were established in Siena, handling trade and loans in both the domestic and international markets. Prominent names include Bonsignori, Gallerani, Ricciardi, Tolomei, Frescobaldi, Bardi, Peruzzi, and Acciaiuoli, who issued loans and performed money transfers for the Holy See, the kings of France and England, and the Flemish counts. Their credit operations were not free of risk. Indeed, in the period between the late-thirteenth and the mid-fourteenth century, quite a few of them failed, particularly those who had lent large sums of money to the English crown, backed by commercial privileges and customs revenues. Unfortunately, the insolvency of the English monarchs and the size of the loans soon drove them into bankruptcy.[5] Nevertheless, the experience illuminated the path for other merchant bankers, who continued the practice of lending to royalty, while wisely diversifying their portfolio.

A number of important "*compagnie*" emerged in the second half of the fourteenth century and grew to dominate the European credit and financial market in the following century. They operated in the major financial marketplaces under the banner of prominent families who had made their names partly through their banking business: the Medici in Florence; Lomellini, Centurione, and Cavallo in Genoa; Borromeo in Milan; and

[4] Bordone (1997, 2007) and Bordone and Spinelli (2005). Regarding the merchants' practices and establishments, see: Favier (1998), Santarelli (1998), Bogaert et al. (1994), Spufford (1988, 2002), and Murray (2005). Regarding the role of Italians in the international fairs: Sayous (1932), Face (1958), Epstein (1994, 2001), Cassandro (1985, 1988, 2001), Bautier (1970), and Gioffrè (1960).

[5] Hunt (1994), Sapori (1926), and Del Punta (2002).

Corner and Soranzo in Venice.[6] Combined banking and trade characterized the business of some of the most important families, such as the Medici in Florence and others in Genoa, who traded principally in silk fabrics and other products, allowing them to consolidate their influence in international markets, which expanded throughout the century.

However, the merchant bankers and *bancherii* could not meet the demands for credit and financing in the last centuries of the Middle Ages in an economy undergoing significant development in trade, political relations, the crafts industry, and the needs of monarchs. The fifteenth century thus witnessed the appearance of the first public banks (discussed in greater detail in Chapter 3) and the *monti di pietà* (institutional pawnbroker), playing distinct yet complementary roles in the field of credit.[7] However, bound by founding charters and legal identities, they occupied a much more restricted credit sphere than the merchant bankers and *bancherii*.

The charting of new commercial horizons, with Genoa playing a leading role both in the Levant and in the Atlantic trade routes, made it possible to consolidate and further strengthen the abilities of the Genoese bankers and money-lenders, who wielded significantly increasing economic power.

Partly in virtue of their mastery of banking techniques, the year 1528 ushered in a very successful season for Genoese capitalists with the institution of the exchange fairs and the *ricorsa*, or exchanges with recourse.[8] The Genoese bankers were the key players in major financial operations with the Spanish Crown at one of its periods of maximum splendor and territorial expansion, acting as their main European financiers. Nevertheless, like their Tuscan counterparts in previous centuries, they were bound via considerable loans and investments to the economic fortunes of their client States and experienced numerous setbacks as a result.

[6] De Roover (1966), Mueller (1979, 1997), Blomquist (2005), Goldthwaite (1968, 1995), Melis (1962), Sapori (1972), Orlandi (2002), and Spufford (2014).

[7] Muzzarelli (2001).

[8] The *ricorsa*, or exchange with recourse, is a lending operation typical of international fairs and widely used by the Genoese. It is based on bills of exchange that are renewed in succession every three months, giving the debtor access to a certain sum of money for a set period of time. The Genoese financiers were thus able to collect considerable sums by borrowing from various savers and offer credit to third parties, particularly the Spanish Crown.

These many innovations elevated Italy to a premier role in credit and finance. Many of them were the products of experience, on the part of both "private bankers" and banking institutions, and would have great relevance throughout the centuries of the Modern era. In Genoa, for example, this background would lay the groundwork for techniques and practices lasting into the nineteenth century.

With its focus on Genoese bankers in the nineteenth century, this book must necessarily make reference to the city's financial leadership dating back to the Middle Ages.[9] Genoa was the first Italian maritime republic to establish trade relations with ports in the British Isles and with China (since the thirteenth century). While the fall of its trade colonies in the eastern Mediterranean and on the Black Sea to the Ottoman onslaught in the fifteenth century interrupted its profitable trade with the Far East, it spurred its merchants to focus their trade and investment in the western Mediterranean, extending to Gibraltar and beyond, setting the scene for future dealings with newly discovered lands. A primary theater of investment was the Iberian peninsula, where Genoese communities had long been established.[10]

These particular conditions allowed Genoese operators to deploy their financial inventiveness in both the public and private sector. Indeed, we may attribute to Genoa the origin of two financial entities that bind together the State, bankers, and investors: public debt and government bonds. The earliest references to public debt are found in Genoese documents dating to the mid-twelfth century. They consist of loans to the state by private citizens with rights to public revenue ("*compere*"[11]) representing variable interest on the borrowed capital. The public debt of the major national monarchies would be based on this financing formula, which has evolved over the centuries into the one currently in use.[12]

[9] Felloni and Laura (2017, 11–12).

[10] Felloni and Laura (2017, 11–12).

[11] The first government loans in Genoa were called "*compere*": the municipality gave its creditors rights to certain municipal tax revenues, the loan thus amounting to the purchase of a revenue stream. The names of the creditors were recorded in a specific registry of "*compere*".

[12] Felloni and Laura (2017, 17–29). Su debito pubblico e titoli si vedano: Fratianni (2006, 497–501), Pezzolo (2005, 2012), Flandreau and Flores (2009), and Chilosi (2017). On the development of financial systems see also: Boyer-Xambeu et al. (1994), Armstrong et al. (2007), and Piola Caselli (2016).

In the first decades of the thirteenth century, we have documentation regarding the subdivision of public debt in Genoa into shares with a nominal value of 100 lire that could be sold to third parties. The introduction of this practice, dictated by the need of a State to obtain loans too large to be provided by a single investor, marked the beginning of a financial technique that paved the way for the advent of government bonds.

Genoa thus represented, as far back as the early Middle Ages, an emblematic case of development in the credit and finance sector induced by factors strictly linked to the availability of economic resources, mainly originating in international-scale trade and finance. This gave impetus to the accelerated development of financial techniques and a regulatory system able to respond to shifting markets in a constantly evolving geopolitical framework.

1.2 Evolution of the Bankers' Activity in the Modern Italian Context

Starting from the evolution of the Italian bankers in the medieval age, as analyzed in Sect. 1.1, I explain how they gained prominence in the modern age in credit and financial activities on a European scale. Long-distance trade requires abundant capital; it must be transferable from one business location to another in order to take full advantage of market opportunities. The direct consequence of such an intense panorama of exchanges is the honing of skills related to credit activities: widespread use of bills of exchange to move capital, the use of customer savings, and contacts and interactions with the political authorities of foreign countries, which often impose taxes on the transactions. The activities of these credit and finance operators are not without risks, including economic cycles, debtor insolvency and political and military situations. While we witness the ruinous fall of many bankers, new players make their way into the market by laying the foundations for great economic fortunes.[13]

In the Genoese scenario of the early sixteenth century, the city is privileged because of its strategic geographic position; because of merchant activities, trade routes, and political alliances, the merchant bankers'

[13] Felloni (2008), Melis (1971, 1972, 1987), Sapori (1982), and García Guerra and De Luca (2010).

success is consolidated further during the course of the modern age, when they specialize in exchange fairs and mortgages stipulated with special contracts called *asientos*.[14] When the exchange fairs come to an end starting in the 1620s, the Genoese were excluded from this leading position in the international financial markets; the precarious conditions of the Spanish tax authorities (which on several occasions interrupt the payment of interest) also contribute to this decline. The direct consequence is that the Genoese divest their capital from the Iberian Peninsula; the new availability of resources gives rise to a diversification of usage, in part taking the form of other States' public securities, or else channeled within the territory of the Republic, favoring residential construction and luxury goods.[15]

In light of new research, a period of economic and financial growth and prosperity can be identified between the end of the seventeenth century and the Napoleonic era. The Genoese specialize in investments intended primarily for public debt securities and loans granted by consortia of Genoese capitalists (not necessarily bankers) in favor of European sovereigns, public bodies, private companies. In this type of loan, known as "interest-bearing mortgages for the use of Genoa",[16] the duration can vary from 8 to 12 years and the real interest accrued is 4–5%; subscribers can sell their shares to third parties.

This second cycle of development ends in the Napoleonic period with the loss of a large part of the capital committed. In the second half of the eighteenth century, investors' favor was especially directed toward the other side of the Alps, in French public securities and in loans to French private individuals. Starting from the last decade of the eighteenth century, there has been a sequence of events and changes in the

[14] Felloni (1997, 109; 2008). Il ruolo dei banchieri genovesi è stato specialmente studiato in relazione a Filippo II: Lapeyre (1953), Neri (1989), Kirk (2005), Kolb (2011), Drelichman and Voth (2014), Homer and Sylla (1996), Morris (1998), Wallerstein (1974), Bernholz and Vaubel (2014), Häberlein (2012), Fusaro (2015), and Parker (2000).

[15] Felloni (1971) and Rollandi and Romani (2018). Per le operazioni creditizie e finanziarie dei banchieri italiani e specialmente dei genovesi nell'età moderna si vedano anche: da Silva (1969), Marsilio (2008, 2012, b, 2017, 2019), Neal (2000), Álvarez Nogal (1997a, b), Sanz Ayán (2005), Rowlands (2015), Stasavage (2011), and Lorenzini et al. (2018).

[16] Felloni (1997, 111–113). Concerning this topic refer: Felloni (1971) and Zanini (2017).

financial-credit dynamics in three specific moments: since 1790, interest on public securities has been paid more and more frequently in nominal assigned value; in 1797 France proceeds to consolidate only one-third of the public debt, reserving the remaining two-thirds for the write-off of paper (bankruptcy of two-thirds); in 1802, at the behest of Napoleon, a third of the capital of Genoese creditors is entered into the Grand Livre de la Dette Publique, removing any possibility of redemption of the remaining two-thirds of mortgages. Giuseppe Felloni observes that the failure of a group of merchant bankers does not lead to the disappearing of the entire category, but begins a new cycle: right at the end of the eighteenth century, we witness the rise of the Rothschild dynasty, the private bankers par excellence of the nineteenth century.[17]

The clear division between the era of Genoese, Genevois, and Dutch bankers and that of new traders especially present on the exchanges of London, Paris, Frankfurt, and Vienna, the Rothschilds' case is exemplary to explain the evolution of the figure of the private banker in the first half of the nineteenth century. Jewish bankers are active in the main European business centers mentioned (to which Naples will be added later) starting at the end of the Napoleonic period. They hold the necessary capital to be investors in the activities that characterize and fuel the cycle of economic growth of the century: placement of state loans on the market; colonial trade; mining industry; investment in railway infrastructure; use of resources in the most innovative financial sectors, including banks and insurance companies in the form of joint stock companies. Participation in these activities represents a multiplier of wealth for this family, which has a network of correspondents and agents spread all over the world. The Rothschilds' fortune peaked in the mid-nineteenth century, after which it suffered a setback due to other fearsome competitors in the international haute banque (Baring, Pereire, Hambro, Blanc Mathieu and C, Hottinguer, Pillet-Will, Gabriel Odier, etc. ...) and, above all, to that deriving from the comparison with anonymous banking companies which are becoming increasingly widespread, and who specialize in new forms of medium and long-term credit to the industrial sector.[18]

[17] Ferguson (1998), Gille (1965), and Bouvier (1968).

[18] Concerning private bankers in the most important european business cities in nineteenth-century refers: Cassis (2006), Cassis and Cottrell (2009), Chapman (1984), Berta (1990), and Conti and Schisani (2011).

With regard to the evolution of the Genoese financial world, however, historiography has not identified a third European cycle, following the Napoleonic experience.

On the contrary, historians have described the first half of the nineteenth century as a period of stagnation, especially in relation to other economies that at that point in time were more dynamic. Fifty years have passed since the publication of Giuseppe Felloni's book on the financial investments of the Genoese between the seventeenth century and the Restoration, in which the historian identifies a series of problems affecting the economy of the Ligurian city at the end of the period he considered, especially from the Restoration until the 1840s.[19]

Referring to the studies of Carlo M. Cipolla, Edoardo Grendi, and Giorgio Doria, Felloni notes that the characteristic financial dynamism of the city leaves room for "a general languor, a heavy atmosphere, a widespread tiredness", producing a period of stagnation.[20]

The most recent historiography, however, has posed new questions and provided new answers precisely regarding this long transition phase of the Genoese economy, as evidenced by the studies of Maria Stella Rollandi and Marco Doria.[21] Taking a cue from these new historiographical perspectives and thanks to the unpublished documentation consulted, I conducted an analysis that has made it possible to shed light on the credit and financial system of Genoa and on its complex national and international relations, right from the pre-unification period.

During this period, some Genoese private bankers continue to maintain a leading role as they retain the skills acquired in previous periods and modify them by adapting them to the new needs of the credit and financial markets. It also emerged that despite the Napoleonic events and the consequent decrease in wealth, there still is a good supply of capital in Genoa, a propensity to save and ability in financial investments. The case of the Parodi bankers in the first half of the nineteenth century fits into this trend: it aligns itself with the international private banks' modus operandi and objectives of the main European business centers. Genoa

[19] Giuseppe Felloni (1971). This argument, connected with the Genovese economy in seventeenth century, is recently studied by Maria Stella Rollandi and Andrea Zanini: Rollandi (1996, 1998, 2019), Rollandi and Marina Romani (2018), and Zanini (2017).

[20] Felloni (1971). The studies to which Felloni refers are: Cipolla (1953), Grendi (1964), and Doria (1969).

[21] Rollandi (2006, 2011, 2012) and Doria (2001, 2007, 2008).

remains an active exchange, responsive to the financial innovations of the time. The presence in the city of the stock exchange also allows us to see how there was a propensity for investment by both bankers and local capitalists.[22]

These skills, combined with their client's confidence as well as their consolidated reputation with other operators in the national and international credit and financial system, allow the Parodis to enjoy competitive advantages over other operators on the Genoa market.

So who was the Genoese banker in the first half of the nineteenth century and how did he distinguish himself from other professionals that dealt with credit?

1.3 The Bankers in Pre-unification Italy

This banker is very different from that of the money changer, both for credit and financial transactions carried out, as for the social role he plays. Gerolamo Boccardo stresses that the main operation carried out by the banker is foreign exchange trading, the willingness to receive deposits and the opening of current accounts.[23] The issue of bearer and on-sight notes is the responsibility of public circulation banks only. Boccardo, who is also Genoese and knows well the Genoese environment, writes his Dictionary in the pre-unification decade; in particular, the picture that he outlines in it is extremely close to the activity of Banca Parodi.

It is a profession that specializes in supporting the country's modernization as well as the need to interact with the international haute banque for public loans and for large financial transactions related to public limited companies (Fig. 1.1).

At the same time, it develops and consolidates the fiduciary relationship with its customers. The banker's reputation is currently at the center of the historiographical debate. It represents one of the fundamental aspects on which financial transactions are developed; according to Boccardo, the

[22] Da Pozzo and Felloni (1964). Regarding economic and financial scenario in Genoa during the first half of nineteenth century see also: Doria (1969) and Rollandi (2006, 2012).

[23] *Banchieri*, in Boccardo (1875, 281–290). Concerning Girolamo Boccardo and in general the development of economic science in Genoa in nineteenth century refer also: Massa (2003). Concerning this argument read also: De Luca and Moioli (2008) and De Simone (1987, 1993).

Fig. 1.1 Italy in the mid-nineteenth century (*Source* Author)

banker's professional success is linked by a double thread to the esteem and consequently to the unlimited trust given to him by his circle of personal contacts.[24] These same contacts as clients, entrust him with their capital in the form of a deposit, allowing him to return it into financial circulation for his personal benefit, and for the benefit of society.

[24] Kobrak (2013).

According to the Genoese economist, the banker is a constantly evolving figure, important for the economic and social development of a nation.

In the first edition of his Dictionary published in 1857, ahead of Schumpeter's model, the banker is described as a heroic entrepreneur; a man who becomes the leader of innovation; he is not simply the process manager, but the real creator of new trends in this field.[25] In the second edition dated 1876, he picked up where he left off with commercial operations as well as banking practice and accounting; however, Boccardo highlights the change in the role of bankers between the 1840s and 1870s.[26]

In fact, in the seventies edition, he underscored how the era of private bankers is in crisis, and the increase of public banks and the general changes in the economic system. Specifically, he observes how the relationship of trust between banker and client has changed. Clients who previously had the opportunity to know in real time their banker's fortune, operating in a context in which information was more accessible, are no longer able to have a relationship of this type; one of the cornerstones supporting the banker's image wavers. Furthermore, with the acceleration of communications (because of railways and telegraphs) and with the recent craving for stock market speculation, everything becomes faster to the point that one wrong financial operation can compromise a large fortune in a short period of time. It is a trend that the economist does not find exclusively in the Genoese context. The spread of this phenomenon is shown clearly with the London situation in Lombard Street: from 40 private banks in 1810 that number dwindled down to 13 despite the size and relevance of business having increased significantly.

The modernization of the production sector encouraged the transformation of the credit and financial field during the nineteenth century. The private bank is not exempt from this evolution. Banks, Boccardo wrote in 1857, "are modern whereas the bankers' profession is ancient". In the centuries-old Italian and Dutch tradition, the private bank retains close links with commerce: merchant banking is the term with which it designates those activities. A variety of functions coexist with a variable degree of intensity in the same House: the colonial merchant pairs with the

[25] *Banchieri*, in Boccardo (1857, 309–318).

[26] *Banchieri*, in Boccardo (1875, 281–290).

banker or the money changer while the international traffic of goods naturally combines with that of coins and metals. The Genoese almanacs of the 1830s fully show these multiple identities in their various nuances. The same company, or the same people, are simultaneously listed in a variety of sections dedicated to administrative institutions or economic activities: bankers, free port shopkeepers, chamber directors, pawnshop administrators, second-class decurions. Each entry refers to a path where the junctions and networks in their segmentations and intersections reveal the alternate pattern of reciprocity or clientelism, interests, business alliances, or rivalries.

1.4 Genoese Private Bankers

Before tackling the case of the Parodi bankers, it is necessary to reference the political and economic context of Genoa, where this family's bank is based. Until 1797, the city was the capital of a small regional state, the Republic of Genoa. Its lasting political independence allowed the growth of a financial system that was refined over time because of the experience, the reputation enjoyed by its economic operators and the development of supranational networks. The exchange joins Amsterdam and Geneva, becoming one of the most respected international finance centers. As already mentioned, the fame of the city is consolidated because of the success enjoyed by the "interest-bearing loan for the use of Genoa", a contract that provides for the borrower on the one hand and on the other "a Genoese capitalist who intervenes in his own name for a share and on behalf of others. "Giuseppe Felloni estimates that between 1686 and 1814 the capital employed by the Genoese in this form amounted to 380 million lire, 80% of which is concentrated between 1755 and 1794.[27] A detailed photograph of the year 1785 allows us to know exactly the resources placed by the Genoese capitalists, which is 342 million lire: 40% in local public debt and the remaining 60% in interest-bearing mortgages with an annual income of 11.55 million lire.[28]

In 1797, with the overthrow of the oligarchic government, a new autonomous republic was born. This republic was linked to France, which annexed it in 1805. Following the Restoration, it did not return to being

[27] Felloni (2016).

[28] Felloni (1971, 477–480).

an independent state, but became part of the Kingdom of Sardinia and subsequently of the Kingdom of Italy. Genoa thus loses its status as a capital city, although it remains an important financial center, albeit in a less prosperous context than in the past due to the losses suffered by the major financial operators during the bankruptcy of the two-thirds to which we referred earlier.[29] Out of a total of 342 million invested in financial assets, the losses amounted to approximately 208 million, almost two-thirds of the committed capital. More generally, the annexation to France and the new administrative organization do not immediately change the economic structure of the territory, which is in a state of crisis. The development opportunities due to entry into the empire are dampened by a variety of factors: by the continental block wanted by Napoleon in 1806, by the French customs administration, by the difficult commercial integration within the empire caused by the bad state of the communication routes and relatively decentralized position.[30] In 1809, the department's prefect described the situation as worrying mainly due to the decrease in the quantity of money available and the speed of its circulation due to trade stagnation and the crisis in manufacturing production.[31] The consequences of the sharp contraction of income from capital invested abroad and the departure of aristocratic families who want to escape high taxation also weigh heavily.[32]

Numerous credit operators have been working in Genoa since the last decades of the eighteenth century: some use only equity capital, others also use funds raised in the form of deposits. The former are mainly the great patrician families; among others there are Houses specialized in giving loans to foreign borrowers, such as the Marchelli brothers and De la Rüe. The main operations they deal with are the trading of goods and precious metals, the purchase and sale of promissory notes, investments in public portfolio securities and the opening of medium-term foreign loans with interest payable in Genoa in six-month installments and in local currency. Starting from this data, Giuseppe Felloni observes how Genoese

[29] Assereto (1975 1994, 2000), Bulferetti and Costantini (1966), and Felloni (1961). Concerning the Italian political context in that period refer: Meriggi (2002).

[30] Piccinno (2013, 43–44).

[31] Doria (1969, 4–24).

[32] Rollandi (2012).

capitalists, like those in Geneva, can be considered "the direct precursors of the high international bank of the early nineteenth century".[33]

These are the forerunners of the new operational model of private bankers, which, however, does not have a clear and tangible explanation in the panorama of the Ligurian exchange. Historiography considers the period of time elapsed between the end of the aristocratic Republic (1797) and national unification (1861) as a "long transition period" where some aspects of the Genoese economy and its credit systems are being redefined due to the ever-changing political and institutional context.[34]

Another important aspect that influences the Genoese credit and financial system is the closure of Banco di San Giorgio in 1805. Due to unemployment, some banking operators become involved in this type of activity such as the Parodis, by taking advantage of their reputation for competence and prudence. An instrument created during those years that helps recognize and define these professional figures is the so-called licensing, regulated by the law 2096 of 22 October 1798 and subsequently supplemented by the laws 264 of 2 October 1800 and 988 of 17 November 1801.[35]

It says that those who exercise a profession related to trade and industry are required to have a "license", i.e., a personal authorization that is therefore useful only to its bearer; consequently every member of a bank or a trading house or other business must have one. From the examination of the tax roles on the licenses relating to the year 1806 and to the year 1811, the following operators were identified: bankers, shopkeepers, and financial brokers. Focusing on the analysis of the first category, in 1806 the following professionals were required to pay for the license: Domenico Celesia, Giuseppe Decamilli, the De La Rüe brothers, Gianluca Durazzo, Giacomo Parodi, and Giovanni Battista Ricci.[36] In 1811 Gerardo Bansa, Domenico Celesia, Giuseppe Decamilli, Jean De Le Rüe, Jean Antoine De Le Rüe, Gianluca Durazzo, Marcello Durazzo, Jonas Hagermann, Giacomo Parodi, Giovanni Quartara, and Giovanni

[33] Felloni (1971, 475).

[34] Rollandi (2006, 41).

[35] *Bulletin des lois* (1801, 576–577).

[36] ASGe, Fondo Prefettura Francese 709, Contribuzione patenti (1806).

Battista Ricci are registered as bankers[37] The patrician citizens who had traditionally engaged in these activities have all but disappeared with the exception of Mr. Durazzo. All the other operators were already active at the end of the eighteenth century, such as the Ricci and the De La Rüe (Table 1.1).

This data shows that in the period from the end of the aristocratic republic to the end of the Napoleonic era, a new class of bourgeois operators is emerging, taking advantage of the opportunities deriving from maritime trade. They begin a process of capital accumulation that allows them to enter the banking sector. Not only did these people never stop operating, directly or through a third party, but they know how to seize the best opportunities: shippers, merchants, grains importers, money handlers, bankers, and army suppliers. Information regarding the socioeconomic junction that existed at the end of the Napoleonic period and information garnered from police inquiries reveal the capital of Genoese merchant and banker families. An Austrian police emissary, whose surname is Frizzi, writes a document titled "The main Individuals of the Ligurian state" (*Quadro caratteristico dei principali individui dello Stato Ligure*). It is not a rigorous document. It is suspect because it is conditioned by judicial and political prejudice; however, it helps us understand how active shopkeepers and bankers with an important turnover and considerable capital are in the city.[38] The report offers a framework and information on many professionals who in the following decades would play an important role in the credit and financial system. Among the bankers mentioned: Lorenzo Boggiano, Giuseppe Decamilli, the De La Rüe brothers, Jonas Hagermann, Giacomo Parodi, Giovanni Quartara, and Giovanni Battista Ricci.[39]

Further information on private bankers operating in the city of Genoa comes from the Napoleonic era *Almanac du commerce*. The names of bankers who are added to the count of the 1805 and 1811 edition of the *Almanac* are registered as dealers or exchange brokers in the lists of licenses contributions (they paid 276 francs instead of 575).[40]

[37] ASGe, Fondo Prefettura Francese 738, Contribuzione patenti (1811).

[38] Rollandi (2012, 17–19).

[39] Vitale (1933, 445–449).

[40] De La Tynna (1805, 1811).

Table 1.1 Private bankers in Genoa during Napoleonic era (1806–1811)

Tax roles for licenses—1806	*Tax roles for licenses—1811*	*Almanach du commerce—1805*	*Almanach du commerce—1811*
Giovanni Battista Ricci	Giovanni Battista Ricci	Giovanni Battista Ricci	Giovanni Battista Ricci
Domenico Celesia	Domenico Celesia	Domenico Celesia	Domenico Celesia
Giacomo Parodi	Giacomo Parodi		Giacomo Parodi
Giuseppe Decamilli	Giuseppe Decamilli		Giuseppe Decamilli
Gianluca Durazzo	Gianluca Durazzo	Gianluca Durazzo	
fratelli De La Rüe	Jean De Le Rüe	fratelli De La Rüe	fratelli De La Rüe
	Jean Antoine De Le Rüe		
	Giovanni Quartara	Giovanni Quartara	Giovanni Quartara
	Gerardo Bansa	Gerardo Bansa	Gerardo Bansa
	Jonas Hagermann		Jonas Hagermann
	Marcello Durazzo		
		Giuseppe Maria Balbi	
		Giacomo Balestrieri	
		Benzi, padre e figlio	
		Giacomo Filippo Durazzo	
		Deluchi e Fossati	
		Health e C.	
		Paul Maystre	Paul Maystre
		Gerolamo e Filippo Morro	Filippo Morro
		Pallavicini, eredi di Nicola	
		Aimé Regny	Regny Cheremond e C.
		Franco Valentino Rossi	
		Domenico Strafforello	Domenico Strafforello
			Baldassarre Castellini

(continued)

Table 1.1 (continued)

Tax roles for licenses—1806	*Tax roles for licenses—1811*	*Almanach du commerce—1805*	*Almanach du commerce—1811*
			Fratelli Charbonnel
			Chiappa Tubino e C.
			L. Degola
			B. Deluchi
			Deluchi e Fossati
			André Doxat
			Fratelli Durazzo
			J. B. Erminio
			Angelo Maria Gnecco
			Nicola Grondona
			P. La Pierre
			Fratelli Oneto
			Giacomo Oneto
			Prat Hortolan e C.
			J. A. Tollot
			Zelvegher e C.

Source ASGe, Fondo Prefettura Francese, 709 and 738; De La Tynna (1805, 1811); Almanach du commerce de Paris, des départements de l'Empire Français et des principales villes de l'Europe, 1805 (Paris, 1805), Almanach du commerce de Paris, des départements de l'Empire Français et des principales villes de l'Europe, 1811 (Paris, 1811)

1.5 New Models of Banking and Finance

It is necessary to trace the coordinates of the international context in relation to the new banking/finance models that developed in the first half of the nineteenth century. Among the elements that characterize the "new model of private banking" are the networks of supranational relationships between the bankers' families, the businesses' longevity, the type of operations carried out, the links between industry and private banks, those between politics and private banks, the amount of resources available.[41] The networks between bankers and the links between politics and private banks are also characteristic of the previous period. In fact, even

[41] Neal (1990), Ugolini (2018), and Bouvier (1957).

though the characteristics of the "new model" are an expression of the intersection of all these elements, the most prominent factors still concern banking and financial operations carried out in support of industry, of the construction of infrastructures, loans to foreign States[42] and international trade.[43]

According to Chapman, however, many typical mechanisms of the "new model" are already present during the eighteenth century; the novelty is rather in the fact that the cohesion and integration between houses belonging to the "haute banque / merchant banking" allow them to significantly expand the range and economic scope of the operations carried out.[44] This is especially true of the massive financial transactions which concern subsidies for the construction of railway infrastructure, as well as loans taken out by the states. In this regard, Jean Bouvier notes that, after 1815 and until the 1840s, the latter represent the high bank's most important operation, contributing to eclipse its commercial function.[45] The French historian also underlines how to a certain extent this type of activity prepares the ground for the further progress of the stock exchange markets also related to industrial development.

In reality, the ways in which the States of the modern age procure the resources to support public spending have already changed since the "financial revolution" that took place in England after 1688, as demonstrated by the now classic study by P. Dickson[46] and the works of DC North and BR Weingast,[47] of P. Termin and H.-J. Voth,[48] of M. Amato and L. Fantacci[49] and of E. Seghezza.[50] In England during the eighteenth century, paths that allowed the reduction of information asymmetries were experimented with. Meanwhile, the coordinates of a more modern and impersonal market were consolidated. The intensification of relations

[42] Cameron (1991, 23–24).

[43] Bouvier (1968, 45–46, 87, 109).

[44] Chapman (1984, 9–15, 34–38).

[45] Bouvier (1968, 109).

[46] Dickson (1967).

[47] North and Weingast (1989).

[48] Temin and Voth (2008).

[49] Amato and Fantacci (2012).

[50] Seghezza (2013, 2015).

between financial operators and the state has positive repercussions also in the area of credit relations between individuals.[51]

Toward the end of the eighteenth century and the beginning of the nineteenth century, the geopolitical upheavals, produced by the French Revolution first and later by the wars of the Napoleonic era, devastated international financial relations, determined inflationary phenomena, and interrupted traditional commercial and financial circuits. The cost of the military campaigns of the Napoleonic era and the compensation payment by France following the Paris Treaty[52] have a very significant influence on the way banking is conducted. In this area, some operators excel, first and foremost the Rothschilds, who know how to organize large international operations aimed at fulfilling the French obligation.[53]

In such a context, the financial intermediary takes action to recover the capital without necessarily committing its resources to the loan. The success of the transaction depends on the intermediary's reputation, which allows it to collect resources from the investing public.[54]

If the operation is successful, in a few years the bankers may be able to retain the sovereigns they serve as clients. In any case, their reputation is strengthened and the foundations are laid for further business expansion. In fact, the "new model" bankers, who in the first decades of the nineteenth century deal mainly with international trade, loans, the sale of public securities[55] and insurance, beginning in the thirties and forties start investing in the industrial sector. This development changes the type and the nature of their business. Industry requires the immobilization of capital in areas that are often innovative but of uncertain economic return even if of great profit potential.

Another area of intervention that has emerged in recent years is the participation in the creation of large joint-stock banking companies, to which private bankers contribute by lending capital and skills; these new

[51] North and Weingast (1989), Pressnell (1956), Cottrell (1980), Mathias (1969), and White (1984).

[52] Cassis (2006) and White (2001).

[53] Cameron (1991, 23–24) and Gille (1965).

[54] Felloni (1971), Dickson (1987, 272–299), and Zanini (2017).

[55] Bouvier (1968, 45–46, 87, 109).

actors in the credit world play an important role in financing capital-intensive productive sectors which have developed since the second half of the nineteenth century.[56]

Bibliography

Archives

Archivio di Stato di Genova (ASGe).
Fondo Prefettura Francese, 709, Contribuzione patenti (1806).
Fondo Prefettura Francese, 738, Contribuzione patenti (1811).

Printed Contemporary and Near Contemporary Sources

Boccardo, Gerolamo. 1857. *Dizionario della Economia Politica e del Commercio.* Torino: S. Franco.

Boccardo, Gerolamo. 1875. *Dizionario universale di economia politica di commercio.* Milano: Treves.

Bulletin des lois de la République Française. 1801. Paris.

De La Tynna, Jean. 1805. *Almanach du commerce de Paris, des départements de l'Empire Français et des principales villes de l'Europe, 1805.* Paris: Au Bureau de l'Almanach du Commerce.

De La Tynna, Jean. 1811. *Almanach du commerce de Paris, des départements de l'Empire Français et des principales villes de l'Europe, 1811.* Paris: Au Bureau de l'Almanach du Commerce.

Secondary Sources

Abulafia, David S. H. 1997. "The Impact of Italian Banking in the Late Middle Ages and the Renaissance, 1300–1500." In *Banking, Trade and Industry: Europe, America and Asia from the Thirteenth to the Twentieth Century*, edited by A. Teichova, G. Kurgan-Van Hentenryk, and D. Ziegler, 17–34. Cambridge: Cambridge University Press.

Álvarez Nogal, Carlos. 1997a. *Los banqueros de Felipe IV y los metales preciosos americanos 1621–1665.* Madrid: Banco de Espania, Servicio de Etudios.

Álvarez Nogal, Carlos. 1997b. *El crédito de la monarquía hispánica durante el reinado de Felipe IV.* Valladolid: Junta de Castilla y León.

Amato, Massimo, and Luca Fantacci. 2012. *The End of Finance.* Cambridge: Polity Press.

[56] Gille (1965) and Bouvier (1968, 45–46, 87, 109; 1970).

Armstrong, Lawrin, Ivana Elbl, and Martin M. Elbl, eds. 2007. *Money, Markets and Trade In Late Medieval Europe: Essays in Honour of John H.A. Munro.* Leiden-Boston: Brill.

Assereto, Giovanni. 1975. *La Repubblica Ligure: lotte politiche e problemi finanziari (1797–1799).* Torino: Fondazione Luigi Einaudi.

Assereto, Giovanni. 1994. "Dall'antico regime all'Unità." In *Storia d'Italia. Le regioni dall'Unità a oggi. La Liguria,* edited by A. Gibelli and P. Rugafiori, 159–215. Torino: Einaudi Editore.

Assereto, Giovanni. 2000. *La seconda repubblica ligure (1800–1805). Dal "18 brumaio genovese" all'annessione alla Francia.* Milano: Selene Edizioni.

Bautier, Robert-Henri. 1970. "The Fairs of Champagne." In *Essays in French Economic History,* edited by R. Cameron, 42–63. Homewood, IL: Richard D. Irwin.

Bernholz, Peter, and Roland Vaubel, eds. 2014. *Explaining Monetary and Financial Innovation: A Historical Analysis.* Cham: Springer.

Berta, Giuseppe. 1990. *Capitali in gioco: cultura economica e vita finanziaria nella City dell'Ottocento.* Venezia: Marsilio.

Blomquist, Thomas W. 2005. *Merchant Families, Banking and Money in Medieval Lucca.* Aldershot: Ashgate.

Bogaert, Raymond, Ginette Kurgan-van Hentenryk, and Herman van der Wee. 1994. *A History of European Banking.* Antwerp-Genève: Mercatorfonds.

Bordone, Renato, ed. 1997. *L'uomo del banco dei pegni. Lombardi e mercato del denaro nell'Europa medievale.* Torino: Scriptorium.

Bordone, Renato, ed. 2007. *Dal banco di pegno all'alta finanza. Lombardi e mercanti-banchieri fra Paesi Bassi e Inghilterra nel Trecento.* Asti: Comune di Asti.

Bordone, Renato, and Franco Spinelli, eds. 2005. *Lombardi in Europa nel Medioevo.* Milano: FrancoAngeli.

Bouvier, Jean. 1957. "Les premiers pas du grand capitalisme, le système de crédit et l'évolution des affaires de 1815 à 1848." *La Pensée* 71–72, no. 2: 3–29.

Bouvier, Jean. 1968. *I Rothschild.* Bari: Laterza.

Bouvier, Jean. 1970. "Rapports entre système bancaires et enterprises industrielles dans la croissance européenne au XIXe siècle." *Studi storici* 11, no. 4: 273–307.

Boyer-Xambeu, Marie-Therese, Delepace Ghislain, and Lucien Gillard. 1994. *Private money & public currencies. The 16th century challenge.* London: Sharpe.

Braudel, Fernand. 1973. *The Mediterranean and the Mediterranean World in the Age of Philip II,* Vol 2. London: Fontana/Collins.

Bulferetti, Luigi, and Claudio Costantini. 1966. *Industria e commercio in Liguria nell'età del Risorgimento.* Milano: Banca Commerciale Italiana.

Cameron, Rondo. 1991. "International Private Banking from the Late Middle Ages to the Mid-nineteenth Century." In *Banchi pubblici, banchi privati e monti di pietà nell'Europa preindustriale. Amministrazione, tecniche operative e ruoli* economici, 17–34. Genova: Società Ligure di Storia Patria.

Cassandro, Michele. 1985. "Strategia degli affari dei mercanti-banchieri italiani alle fiere internazionali d'Oltralpe (secoli XIV–XVI)." In *Aspetti della vita economica medievale*, 140–50. Firenze: Università degli Studi di Firenze.

Cassandro, Michele. 1988. "Credito e banca in Italia tra Medioevo e Rinascimento." In *Credito e sviluppo economico in Italia dal Medioevo all'età contemporanea*, 131–45. Verona: Sise.

Cassandro, Michele. 2001. "Le fiere nell'economia europea medievale e della prima età moderna." *Studi storici Luigi Simeoni* 51: 9–27.

Cassis, Youssef. 2006. *Capitals of Capitals. The Rise and Fall of International Financial Center 1780–2009.* Cambridge: Cambridge University Press.

Cassis, Youssef, and Philip Cottrell, eds. 2009. *The World of Private Banking.* Farnham-Burlington: Ashgate.

Chapman, Stanley D. 1984. *The Rise of Merchant Banking.* London: Allen & Unwin.

Chilosi, David. 2017. "Revisiting the Notes on the History of Interest Rates: Bonds' Markets in the Republic of Genoa." In *State Cash Resources and State Building Activities in Europe, 13th-18th century, Institut de la gestion publique et du developpement economique*, edited by K. Beguin and A. L. Murphy, 167–78. Paris: Institut de la gestion publique et du développement économique.

Cipolla, Carlo M. 1953. "Agli inizi della rivoluzione industriale nell'economia ligure." In *Genova. Uomini e fortune*, 3–24. Genova: Levante, Società di Assicurazioni e Riassicurazioni.

Cipolla, Carlo M. 1956. *Money, Prices, and Civilization in the Mediterranean World: Fifth to Seventeenth Century.* Princeton: Princeton University Press.

Cipolla, Carlo M. 1976. *Before the Industrial Revolution: European Society and Economy, 1000–1700.* London: Methuen.

Conti, Giuseppe, and Maria Carmela Schisani. 2011. "I banchieri italiani e la *haute banque* nel Risorgimento e dopo l'Unità." *Società e storia* 131, no. 1: 133–70.

Cottrell, Philip L. 1980. *Industrial Finance 1830–1914. The Finance and Organization of English Manufacturing Industry.* London-New York: Methuen.

Da Pozzo, Mario, and Giuseppe Felloni. 1964. *La borsa valori di Genova nel secolo XIX.* Torino: ILTE.

Da Silva, José-Gentil. 1969. *Banque et crédit en Italie au XVIIe siècle*, 2 vols. Paris: Klincksieck.

De Luca, Giuseppe, and Angelo Moioli. 2008. "Il potere del credito. Reti e istituzioni in Italia centro-settentrionale fra età moderna e decenni preunitari."

In *Storia d'Italia*, *Annali 23*, *La Banca*, edited by C. Bermond, A. Cova, A. Moioli and S. La Francesca, 212–55. Torino: Einaudi.

De Simone, Ennio. 1987. *Storia della banca dalle origini ai nostri giorni*. Napoli: Arte Tipografica.

De Simone, Ennio. 1993. *Alle origini del sistema bancario italiano (1815–1840)*. Napoli: Edizioni Scientifiche Italiane.

De Simone, Ennio. 2011. *Moneta e banche attraverso i secoli*. Milano: FrancoAngeli.

Del Punta, Ignazio. 2002. "Il fallimento della compagnia Ricciardi alla fine del secolo XIII: un caso esemplare?" *Archivio Storico Italiano* 160, no. 2: 221–67.

De Roover, Raymond. 1948. *Money, Banking and Credit in Mediaeval Bruges. Italian Merchant Bankers, Lombards and Money-Changers. A Study in the Origins of Banking*. Cambridge, MA: The Mediaeval Academy of America.

De Roover, Raymond. 1953. *L'evolution de la lettre de change, XIVe–XVIIIe siècles*. Paris: Librairie Armand Colin.

De Roover, Raymond. 1966. *The Rise and Decline of the Medici Bank: 1397–1494*. New York: W. W. Norton.

Dickson, Peter G. 1967. *The Financial Revolution in England. A Study in the Development of Public Credit, 1688–1756*. London: Macmillan.

Dickson, Peter G. 1987. *Finance and Government Under Maria Teresa, 1740–1780, II*, *Finance and Credit*. Oxford: Clarendon Press.

Doria, Giorgio. 1969. *Investimenti e sviluppo economico a Genova alla vigilia della Prima Guerra Mondiale* (1815–1882). Milano: A. Giuffrè Editore.

Doria, Marco. 2001. "Un'economia in trasformazione tra progetti e realtà. Genova nella prima metà del XIX secolo." *Atti della Società Ligure di Storia Patria* 41, no. 2: 171–92.

Doria, Marco. 2007. "Da un'economia di antico regime all'industrializzazione." In *Storia della Liguria*, edited by G. Assereto and M. Doria, 211–28. Roma-Bari: Laterza.

Doria, Marco. 2008. "Economia e investimenti finanziari a Genova nell'età cavouriana." *Atti della Società Ligure di Storia Patria* 48, no. 1: 225–51.

Drelichman, Mauricio, and Hans-Joachim Voth. 2014. *Lending to the Borrower from Hell. Debt, Taxes, and Default in the Age of Philip II*. Princeton-Oxford: Princeton University Press.

Epstein, Stephan R. 1994. "Regional Fairs, Institutional Innovation, and Economic Growth in Late Medieval Europe." *Economic History Review* 47: 459–62.

Epstein, Stephan R. 2000. *Freedom and Growth. The Rise of States and Markets in Europe 1300–1750*. London: Routledge.

Epstein, Stephan R. 2001. "Fairs, Towns, and States in Renaissance Europe." In *Fiere e mercati nella integrazione delle economie europee, secc. XIII–XVIII*, edited by S. Cavaciocchi, 71–90. Florence: Le Monnier.

Face, R. D. 1958. "Techniques of Business in the Trade Between the Fairs of Champagne and the South of Europe in the 12th and 13th centuries." *Economic History Review* 10: 427–39.

Favier, Jean. 1998. *Gold & Spices. The Rise of Commerce in the Middle Ages*. New York: Holmes and Meier.

Felloni, Giuseppe. 1961. *Popolazione e sviluppo economico della Liguria nel secolo XIX*. Torino: ILTE.

Felloni, Giuseppe. 1971. *Gli investimenti finanziari genovesi in Europa tra il 1600 e la Restaurazione*. Milano: A. Giuffrè.

Felloni, Giuseppe, ed. 1997. *Moneta, credito e banche in Europa: un millennio di storia*. Genova: Brigati.

Felloni, Giuseppe. 2008. "Dall'Italia all'Europa: il primato della finanza italiana dal Medioevo alla prima età moderna." In *Storia d'Italia, Annali 23, La Banca*, edited by C. Bermond, A. Cova, A. Moioli and S. La Francesca, 93–149. Torino: Einaudi.

Felloni, Giuseppe. 2016. "Genova e il capitalismo finanziario dalle origini all'apogeo (secc. X-XVIII)." *Atti della società ligure di storia patria* 56: 71–79.

Felloni, Giuseppe, and Guido Laura. 2017. *Genoa and the History of Finance: Twelve First?* Genova: G. Brigati.

Ferguson, Niall. 1998. *The World's Banker. The History of the House of Rothschild*. London: Weidenfeld & Nicolson.

Ferguson, Niall. 2008. *The Ascent of Money: A Financial History of the World*. New York: Penguin books.

Flandreau, Marc, and Juan H. Flores. 2009. "Bonds and Brands: Foundations of Sovereign Debt Markets." *Journal of Economic History* 69, no. 3: 646–84.

Fornasari, Massimo. 2017. *La banca, la borsa, lo Stato. Una storia della finanza (secoli XIII-XXI)*. Torino: Giappichelli.

Fratianni, Michele. 2006. "Government Debt, Reputation and Creditors' Protections: The Tale of San Giorgio." *Review of Finance* 10, no. 4: 497–501.

Fusaro, Maria. 2015. *Political Economies of Empire in the Early Modern Mediterranean: The Decline of Venice and the Rise of England, 1450–1700*. Cambridge: Cambridge University Press.

García Guerra, Elena M., and Giuseppe De Luca, eds. 2010. *Il mercato del credito in età moderna. Reti e operatori finanziari nello spazio europeo*. Milano: FrancoAngeli.

Gille, Bertrand. 1965. *Histoire de la Maison Rothschild, 1, Des origines a 1848*. Genève: Droz.

Gioffrè, Domenico. 1960. *Gênes et les foires de change: de Lyon à Besançon*. Paris: S.E.V.P.E.N.

Goldthwaite, Richard A. 1968. *Private Wealth in Renaissance Florence: A Study of Four Families*. Princeton: Princeton University Press.

Goldthwaite, Richard A. 1995. *Banks, Palaces and Entrepreneurs in Renaissance Florence*. Aldershot: Variorum.

Grendi, Edoardo. 1964. "Genova nel Quarantotto." *Nuova Rivista Storica* 48, no. 3–4: 307–49.

Häberlein, Mark. 2012. *The Fuggers of Augsburg: Pursuing Wealth and Honor in Renaissance Germany*. Charlottesville-London: University of Virginia Press.

Heers, Jacques. 1961. *Gênes au XVe siècle. Activité économique et problems sociaux*. Paris: S.E.V.P.E.N.

Homer, Sidney, and Richard E. Sylla. 1996. *A History of Interest Rates*. New Brunswick: Rutgers University Press.

Hunt, Edwin S. 1994. *The Medieval Super-Companies: A Study of the Peruzzi Company of Florence*. Cambridge: Cambridge University Press.

Hunt, Edwin S., and James M. Murray. 1999. *A History of Business in Medieval Europe, 1200–1550*. Cambridge: Cambridge University Press.

Kindleberger, Charles P. 1984. *A Financial History of Western Europe*. London: Allen & Unwin.

Kirk, Thomas Allison. 2005. *Genoa and the Sea: Policy and Power in an Early Modern Maritime Republic, 1559–1684*. Baltimore-London: Johns Hopkins University Press.

Kobrak, Christopher. 2013. "The Concept of Reputation in Business History." *Business History Review* 87, no. 4: 763–86.

Kolb, Robert W., ed. 2011. *Sovereign Debt: From Safety to Default*. New York: Wiley.

Lapeyre, Henri. 1953. *Simon Ruiz et les 'Asientos' de Philippe II*. Paris: Libraire Armand Collin.

Le Goff, Jacques. 1956. *Marchands et banquiers du moyen age*. Paris: Presses Universitaires de France.

Lopez, Roberto S. 1956. *La prima crisi della Banca di Genova, 1250–1259*. Milano: Università Bocconi.

Lopez, Roberto S., et al. 1982. *L'alba della banca. Le origini del sistema bancario tra Medioevo ed età moderna*. Bari: Dedalo.

Lorenzini, Marcella, Cinzia Lorandini, and D'Maris Coffman, eds. 2018. *Financing in Europe. Evolution, Coexistence and Complementarity of Lending Practices from the Middle Age to Modern Time*. London: Palgrave Macmillan.

Marsilio, Claudio. 2008. *Dove il denaro fa denaro. Gli operatori finanziari genovesi nelle fiere di cambio del XVII secolo*. Novi Ligure: Città del Silenzio.

Marsilio, Claudio. 2012a. "Genoese Finance, 1348–1700." In *Handbook of Key Global Financial Markets, Institutions, and Infrastructure, Vol. 1*, edited by G. Caprio, 123–32. Oxford: Elsevier.

Marsilio, Claudio. 2012b. "The Genoese and Portuguese Financial Operators' Control of the Spanish Silver Market (1627–1657)." *Journal of European Economic History* 41, no. 3: 67–89.

Marsilio, Claudio. 2017. "A Wise Man Is Always Ready to Face a Disaster. The Professional Skill of Genoise, Florentine and Portuguese Financial Operators in Seventeenth-Century Exchange Fairs." In *State Cash Resources and State Building Activities in Europe, 13th-18th Century, Institut de la gestion publique et du developpement economique*, edited by K. Beguin and A. L. Murphy, 179–94. Paris: Institut de la gestion publique et du développement économique.

Marsilio, Claudio. 2019. "Exchange Fairs and the International Credit Market. The Genoese Financial Operators' Professional Skills (XVII century)." *Storia economica* 22, no. 2: 273–90.

Marzo Magno, Alessandro. 2013. *L' invenzione dei soldi: quando la finanza parlava italiano.* Milano: Garzanti.

Massa, Paola, ed. 2003. *Economisti liguri dell'Ottocento. La dottrina economica nell'Ateneo genovese e in Liguria.* Genova: Accademia Ligure di Scienze e Lettere.

Mathias, Peter. 1969. *The First Industrial Nation. An Economic History of Britain 1700–1914.* London: Methuen.

Melis, Federigo. 1962. "Francesco Datini come operatore economico." *Economia e storia* 9: 195–98.

Melis, Federigo. 1971. "Orígines de la banca moderna." *Moneda y Credito* 116: 3–18.

Melis, Federigo. 1972. *Documenti per la storia economica dei secoli XIII-XVI.* Firenze: Olschki.

Melis, Federigo. 1987. *La banca pisana e le origini della banca moderna.* Firenze: Le Monnier.

Meriggi, Marco. 2002. *Gli Stati italiani prima dell'Unità. Una storia istituzionale.* Bologna: Il Mulino.

Morris, Terence Allan. 1998. *Europe and England in the Sixteenth Century.* London-New York: Routledge.

Mueller, Reinhold C. 1997. *The Venetian Money Market: Banks, Panics, and the Public Debt, 1200–1500.* Baltimore: Johns Hopkins University Press.

Mueller, Reinhold C. 1979. "The Role of Bank Money in Venice, 1300–1500." *Studi veneziani* 3: 47–96.

Murray, James. M. 2005. *Bruges, Cradle of Capitalism, 1280–1390.* Cambridge: Cambridge University Press.

Muzzarelli, Maria Giuseppina. 2001. *Il denaro e la salvezza: l'invenzione del Monte di pietà.* Bologna: Il Mulino.

Neal, Larry. 1990. *The Rise of Financial Capitalism. International Capital Markets in the Age of Reason.* Cambridge: Cambridge University Press.

Neal, Larry. 2000. "How It All Began: The Monetary and Financial Architecture of Europe During the First Global Capital Markets 1648–1815." *Financial History Review* 7, no. 2: 117–40.

Neal, Larry. 2015. *A Concise History of International Finance: From Babylon to Bernanke*. Cambridge: Cambridge University Press.

Neri, Enrica. 1989. *Uomini d'affari e di governo tra Genova e Madrid: secoli 16. e 17.* Milano: Vita e Pensiero.

North, Douglass C., and Barry R. Weingast. 1989. "Constitutions and Commitment: The Evolution of Institutions Governing Public Choice in Seventeenth-Century England." *The Journal of Economic History* 49, no. 4: 803–32.

Orlandi, Angela. 2002. *Le grand parti: fiorentini a Lione e il debito pubblico francese nel XVI secolo*. Firenze: L. S. Olschki.

Palermo, Luciano. 2008. *La banca e il credito nel Medioevo*. Milano: Bruno Mondadori.

Parker, Geoffrey. 2000. *The Grand Strategy of Philip II*. New Haven: Yale University Press.

Pezzolo, Luciano. 2005. "Bonds and Government Debt in Italian City-States 1250–1650." In *The Origins of Value: The Financial Innovations That Created Modern Capital Markets*, edited by N. Goetzmann and K. G. Rouwenhorst, 145–63. Oxford: Oxford University Press.

Pezzolo, Luciano. 2012. "Republics and Principalities in Italy." In *The Rise of the Fiscal States. A Global History 1500–1914*, edited by P. K. O'Brien and B. Yun-Casalilla. Cambridge: Cambridge University Press.

Piccinno, Luisa. 2013. *I trasporti in Liguria all'inizio dell'Ottocento. Nuove dimensioni e modelli operativi*. Milano: FrancoAngeli.

Piola Caselli, Fausto. 2016. *Government Debts and Financial Markets in Europe*. London: Pickering & Chatto.

Pressnell, Leslie S. 1956. *Country Banking in the Industrial Revolution*. Oxford: Clarendon Press.

Rollandi, Maria S. 1996. *A Groppoli di Lunigiana. Potere e ricchezza di un feudatario genovese (secc. XVI-XVIII)*. Genova: Società Ligure di Storia Patria.

Rollandi, Maria S. 1998. "Da mercanti a «rentiers» . La famiglia genovese dei Brignole Sale (secc. XVI-XVIII)." In *Tra rendita e investimenti. Formazione e gestione dei grandi patrimoni in Italia in età moderna e contemporanea*, 105–24. Bari: Cacucci.

Rollandi, Maria S. 2006. "Da «negozianti» a banchieri. La famiglia Oneto nell'Ottocento." In *Ottocento in salotto. Cultura, vita privata e affari tra Genova e Napoli*, edited by C. Olcese Spingardi, 41–47. Firenze: Maschietto.

Rollandi, Maria S. 2011. "Navigazione e porto. Progetti e realizzazioni della politica cavouriana." In *Cavour e Genova. Economia e politica*, edited by M. E. Tonizzi, 61–74. Genova: De Ferrari.

Rollandi, Maria S. 2012. "Patrimoni e spese della nobiltà genovese nella Restaurazione." In *Gio. Carlo di Negro (1769–1857). Magnificenza, mecenatismo, munificenza*, edited by S. Verdino, 9–28. Genova: Accademia Ligure di Scienze e Lettere.

Rollandi, Maria S. 2019. "«Andare a nozze» a Genova nel Settecento. Note da un archivio familiare." In *Le vocazioni di un territorio. Saggi di Storia economica per Paola Massa*, edited by M. Doria, L. Piccinno, G. L. Podestà, M. S. Rollandi and A. Zanini, 43–87. Genova: De Ferrari.

Rollandi, Maria S., and Marina Romani. 2018. "Tesori ovvero beni denaro-equivalenti. Considerazioni sulle funzioni degli oggetti nell'antico regime (secoli XV-XVIII)." *Società e Storia* 159, no. 1: 1–34.

Rowlands, Guy. 2015. *Dangerous and Dishonest Men: The International Bankers of Louis XIV's France*. Basingstoke: Palgrave Macmillan.

Santarelli, Umberto. 1998. *Mercanti e società tra mercanti*. Torino: Giappichelli.

Sanz Ayán, Carmen. 2005. "Presencia y fortuna de los hombres de negocios genoveses durante la crisis hispana de 1640." *Hispania* 65: 91–114.

Sapori, Armando. 1926. *La crisi delle compagnie mercantili dei Bardi e dei Peruzzi*. Firenze: L. S. Olschki.

Sapori, Armando. 1972. *La Mercatura Medievale*. Firenze: Sansoni.

Sapori, Armando. 1982. *Studi di Storia economica. Secoli XIII-XIV-XV*. 2 vols. Firenze: Sansoni.

Sayous, André. 1932. "Les opérations des banquiers italiens en Italie et aux foires de Champagne pendant le XIIIe siècle." *Revue historique* 170, no. 1: 1–31.

Seghezza, Elena. 2013. "La Rivoluzione Gloriosa: riforma costituzionale e distribuzione del reddito." *Rivista di storia economica* 29, no. 1: 55–86.

Seghezza, Elena. 2015."Fiscal Capacity and the Risk of Sovereign Debt After the Glorious Revolution: A Reinterpretation of the North–Weingast Hypothesis." *European Journal of Political Economy,* 38: 71–81.

Spufford, Peter. 1988. *Money and Its Use in Medieval Europe*. Cambridge: Cambridge University Press.

Spufford, Peter. 2002. *Power and Profit: The Merchant in Medieval Europe*. London: Thames & Hudson.

Spufford, Peter. 2014. "The Provision of Stable Moneys by Florence and Venice, and North Italian Financial Innovations in the Renaissance Period." In *Explaining Monetary and Financial Innovation: A Historical Analysis,* edited by P. Bernholz and R. Vaubel, 227–51. Cham: Springer.

Stasavage, David. 2011. *States of Credit: Size, Power and the Development of European Polities*. Princeton: Princeton University Press.

Taviani, Carlo. 2018. "Companies, Commerce and Credit." In *A Companion to Medieval Genoa*, edited by C. E. Beneš, 427–47. Leiden-Boston: Brill.

Temin, Peter, and Hans-Joachim Voth. 2008. "Private Borrowing during the Financial Revolution: Hoare's Bank and Its Customers, 1702–24." *The Economic History Review* 61, no. 3: 541–64.

Ugolini, Stefano. 2018. "The Origins of Swiss Wealth Management? Genevan Private BANKING, 1800–1840." *Financial History Review* 25, no. 2: 161–82.

Vannini Marx, Anna, ed. 1985. *Credito, banche e investimenti: secoli 13.-20.* Firenze: Le Monnier.
Vitale, Vito. 1933. "Informazioni di polizia sull'ambiente ligure (1814–1826)." *Atti della Società Ligure di Storia Patria* 61: 419–49.
Wallerstein, Immanuel. 1974. *The Modern World-System.* I. *Capitalist agriculture and the origins of the European world-economy in the sixteenth century.* Orlando: Academic Press.
White, Eugene N. 2001. "Making the French Pay: The Cost and Consequences of the Napoleonic reparations." *European Review of Economic History* 5, no. 3: 337–65.
White, Lawrence H. 1984. *Free Banking in Britain. Theory, Experience and Debate (1800–1845).* Cambridge: Cambridge University Press.
Zanini, Andrea. 2017. *Impresa e finanza a Genova. I Crosa (secoli XVII-XVIII).* Genova: Sagep.

CHAPTER 2

The Parodi Bankers

2.1 The Parodi Bank in the Pre-unification Period

The Parodi family, originally from Albisola, became economically established in the early nineteenth century in a period of great transformation in Genoa. During this period, many of the wealthy families suffer financial losses. Documents we studied, in fact, trace the credit activity of the Parodis back to the end of the eighteenth century. Giacomo (1754–1830) continued his father Bartolomeo's profession (Fig. 2.1). He owns a "banking shop" at first with his brother Francesco, and subsequently, in 1792, he manages it on his own.[1] A moderate debut, with the "small bank of promissory notes" near the Royal Bridge. Parodi lives in a modest house in the popular Coltelleria alley, located in the Molo district.[2] He is married to Marianna Casareto and has four children. In the 1850s, his only son, Bartolomeo (1789–1865), was defined by the count of Cavour

[1] ADG, FP, 4/31, Atto notarile contenente la divisione di beni fra Giacomo e Francesco Parodi (1792). Rollandi (2014).

[2] ADG, FP, 6/50, Tribunale Civile di Genova e Corte d'Appello di Genova, causa Parodi-Castagnola (1852).

L. Maffi, *Private Bankers in the Italian 19th Century*, Palgrave Studies in Economic History, https://doi.org/10.1007/978-3-030-63361-5_2

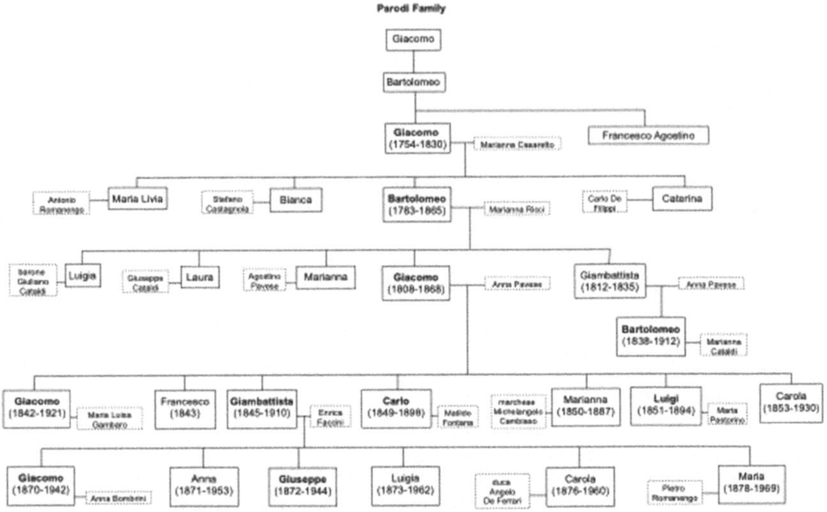

Fig. 2.1 Parodi family tree (*Source* Author elaboration)

as the wealthiest banker in the Kingdom of Sardinia.[3] He has three daughters Bianca, Livia, and Caterina who have no interest in banking, but who indirectly allow us to understand how successful their father's business is.[4] His business grows steadily and within twenty years during the last decade of the eighteenth century and the early 1820s of the following century.

From a lawsuit filed by Bianca's heirs relating to her dowry, we are aware of the fact that these instruments (dated 1796) were modified with subsequent annotations in 1816, precisely because Giacomo wants to share with his daughter his growing prosperity.[5]

[3] Cavour (1889, 511).

[4] ADG, FP, 6/50, Tribunale Civile di Genova e Corte d'Appello di Genova, causa Parodi-Castagnola (1852).

[5] ADG, FP, 6/50, Tribunale Civile di Genova e Corte d'Appello di Genova, causa Parodi-Castagnola (1852).

Table 2.1 Employees Banco Parodi in 1828

	Name	*Job*
1	Giacomo Parodi	Banker
2	Bartolomeo Parodi	Banker's son
3	Pietro Bado	Assistant
4	Carlo Olivari	Assistant
5	Vincenzo Saettone	Assistant
6	Carlo Bombrini	Assistant
7	Sacco	Assistant
8	Lorenzo Dias	Assistant

Source 4/37, Atti causa giudiziaria, Bartolomeo Parodi Carlo Odino e Antonio Romanengo (1833)

A further tangible sign of the banker's success is the purchase of real properties in Via Luccoli in 1818,[6] which is where his son Bartolomeo's home will eventually be located (in 1838).[7]

In the 1820s, the rise of the banker was complete, as well as his specialization in credit activities, his skills, and his reputation. In the last years of his life, Giacomo largely lost his sight. By the end of 1827, he needs the support of his most trusted assistants in the most delicate phases of his work. Carlo Bombrini in particular is the one who often guides his hand in placing his signature.[8]

In 1828, six clerks work in the bank, located in Piazza della Posta Vecchia, in addition to Giacomo and his son Bartolomeo (Table 2.1).

It is precisely with Bartholomeo that the Parodi family business marks the transition from the emerging Genoese bourgeoisie and its liquidity, relationships, and credit skills, to a banking approach adhering to the credit/financial models typical of the European haute banque, thus taking advantage of the ability to organize in the new operational horizons of the national and international economy.

As emerges from documentary sources, whether financial, political, or judicial, the Parodi name occurs frequently in the pre-unification

[6] ADG, FP, 4/31, Atto relativo all'acquisto di immobili in via Luccoli (1818).

[7] ADG, FP, 4/39, Patto di famiglia tra Bartolomeo Parodi e il figlio Giacomo, relativo alla ditta bancaria Parodi (1837).

[8] ADG, FP, 4/37, Atti causa giudiziaria, Bartolomeo Parodi contro Carlo Odino e Antonio Romanengo (1833): "Giacomo Parodi's hand was guided for the signature by Mr. Carlo Bombrini".

decades, confirming the extraordinary credibility and value of the bankers' name. Some of the protagonists of the haute banque and international finance appear in the Parodi network. These include James de Rothschild, Alessandro Torlonia[9] banker to the Holy See, Raffaele De Ferrari, an important European entrepreneur and financier,[10] as well as statesmen such as Camillo Benso di Cavour and Cardinal Giacomo Antonelli the Holy See's Secretary of State.[11] In 1834, the Parodis, who already represent the Rothschilds of Naples, also offered their services to the Rothschild house in London, offering the same conditions extended to the Rothschild house in Naples[12]: "Courtage de bours reels à v.s charge à ½ per mille. Interets reciprocals 4% an".

On October 18, 1838, James de Rothschild, traveling to Italy in search of counterparts with whom to grow his business, sent a letter from Genoa to his Paris house in which he identified in the Parodi house the most important company in the city, with a business of 3–4 million francs at the time.[13] It is Rothschild himself who defines the Ricci and Hagerman[14] as well as Parodi bank houses as haute banque. The same day Bartolomeo Parodi sent a letter to the Rothschilds of Paris in which he wrote: "Je viens vous parteciper d'avoir eu l'honneur de presenter mes hommages à M. le Baron Jacques de vs. maison qui m'a invité à vous faire des remises en compte à demi en case de convenience", claiming to be in favor of this opportunity.[15] Parodi is therefore a reference banker in Genoa for

[9] Felisini (1990, 2016).

[10] Bergeron (1991) and Doria (1991).

[11] Coppa (1990).

[12] RAL, XI/112/116, Parodi (1834).

[13] Gille (1965, 425–426).

[14] Giovanni Battista Ricci and Jonas Hagermann were two bankers working in Genoa in the first half of the nineteenth century. Both of them were presented in the tax roles on the contribution of licenses [contribuzione delle patenti] relating to the year 1811 (ASGe, Fondo Prefettura Francese, 738).

[15] ANMT, BR, 132 AQ 9 P 095, Parodi (1838–1847). The relations between Parodi bank and the Rothschild bank in Paris have been mentioned since 1838. The relations between the two banking houses will be uninterrupted until 1914; the most important credit and financial affairs, however, occurred in the 1840s, 1850s, and 1860s.: ANMT, BR, 132 AQ 9 P 095, Parodi (1838–1847), 132 AQ 9 P 096, Parodi (1848–1851), 132 AQ 9 P 097, Parodi (1852–1855), 132 AQ 9 P 099, Parodi (1860–1863), 132 AQ non coté 145, Parodi (1852–1868), 132 AQ 9 P 207, Parodi (1868–1873), 132 AQ 9 P 208, Parodi (1874–1877), 132 AQ 9 P 209, Parodi (1878–1883), 132 AQ 9 P 210,

the Rothschild houses in Naples, London, and Paris, a role that implicitly certifies credit and financial skills that are up to the major European bankers' standards.

Regarding the family's and the bank's assets, we should note the difficulty of interpreting the available data. First of all, it is difficult to evaluate and distinguish the family's assets from the bank's, especially regarding financial transactions. This difficulty emerges clearly from a lawsuit dated 1839, filed by the heirs of Maria Livia Parodi Romanengo (daughter of Giacomo) against their uncle Bartolomeo Parodi, where regarding family property it is specified that *facilius est extorquere clavam de manu Herculis* to obtain from the banker the real value of the legacy left by her father Giacomo. From the survey carried out on the occasion of the judicial proceeding, it appears that in 1833 the fortune of the late Giacomo amounted to over 3,300,000 lire; the holding in the Asti area, purchased for the price of 518,562 lire, and a large part of the profits from banking activities are excluded from this assessment, since the accounting books are not made available.[16] During the first half of the century, the Parodi family also accumulated huge real estate investments in Genoa, Sestri Ponente, and Monferrato.[17]

The reputation and wealth of these bankers grew in the 1940s, both because of investments in joint stock companies, mostly banks, that were created in Genoa, and as underwriters of loans to the Holy See (1846, the Parodi-Torlonia loan).[18] Already in the early years of this decade, in his correspondence with Emile De La Rüe, Cavour, besides dwelling on political, financial, and economic issues, also inquired about banking activities in Genoa. The indications provided by the Genoese banker De La Rüe originally from Geneva give the statesman the opportunity to describe the substance and reputation of the Parodi. That convinces him that Parodi will be the ideal partners to establish modern banking activities

Parodi (1884–1887), 132 AQ 9 P 318, Parodi (1888–1892), 132 AQ 9 P 319, Parodi (1893–1897), 132 AQ 9 P 320, Parodi (1898–1901) and 132 AQ 9 P 321, Parodi (1902–1914).

[16] ADG, FP, 4/38 Atti causa giudiziaria Romanengo contro Bartolomeo Parodi (1839).

[17] Doria (1969, 96).

[18] Mancardi (1874, 47–48, 460, 485).

Table 2.2 Evolution of the Name and Capital of the Parodi Bank

Years	*Name*	*Capital (lire)*
ante 1830	Giacomo Parodi q. Bartolomeo (ragione di commercio)	n.d.
1830–1837	Bartolomeo Parodi q. Giacomo (ragione di commercio)	n.d.
1837	Ditta Bartolomeo Parodi e Figlio	400,000
1868	Ditta Bartolomeo Parodi e Figlio	2,200,000
1874	Ditta Bartolomeo Parodi e Fratelli	3,200,000
1913	Ditta Bartolomeo Parodi e Fratelli	400,000

Source ADG, FP, 4/38, 4/39, 11/116 and 12/127

in the Kingdom of Sardinia and to subsequently support the unification project.[19]

In 1843 for the foundation of the Banca di Genova, which would become, in 1844, the first issuing bank of the Sardinian states, Cavour wrote to Emile De La Rüe that: "deux ou trois des premières maisons de votre ville, vous, Parodi, Ricci par exemple offerent au ministre de se charger de toutes les actions qu'il a à sa disposition (soit 2/3), en payant un prime au gouvernement".[20] Later, Raffaele De Ferrari will confirm the house's reputation as the only reliable one. By the end of 1847, he is in Paris. He is very worried by the economic situation that is emerging in France, so the duke tried to monetize credits, securities, and shares in Genoa to buffer the chasm of the losses he suffered. He gives the mandate to sell all Piedmontese, Roman, Milanese, and Neapolitan public securities and the shares of the Bank of Genoa and the Neapolitan railway. A few months later, on February 27, 1848, in relation to the transfer of the money obtained from the sale, he wrote to Bernardo Pellegrini, his assiduous correspondent: "I believe that in Genoa you can only trust Parodi and no one else".[21] With regard to the company's evolution in terms of the business name, there have been changes over the course of the century for opportunity reasons or because of adjustments to family history (Table 2.2). Before 1830, the name was "Giacomo Parodi q. Bartolomeo." From 1830, the year of Giacomo's

[19] Aubert (1984).

[20] Cavour (1973, 56). Regarding the cotext refer (Bachi 1933).

[21] Doria (1991, 460).

death, it became "Bartolomeo Parodi q. Giacomo." In 1837, because of the agreement between Bartolomeo and his son Giacomo (1808–1868), the "Bartolomeo Parodi & Son Company" was born with a capital of 400,000 lire, for the duration of five years, renewable unless canceled by one of the members with notice to be given three months before the deadline.[22] This company remained active until Giacomo's death. His heirs in 1868 reconstituted the "Bartolomeo Parodi & Son Company" with capital of 2,200,000 lire.[23]

The business, which since 1874 has taken on the name "Bartolomeo Parodi & Brothers' Company" with share capital of 3,200,000 lire,[24] continues until the bank's liquidation in 1928. A document, kept in the archive and belonging to one of the last years of business, illustrates the long history of the Parodi bank.[25]

[22] ADG, FP, 4/39, Patto di famiglia tra Bartolomeo Parodi e il figlio Giacomo, relativo alla ditta bancaria Parodi (1837). The banking business of the Parodi is mentioned over the years in the Genoese trade almanacs (in the same almanacs, there are also the other private bankers working in the city) *Almanacco* (1822), *Lunario genovese* (1830), *Lunario genovese* (1881), *Almanacco* (1837), *Il Cicerone* (1845), *Il Cicerone* (1855), *Il Cicerone* (1857), *Annuario* (1870), Lossa (1868, 1874) and Chiozza (1874–1875).

[23] ADG, FP, 4/39, Atto costitutivo della ditta bancaria "Ditta Bartolomeo Parodi e figlio" (1868).

[24] ADG, FP, 11/116, Atto costitutivo ditta "Ditta bancaria Bartolomeo Parodi e Fratelli" (1874).

[25] ADG, FP, 12/127, Richiesta relativa al controllo dell'imposta sui redditi di ricchezza mobile (1926): It is a letter addressed to the Minister of Finance on June 6, 1925, which makes clear the subsequent steps of the bank's name. In the letter, there is the following description: "The Bank Bartolomeo Parodi and Fratelli, the brothers were the only partners, owners and signatory representatives, was established on August 14th, 1874, registered in Genoa on the same month and year in register 103, No. 7644 transcribed on September 1st, 1874 to No. 68 of register No. 1 of transcription of "Atti di Società" of the year 1874 at the commercial court of Genoa".

The bank worked up to the present, through transformations that became necessary in such a long period of time. The transformations were as follows:

private act authenticated by the notary Gian Carlo Besio of Genoa on March 17, 1894, registered in Genoa on the 23rd of the same month in register 245 No. 10,383; act of the notary Gian Carlo Besio predicted on August 30, 1894, registered in Genoa on September 6 the same year in register 223 No. 1190. Notarial act of Gian Carlo Besio, registered in Genoa in the same month and year at n° 4.484 volume 367. Notarial act Gian Carlo Besio January 11, 1913, registered in Genoa 17th the same month and year at volume 383, No. 3795.

The Bartolomeo Parodi and Fratelli Bank, which has lived for over half a century, from 1874 until now, was the continuation and transformation of the banking activities of the "Bartolomeo Parodi e Figlio" Bank established with writing on November 30, 1868. This

Table 2.3 Credit operations handled by private bankers

1	Trade in precious metals
2	Exchange of currencies
3	Deposits
4	Credit transfers
5	Recoveries, receipts and payments
7	Arbitrages
8	Discounts
9	Bank accounts
10	Loans with security

Source Boccardo, Dizionario universale, 281–290

2.2 The Credit Operations Carried Out by the Parodis

The private banker operates basically within two economic spheres: credit and finance. As mentioned earlier, a banker's reputation is closely linked to his ability to attract deposits, the cornerstone of all of the private bank's operations. The deposits represent the nexus between the banker's need to constantly have capital, and any and all client benefits. These derive from the deposit itself along with the opportunity of using the services made available by the bank. In the pre-unification period, deposits are of two types: repayable on demand or at a fixed term. The former, due to their temporary nature, which allows them to be collected at any time, do not flow into the capital available to the banker for his business. The fixed term deposits, on the other hand, allow the banker to dispose of them according to the opportunities and strategies deemed most advantageous for the company's business.

Boccardo, studying the activity relating to commercial credit practices, identifies ten main banking operations (see Table 2.3)[26]; with regard to financial investments, it clearly distinguishes two phases: an earlier period mainly sees banking operations on national and foreign public debt; since the 1940s, they added investments relating to the purchase of

also was the continuation of the previous centuries-old banking business of the Parodi family. About long-term businesses, compare: Ferrandino and Napolitano (2014).

[26] *Banchieri*, in Boccardo (1875, 281–290). Concerning the most important credit operations refer: Felloni (1997, 80–84). Regarding credit operations of private bankers read also: Segreto (2001), Scatamacchia (2013), and Balbo (2000).

shares of listed companies, particularly in banking, insurance, and railway companies.

The consultation and study of the Parodi Archive have revealed documents which in a more detailed manner and through reports related to procedures or practices confirm the professional path of the banking sector as described by the Genoese economist according to more general parameters. As regards the credit and financial activities carried out in the Parodi bank, there is valuable information in the general power of attorney given by Bartolomeo to his son Giacomo in 1833.[27] Already in itself, the list of managerial and decision-making functions linked to the role of the private banker defines a profile that brings together skills, responsibilities, and abilities that are very much in line with the description made by Boccardo in his Dictionary.

In the activities registered in the 1865 general power of attorney, given by Giacomo to his sons Giacomo and Bartolomeo, some new information is found when compared with the same document of thirty years earlier, such as the reference to the National Bank, discount banks, and other financial transactions.[28]

Financial operations, activities that distinguish and place the Parodi bank in the circuit of national and international private bankers, are examined in the chapter dedicated to financial intermediation skills.

2.3 Accounting Management of the Parodi Bank

In the aforementioned court case between Antonio Maria Romanengo and Bartolomeo Parodi, the latter is called upon to provide plenty of information on banking, corporate accounting, and business.[29] Here the banker is reluctant to hand over the documents relating to the management of his business. That said, however, an excellent picture emerges of the operations carried out and the management of a banking company in Genoa in the early decades of the nineteenth century. This happens thanks to the following accounting documents produced by the two bankers and by the six "clerical and computational" clerks present in the company:

[27] ADG, FP, 6/51, Procura di Bartolomeo Parodi nei confronti del figlio Giacomo per l'attività bancaria (1833).

[28] ADG, FP, 6/51, Procura di Giacomo Parodi nei confronti di Giacomo e Bartolomeo Parodi per l'attività bancaria (1865).

[29] ADG, FP, 4/38 Atti causa giudiziaria Romanengo contro Bartolomeo Parodi (1839).

cash books; current accounts books; books on routes and remittances; copybooks; book of purchases and sales, containing the negotiation of bills both abroad and on the exchange; book with the bills of exchange on the foreign exchange that circulate in the bank, both those bought on the exchange and those received from the correspondents; book of bills in the square or on the square[30]; deadline book, containing the deadlines for bills to be collected or paid; book with the deadlines of the matches that must be requested and the payments that must be made; book with uses in public funds; budget books.

Bartolomeo Parodi initially admits the existence of only the following materials: two books of financial statements, the first from 1806 to 1816 and the second from 1816 to 1825; a book with the promissory notes bought in the square and resold (from 1824 to 1829); the schedule of bills of exchange from 1818 to 1822. However, pursued by the counterpart, he subsequently reveals 34 additional books, which contain the accounts of the credit and financial transactions indicated above.[31]

However, he does not deliver the book of purchases and sales, containing the negotiation of bills both abroad and in the square, nor the cash book. He makes a statement on the amount of cash, which he says is 710,502 lire (as of September 13, 1833). Also in these cases the counterparty specifies that

> where the Italian language is spoken, the cash, meaning species that can be counted, of a material with weight be it gold, silver or mixed metals which can be spent, represent credits. They can be demanded or not, at which point do they cease being credits?

Precisely because of this aspect, the document also clarifies the non-coincidence between money changers and bankers, giving us a further valuable description of these activities. The difference lies in the credit and financial transactions carried out, but this difference comes from the greater amount of cash that the banker has available. This reserve allows

[30] ADG, FP, 4/38 Atti causa giudiziaria Romanengo contro Bartolomeo Parodi (1839). In the document is written: "In this book the daily operations on the purchase of commercial contact details are marked, the bills of exchange are registered with the name of the tractors, brokers, indicating the amount of letters in foreign currency, fixed exchange rate, and valuation in our currency".

[31] Sebbene menzionato nel fascicolo il materiale documentario non è conservato nell'attuale archivio.

him to carry out operations that require technical times in the flow of capital between one place and another, times that a currency exchange cannot guarantee. The banker also uses the money he has on deposit for loan or investment activities. The consistency of the reserve in coins and precious metals can be seen from the text in the following passage:

> For example, on one occasion he found himself so flush with cash, that Mr. Parodi had to shore up the floor of the room in which he kept the cash; on another occasion of some fear of public calamity, he invited those who had money deposited with him to withdraw it.

In support of how renowned the reserves of Parodi were, in 1839, he was defined in documentation as "one of the primary bankers, the largest consignor, and receiver of groups, currencies, gold and silver rods"[32] of the Kingdom of Sardinia.

From the examination of the documents mentioned in the aforementioned case and from the books required for the relative judgment, it can be observed how they correspond to the indications provided by Boccardo in his Dictionary, where it is stated that, being that of the banker a commercial activity, it is necessary to keep regular accounts, which are made indispensable by the complexity and frequency of credit and financial affairs.[33] The essential books for bank accounting, according to the Genoese economist, can be divided into two categories. Four main instruments should be included in the first category: the bank's journal, which transcribes transactions in chronological order; the book of current accounts, which contains the operations associated with the names of the people registered in alphabetical order; the ledger, a classification by order of subjects under the title of general accounts; the inventory of activities.

In the second category, also called subsidiary books for accounting, four types of instruments are included: the letter copier which reports daily all correspondence sent by the company; the "batch" of letters received; the book of debtors; the book of signatures of account holders to be used as a comparison for cases of doubt. In addition to these, the cash book, the deposits book, and the book of withdrawals are fundamental.

[32] ADG, FP, 4/38 Atti causa giudiziaria Romanengo contro Bartolomeo Parodi (1839).

[33] *Banchieri*, in Boccardo (1875, 309–318).

Bibliography

Archives

Archivio di Stato di Genova (ASGe).

Fondo Prefettura Francese, 738, Contribuzione patenti (1811).

Archivio Doria di Genova (ADG).

FP, 4/31, Atto notarile contenente la divisione di beni fra Giacomo e Francesco Parodi (1792).

FP, 4/31, Atto relativo all'acquisto di immobili in via Luccoli (1818).

FP, 4/37, Atti causa giudiziaria, Bartolomeo Parodi Carlo Odino e Antonio Romanengo (1833).

FP, 4/38 Atti causa giudiziaria Romanengo contro Bartolomeo Parodi (1839).

FP, 4/39, Patto di famiglia tra Bartolomeo Parodi e il figlio Giacomo, relativo alla ditta bancaria Parodi (1837).

FP, 4/39, Atto costitutivo della ditta bancaria "Ditta Bartolomeo Parodi e figlio" (1868).

FP, 4/39, Atto costitutivo ditta "Ditta bancaria Bartolomeo Parodi e Fratelli" (1874).

FP, 6/50, Tribunale Civile di Genova e Corte d'Appello di Genova, causa Parodi-Castagnola (1852).

FP, 6/51, Procura di Bartolomeo Parodi nei confronti del figlio Giacomo per l'attività bancaria (1833).

FP, 6/51, Procura di Giacomo Parodi nei confronti di Giacomo e Bartolomeo Parodi per l'attività bancaria (1865).

FP, 12/127, Richiesta relativa al controllo dell'imposta sui redditi di ricchezza mobile (1926).

Rothschild Archive London (RAL).

XI/112/116, Parodi (1834).

Archives Nationales du Monde du Travail – Banque Rothschild (ANMT, BR).

BR, 132 AQ 9 P 095, Parodi (1838–1847).

BR, 132 AQ 9 P 096, Parodi (1848–1851).

BR, 132 AQ 9 P 097, Parodi (1852–1855).

BR, 132 AQ 9 P 099, Parodi (1860–1863).

BR, 132 AQ non coté 145, Parodi (1852–1868).

BR, 132 AQ 9 P 207, Parodi (1868–1873).

BR, 132 AQ 9 P 208, Parodi (1874–1877).

BR, 132 AQ 9 P 209, Parodi (1878–1883).

BR, 132 AQ 9 P 210, Parodi (1884–1887).

BR, 132 AQ 9 P 318, Parodi (1888–1892).

BR, 132 AQ 9 P 319, Parodi (1893–1897).

BR, 132 AQ 9 P 320, Parodi (1898–1901).

BR, 132 AQ 9 P 321, Parodi (1902–1914).

Printed Contemporary and Near Contemporary Sources

Almanacco del Ducato di Genova per l'anno 1822. 1822. Genova: Frugoni.

Almanacco del Ducato di Genova per l'anno 1837. 1837. Genova: Frugoni.

Annuario della provincia di Genova pel 1869–1870. 1870. Genova: Ferrando.

Boccardo, Gerolamo. 1857. *Dizionario della Economia Politica e del Commercio*. Torino: S. Franco.

Boccardo, Gerolamo. 1875. *Dizionario universale di economia politica di commercio*. Milano: Treves.

Cavour, Camillo. 1889. *Nouvelles lettres inédites*, edited by Amédée Bert. Torino: L. Roux et C.

Chiozza, Edoardo M. 1874–1875. *Guida commerciale descrittiva di Genova, I*. Genova: C. D'Aste.

Il Cicerone ossia guida di Genova per l'anno 1855. 1855. Genova: Tip. di G. Schenone.

Il Cicerone ossia guida di Genova per l'anno 1857. 1857. Genova: Tip. di G. Schenone.

Il Cicerone, ossia guida in Genova. 1845. Genova: Stamperia Casamara.

Lossa, Augusto. *Annuario Lossa del commercio e dell'industria del Regno d'Italia*. 1868. Firenze.

Lossa, Augusto. *Annuario Lossa del commercio e dell'industria del Regno d'Italia*. 1874. Firenze.

Lunario genovese compilato dal signor Regina e soci. 1830. Genova: Tipografia dei Fratelli Pagano.

Lunario genovese compilato dal signor Regina e soci. 1881. Genova: Tipografia dei Fratelli Pagano.

Mancardi, Francesco. 1874. *Cenni storici sull'amministrazione del debito pubblico del Regno d'Italia e sulle amministrazioni annesse offerti al Parlamento nazionale*, vol. 1. Roma: Stamperia Realeaubert.

Secondary Sources

Aubert, Charles. 1984. *Les De La Rüe. Marchands, magistrats et banquiers. Genève, Gênes (1556–1905)*. Genève: Édition Payot.

Bachi, Riccardo. 1933. "La formazione e l'opera della banca di emissione nel Regno di Sardegna dalla Restaurazione al 1859." *Rivista Bancaria* 14: 899–911.

Balbo, Ivan. 2000. "Banche e banchieri a Torino: identità e strategie (1883–1896)." *Impresa e storia* 21, no. 1: 61–101.

Bergeron, Louis. 1991. "Le premier duc de Galliera dans la Haute Banque parisienne du XIXe siècle." In *I duchi di Galliera. Alta finanza, arte e filantropia tra Genova e l'Europa nell'Ottocento*, 1, edited by G. Assereto, G. Doria, P. Massa Piergiovanni, L. Saginati and L. Tagliaferro, 329–39. Genova: Marietti.

Cavour, Camillo. 1973. *Epistolario*, III (1844–1846), edited by Carlo Pischedda. Firenze: Olschki.bachi.

Coppa, Frank J. 1990. *Cardinal Giacomo Antonelli and papal politics in European affairs*. Albany: State University of New York Press.

Doria, Giorgio. 1969. *Investimenti e sviluppo economico a Genova alla vigilia della Prima Guerra Mondiale* (1815–1882). Milano: A. Giuffrè Editore.

Doria, Giorgio. 1991. "La strategia degli investimenti finanziari di Raffaele De Ferrari dal 1828 al 1876." In *I duchi di Galliera. Alta finanza, arte e filantropia tra Genova e l'Europa nell'Ottocento, 1,* edited by G. Assereto, G. Doria, P. Massa Piergiovanni, L. Saginati and L. Tagliaferro, 449–510. Genova: Marietti.

Felisini, Daniela. 1990. *Le finanze pontificie e i Rothschild. 1830–1870.* Napoli: Edizioni Scientifiche Italiane.

Felisini, Daniela. 2016. *Alessandro Torlonia. The Pope's Banker.* London: Palgrave Macmillan.

Felloni, Giuseppe, ed. 1997. *Moneta, credito e banche in Europa: un millennio di storia.* Genova: Brigati.

Ferrandino, Vittoria, and Maria Rosaria Napolitano, eds. 2014. *Storia d'impresa e imprese storiche. Una visione diacronica.* Milano: FrancoAngeli.

Gille, Bertrand. 1965. *Histoire de la Maison Rothschild, 1, Des origines a 1848.* Genève: Droz.

Rollandi, Maria S. 2014. "Parodi." In *Dizionario biografico degli italiani* 81, 401–5. Roma: Treccani.

Scatamacchia, Rosanna. 2013. "I banchieri questi sconosciuti. Appunti di ricerca (XIX-XX secolo)." In *Studi in ricordo di Tommaso Fanfani*, edited by M. Berti, A. Bianchi, G. Conti, D. Manetti, M. Merger and V. Pinchera, 793–800. Pisa: Pacini.

Segreto, Luciano. 2001. "I banchieri privati e l'industrializzazione italiana." *Impresa e storia* 24, no. 2: 273–306.

CHAPTER 3

Banking Institutions

3.1 Evolution of Banking Institutions

The figure of the banker must be correlated with the analysis of the credit systems. Already since the late Middle Ages, bankers have not been able to satisfy the complex needs linked to the credit market; here, for the purpose of market integration, public stalls and pawnshops take on importance through activities regulated by statutes. The first evidence of these dates back to the fifteenth century and can be identified with the public benches: in Barcelona, the Taula de canvi (1401) and then in Genoa the Banco di San Giorgio (1408).[1] The latter, in addition to handling deposits and transfers, also grants loans guaranteed to the state and to individuals in the form of credit openings in the current account.[2] During the modern age, there was an increase in the number of public banks, both in Italy and abroad, so much so that around 1640 there were 21 in

[1] Felloni (2010), Fratianni (2006, 497–501), and Sieveking (1906).

[2] Felloni (1997, 116; 2008). Felloni points out that the public bank: "it always allows to avoid the use of metallic money thanks to the giro account service offered by the bank to its customers;—very often the bank provides the market with an additional mass of types of payment in the form of a still primitive paper currency, payable on demand. This paper currency is issued to the holder of the deposit in the denominations preferred (and not in fixed denominations), it is nominative and it is transferable only by endorsement (and not by simple delivery)". Concerning this topic read also: De Luca (2003).

L. Maffi, *Private Bankers in the Italian 19th Century*, Palgrave Studies in Economic History, https://doi.org/10.1007/978-3-030-63361-5_3

Italy. In addition to accepting money on deposit, these institutions repay it or transfer it to third parties and perform additional functions in the economic context.[3]

The evolution of these credit systems has led to the development of a more modern banking activity in which convertible banknotes are used, issued in fixed denominations and payable to the bearer, and which provides for the systematic extension of credit to individuals.[4] Exemplary, in this regard, is the role played by the Bank of England, founded in 1694, which can perform the following activities: acceptance and reimbursement of interest deposits, funds reallocation, discount of commercial bills, advances on goods, mortgage loans, trade in precious metals. The Bank can also issue various types of securities (bills, bills of credit, accomptable notes, banknotes) and during the eighteenth century it came to have exclusive rights on the issue of banknotes. The evolution of the banking system is correlated with the new financial needs that developed during the eighteenth century and then even more so in the nineteenth century. There is a strong correlation that economic growth is conditioned by the ability of the banking systems to respond to new needs; it follows that the various European areas develop different models that relate to one another and integrate over time.[5]

By limiting attention to the Italian context, the Napoleonic climate impoverished its financial fabric, particularly affecting private securities, thus distorting the process of capital accumulation of the wealthiest urban classes, linked to investments in government securities.[6] This phenomenon, already mentioned previously, is manifested in a dramatically evident way in Genoa, the most important banking center of the Peninsula. However, the panorama is different in the various pre-unification states and changes from urban to rural contexts. In general,

[3] Concerning public banks: Ugolini (2017). Regarding the financial context read also: Fratianni (2010).

[4] Felloni (1997, 120).

[5] Felloni (1997, 130–132). In France in the mid-nineteenth century, when the Bank of France obtained the role of central bank, the banking system was divided into four types of banks: haute banque or private bank; big credit institutions; banque universelle; land credit bank, cooperative credit bank and colonial credit bank.

[6] Concerning the development of credit systems in Peninsula read: De Luca and Moioli (2008), De Simone (1993), Bernardello (2002), Felisini (2016), Strangio (2001, 2006, 2013), Pinchera (1961), De Luca (2007, 2013a), Piluso (2000, 2002), Levati (1997), and Angeli (1982).

the groups of merchant-bankers, shopkeeper-bankers and private bankers of the main Italian cities have declined and, moreover, many of these actors are newcomers. For the same period, the surviving Banco della Due Sicilie remained the only representative of the public banks.

The credit and financial systems of the pre-unification States have changed since the 1820s both for the use of foreign *haute banque* (which begins to intervene in public finance) and for the establishment of new credit institutions.

After the difficulties of the Napoleonic period, therefore, under the impulse of changed social and economic needs, the credit systems are regenerated by finding new expressions. In the north of the Peninsula, for example, the innovative credit institutions that are developing are destined to spread. First of all, the Savings Banks, which first appeared in Veneto and Lombardy starting in the 1820s. They are institutions aimed at promoting savings in the less well-off classes, through the investment of deposits in safe operations, even if they are not very profitable. As evidence of the social value of these banking activities, profits are used in social assistance and social support activities.[7] At the time of national unification, the most important Savings Banks are those of Milan, Florence, Rome, and Bologna. Essential for the modernization of the country and for its infrastructural, industrial, and commercial development are the credit institutions which, starting from the 1840s and 1850s, were founded, in the form of a joint-stock company, first in Genoa, Turin, and Milan (Commerce and Industry Fund, Sete Bank, General Fund, Discount Fund). These institutions, despite the differences found in their various statutes, accept sums in current accounts and can use the available resources of deposits, funds in bonds and securities, coins and precious metals for invoice financing, advances, purchase and sale of private shares and public securities.

Of fundamental importance for the development of this sector and more generally for the economy is the appearance in Italy of the issuing bank, in the form of a joint-stock company on the initiative of private individuals. In Rome in 1825, a Discount Bank was born, with the possibility of issuing throughout the Papal States, which deals with the discount of bills, mandates, and bonds using tickets payable on sight for the discount. The Bank was short-lived and closed at a loss in 1831.

[7] Cafaro (2000), Cova and Galli (1991), and De Bonis et al. (2012).

Subsequently, in 1834 the Banca Romana was founded by French joint-stock company, which assumed the issuance right and was absorbed in 1850 by the Bank of the Papal States.[8] If the initial experiences in the State of the Church have not had particular success, more satisfactory results are obtained in areas with more lively economies, even if characterized by a shortage of monetary means. This is the case in the Grand Duchy of Tuscany with the Discount Bank of Florence (1826) and in the Kingdom of Sardinia, where the Bank of Genoa was founded in 1844 and the Bank of Turin in 1847, respectively.[9] In 1849, the two banks merged to give rise to the National Bank.[10] Finally, before Italian unification, the Tuscan National Bank (1857) was founded, with functions similar to the equivalent institution already active in the Sardinian state.

In those decades in the Kingdom of Sardinia, there is a structural change, an evolutionary process that has already matured in numerous other economically more advanced European countries. The changes involve public debt management, credit and financial institutions and the money supply.[11] The causes can be traced back to the increase in national and international commercial traffic, to industrial and infrastructure development: new dynamisms that require complex intermediation systems for payments. The market integration and guarantee functions are carried out by the issue and discount banks created in Italy in those decades, performing the function of "lender of last resort" and managing

[8] Graziani (1995).

[9] Felloni (1997, 138). Other issuing banks are also established in the Grand Duchy of Tuscany in Livorno, Siena, Pisa, Arezzo, and Lucca.

[10] Podestà (2004) and Felloni (1997, 138–139). The banking activities that the Bank of Genoa can carry out are: "discount commercial effects in Genoa or Turin, collect bills due in Genoa from private individuals and public administrations, receive free deposits of money in a current account, grant advances against deposit of securities of state, valuable materials, currencies and use of funds in public securities". When the National Bank is founded, the type of operations increases and transforms, especially in relation to the geographic area in which banking activities can take place: "possibility of discounting bills also in other places in the state and abroad; the strict three-month limit for advances and the permission to grant them also on the deposit of raw silks, worked silks and bills payable on other markets".

[11] The French credit and financial system was considered as a model for the economic activities in the period of Italian unification. Gille (1959a), Bouvier (1961), Plessis (1982, 1985), and Cameron (1953). Concerning the books and articles published in nineteenth century: Aycard (1867), Bailleux de Marisy (1872), Bonnet (1864), Coquelin (1848), and Pereire (1866).

liquidity through the issue of paper money.[12] The actors involved in these transformations are numerous, ranging from the central authorities that have to define the economic and financial policies to the economic operators of the credit sector and to the entrepreneurs who, in a changed commercial and industrial context, need capital for development. However, prior to national unification, the economic fragmentation of regional markets, whose operating models are manifold, compounded that in the political arena.[13] In this situation, Genoa develops a modern payment and brokerage system, ahead many other Italian cities, including Milan itself.[14] The Ligurian capital experiments with its own issuing bank and the related technical, money management, and liquidity skills.

A central body for the feedback and guarantee of stability, the Bank of Genoa provides economic operators with an institution of reference in case of liquidity crises, which were not uncommon in that type of economic and financial context.

The early specialization of Genoese credit operators and the commitments made in setting up discount and issue banks are a direct consequence of the skills acquired and accumulated over time in terms of banking, finance, commercial activities and, of course, the presence of capital. Let's remember that the operators of the city have consolidated their international relations since the Ancien Régime.

It is therefore essential to study the role of Genoese bankers to identify the aspects of innovation and modernization, but also to detect their persistence or inertia with respect to change.

The banker systematically interprets the market mechanisms and, in the contractual aspects of banking operations, combines the fiduciary factor with customers and other bankers. It is a mixture of theoretical reflection and practical rules that also outlines the profile of "central bankers", that is, those who have responsibility for governing currency and guaranteeing the entire credit system.[15]

In this regard, an aspect that historiography has not yet investigated in detail on the Italian scene is represented by the relations between

[12] Piluso (1999, 9–16) and Landes (1956), "Vieille banque," 202–222.

[13] De Luca and Moioli (2008), De Simone (1993), Bertini (1994), De Rosa (2004), Avallone (2014), Polsi (1993), and De Luca (2013b).

[14] Piluso (1999, 10), Cafaro (1990, 159–168), Licini (1997), and De Luca (2007).

[15] Ugolini (2017), Goodhart (1988), Toniolo (1995), and Hawtrey (1932). Concerning Italian monetary history read: Fratianni and Spinelli (1997).

private bankers and the foundation of issuing and credit institutions, in a process of integration of Italian credit systems which began in the decades preceding national unification.[16]

Giandomenico Piluso, inspired by international historiographic literature, observes that there is an important two-way link between central bankers and private bankers, mainly resting on two dynamics. On the one hand, the arrival of private bankers to manage money and the system (as in the English case)[17]; on the other, the central banker, having to govern the entire system, is required to reflect on the fundamental mechanisms of money and credit and, in order to do this, he needs close relationships with private bankers with their fingers the pulse of the real market.

Genoese bankers, therefore, are able to found an Issue and Discount Bank and to become "proto" central-bankers.[18] This bank is not only relevant in the context of the city, but it is relevant for the entire Kingdom of Sardinia and subsequently for the Kingdom of Italy, thanks to Genoese professionals of the caliber of Carlo Bombrini, General Manager.

3.2 The Context of the Kingdom of Sardinia

In the first half of the nineteenth century in the Sardinian states, the change in the credit and payment systems began in 1816, in full Restoration period. A monetary reform took place that introduced the decimal system and bimetallism. However, the development path becomes more evident since the 1940s: the creation of discount and circulation banks is flanked by the implementation of a new commercial code and reforms in the payment system.[19] All of the Kingdom's private banks are organized with family-owned capital and small investment activities. They specialize in credit and commercial activities and are run for a specific

[16] Conte (1990, 13–24) and Scatamacchia (2008).

[17] Cassis (1984, 2006) and Cassis and Cottrell (2009).

[18] Conte (1990) and Doria (1969). It is not possible to define the Bank of Genoa as a central bank and it is not possible to define its chief as a centrale banker in a contemporary way. The Bank of Genoa does not have all the control and inspection functions typical of all the contemporary central banks. For this reason, I use proto-bank and proto-central banker to describe this type of process.

[19] Conte (1990, 13–24). Concerning the economic development of the Kingdom of Sardinia: Cibrario (1852), Rosselli (1954), Romeo (1975), and Castronovo (1965). Regarding the economic context of Genoa in that period refer: Quaglia (1846), Bertolotti (1834), and Cevasco (1838).

profit purpose. Therefore, most of them are not suited to support innovations for modernization (the aforementioned investments in railway construction companies and public loan financial operations). The most important banks in the state are Parodi and De La Rue in Genoa (with a turnover of ten and three million, respectively), Nigra, Bolmida, and Barbaroux in Turin.[20]

As mentioned earlier, the increase in transactions and changes in payment methods and the opening of new credit disbursement scenarios encourage innovation. In some European areas, the changes are more rapid, in others they have difficulty manifesting themselves: in both cases, the positive trend of trade and the development of the industrial sector stimulate the dynamics of improvement.

The Genoese protectionist trade policy was characteristic of the thirty years following the end of the Napoleonic age.[21] In addition to damaging exchange activities, it inhibits the credit system renewal. On the other hand, it should be noted that public institutions, such as the Cassa de' Censi, the Compagnia di San Paolo, and some pawnbrokers, only indirectly play the role of supporting production activities. In addition to the most important bankers in the Kingdom, some international businessmen operating in Genoa and Turin also have relationships with the most important European haute banques involved in the most modern financial enterprises: Luigi and Vincenzo Bolmida and Raffaele de Ferrari Duke of Galliera.

[20] Doria (2001, 171–173).

[21] Concerning the economic context of the Kingdom of Sardinia, with focus on Liguria, the observations of Leandro Conte are important, because they underline how economic stagnation initially disadvantaged the development of significant innovations in the credit and payment systems. Conte also describes the credit and financial transactions of these private bankers of the Kingdom of Sardinia: "Working almost exclusively on the main cities, the function performed by these institutes was the following: regulation of the offer of international payment services operated in the transfer bill of exchange; transfer precious metal to discount of bills of exchange; advances on public securities; credit openings to a limited number of customers. The economic culture behind these choices was based on the acquisition of profit and not on the operational qualitative growth of credit. It looked at the sum of the financial speculations of each individual bank deal. Due to this way of operating, the main activities were: buying and selling of public debt securities issued by European states; currency transactions; financing of production activities that required seasonal increases of financial liquidity (e.g. silk); of individual financial projects. It was a credit activity that maintained expectations of other short-term profits, which could be carried out by mobilizing relatively small capital": Conte (1990, 23–24). A different point of view regarding this topic: Bergier (1985).

In the early 1840s, awareness of the need to overcome the sector's limits grew among private and financial bankers, the protagonists of the Kingdom's credit system. This need derives from the absence of an issue and discount bank similar to those present in France and England.[22]

The three decades of stagnation between the end of the Napoleonic era and the 1940s aren't encouraging for Genoa. However, if attention is focused on the final period of the thirty years in question, one may be surprised at the abundance of capital which was present in the city. The opening of the Banca di Genova (1844) is the demonstration that in the first half of that decade sufficient resources are available in the Ligurian capital to start considerable credit and financial transactions.[23]

The abundance of capital on the exchange is well known to the protagonists of the Genoese credit and financial system of that time, so much so that Bartolomeo Parodi himself, as president of the regency council of the Bank of Genoa, in a speech dated 13 July 1847 says that in Genoa there is such a large amount of money that "if it were paid into the bank's coffers it would greatly increase the number of bank notes in circulation".[24]

The immobility of that period, understood as the apparent absence of capital, attributable to the financial distress of the Napoleonic era, is interpreted by the historian Carlo M. Cipolla in the key of "collective propensity to treasure", a fruitless saving that is "a tremendously depressive force on the Ligurian economy" and, therefore, one of the foremost reasons for the stagnation of the productive sectors and trade in those three decades. However, such an assumption does not fully explain the causes of the phenomenon.[25] Giorgio Doria specifies how it is necessary to investigate the origin of this propensity and to figure out the possible reasons that predispose it to the accumulation of gold and silver.[26] The establishment of these significant financial reserves can, in retrospect, be considered a positive aspect as these resources prove necessary for the leap that will characterize the development of the Genoese economy in the

[22] This legal form allowed the new bank to have sufficient capital to carry out financing activities suited to the needs of the commercial background; it also allowed the bank to ensure liquidity in the business market by issuing banknotes, whose convertibility was guaranteed.

[23] Doria (1969, 6–10; 2001, 171–173).

[24] Doria (1969, 9–10).

[25] Cipolla (1953) and Grendi (1964).

[26] Doria (1969).

Cavour decade. Indeed, this capital is already fundamental in the previous decade, effectively constituting the basis for the development of those financial and credit institutions capable of making Genoa the protagonist of the foundation of the issuing bank. In this context, private bankers are configured as promoters of the establishment of a "proto central bank" in the Kingdom of Sardinia and, at the same time, offering themselves as bankers at the helm of the same bank. The economic and financial situation outlines their role as guarantors of the system. The formation of capital and the propensity to save by the Genoese are therefore useful for the development of the city, and also for that of the entire country.

In Genoa, interest in the issuing bank develops as a consequence of the growing demand for money, due to the difficulty in payments, which leads to an increase in gold imports from France.[27] Coin minting in the city mint increased by 15.67% in the early 1940s compared to the five-year period 1835–1839. The opening of the Bank of Genoa, on the other hand, decreases coinage: from around 6 million in 1844 to 2.5 million in 1845 to 1.9 million in 1846 to 1.7 million in 1847.

The commercial code in force since 1842 provides that the foundation of anonymous companies is authorized through the Regie Patenti, after a positive opinion from the Council of State.[28] The Marquis Carlo Alfieri di Sostegno, in charge of studying and discussing the project, in his Report highlights some significant aspects to understand the economic culture of those who propose the foundation of the institute.[29] He focuses on how the project is presented by the "main bankers and shopkeepers of the city of Genoa", who propose the creation of an institution "recognizing the advantages that the existence of a deposit, discount and current accounts institution. It points to the main exchanges in Europe both for the ease of doing business and the increase in commercial affairs, and to ease the frequent shortages of gold and silver coins with the ability of printing paper currency". Furthermore, he observes how important it is to insert paper currency into payment systems by discounting bills. Genoese bankers clearly have an interest in setting up the bank because an increase in liquidity is triggered by the very operations they are called upon to carry out. Being themselves the main economic operators of the

[27] Felloni (1956).

[28] *Codice di Commercio* (1842, art. 46).

[29] Conte (1990, 29–30).

exchange, this foundation allows the increase of their profits as private bankers.[30]

It is precisely in this context of renewed capitaly availability and propensity to save, related to the growth of capital itself, that in the first half of the 1840s, at the end of the bureaucratic process, the Banca di Genova was established. The founders are private bankers, shopkeepers, entrepreneurs, and financiers: Giuliano Cataldi, Giacomo Oneto, Pellegrino Rocca, Marco Massone, Francesco Pavese, Giuseppe Carmignani, Raffaele de Ferrari duke of Galliera, Bartolomeo Parodi (owner of the main private city bank). In the first years of the bank's life, they hold the main roles, from the office of president to those of regency advisers. Citizen private bankers therefore play a decisive role in establishing the Issuing Bank.

The founders of the bank act on their own experience and personal interests with the aim of absorbing the innovations that run through the contemporary and European credit and financial world, exploiting their implicit impulses, thus leading the Genoese market toward new current strategies.

The first years of the institute's life are influenced by two currents of thought regarding the line of management to be implemented: one privileges the territoriality of action, concentrating operations in the local area and ensuring the achievement of results in terms of substantial share dividends. The second strategic line of thought, which is destined to prevail, is more focused on guaranteeing liquidity to the economic system that the institution is called upon to provide, while running the risk of placing the bank in a debt position and, consequently, guaranteeing lower profits than those that could be obtained with more lucrative investments. Its direct implementation is clearly recognizable in the management of Carlo Bombrini, director of the institute. He expands the bank's activities to the main business areas of the Kingdom, making it an active party in favor of the silk market by giving loans according to the planned strategies, at the Regie Finanze both in 1846 and in 1847.

The Banca di Genova therefore began its business with national scope. In September 1848, it proceeded to issue non-convertible paper currency to implement a 20 million lire loan to the state; this loan was exacted

[30] Conte (1990, 28).

by decree following the emergency caused by the ongoing War of Independence. A measure of this magnitude naturally provokes hostile and worried reactions among the board members. But management's philosophy, backed by an influential political framework, held sway. The merger between the "Banca di Genova" and the "Banca di Torino" was implemented in December 1849: the National Bank, with headquarters in Genoa, has shown since its inception the importance of the Genoese capital in the new credit and issuing institution.[31]

3.3 Genoa During the Cavour Decade

During the 1850s, Genoa witnessed notable economic development accompanied by strong demographic growth. The population grew by over 27.5% from 100,184 in 1849 to 127,735 in 1861.[32] The relative stability over the previous thirty years had gradually laid the groundwork for growth during the decade under Cavour (1852–1861). Capital accumulation and the development of credit and finance systems were fundamental elements in enabling subsequent transformations. New ideas both within and outside of the Genoese economic and political sphere began to take form starting especially in the 1840s, with Genoa playing an important role in development of the Kingdom of Sardinia.[33] External impulses came from Carlo Cattaneo, Camillo Benso di Cavour, and Ilarione Petitti di Roreto, who all agreed that Genoa played an indispensable role in commerce and banking, that the Kingdom's customs policies needed reworking, and that the need to build modern terrestrial infrastructure to connect Genoa to the Po River Valley could no longer be put off.[34] The implementation of concrete plans that allowed the city to capitalize on its strategic role became possible with Cavour in government aiming to modernize the State, giving a strong boost to the construction of railways, with the Genoa-Turin line one of the

[31] Doria (1991), Calzavarini (1969), and Coppini (1994).

[32] Doria (2001, 171–173). For the political and social context: Montale (1999), Felloni (1961), and Guglielmino (1940).

[33] Marongiu (2011).

[34] Doria (2001, 184–185), Marchese (1957a, b, 1959), Abrate (1961), Grendi (1964), Doria (1969, 120–124), Giacchero (1980, 126–137), Rollandi (1991), and Virgilio (1869).

prime objectives.[35] This infrastructure also meant more business for the port, with prospects for direct connections to France and Switzerland. Cavour's plans also called for dedicating the port of Genoa exclusively to commercial purposes, moving the navy to La Spezia and redeveloping the Genoa harbor by building docks. The demilitarization of the entire Genoa area, including the decommissioning of the forts surrounding the city and the transfer of the naval arsenal, met with resistance from the main players in the Ligurian economy, who were quite understandably alarmed at the potential upheaval of their local interests. The merchants and entrepreneurs associated with the Chamber of Commerce, who were in favor of the initiatives on the table, were opposed by forces characterized by provincialism and strong hostility toward Turin.[36]

The more favorable economic conditions and renewed dialogue with the Piedmont government allowed the development of new business ventures. This took place in a number of sectors, first among them steam shipping and transportation.[37] One of the major players in the latter sector was Raffaele Rubattino, a pioneering entrepreneur who had founded the "Compagnia lombarda d'assicurazione marittima" [Lombard Maritime Insurance Company] in 1837 with the support of capital from Milan. He had use of two steamships in 1839 and added five more by 1845, providing regular service between Genoa, Marseille, and other ports in Italy. Plans also called for routes to Sardinia, a project that enjoyed strong support in the press from the Genoa Chamber of Commerce. Rubattino also presented the project to Prince Eugenio di Savoia Carignano with a request for public funding. As regards land transport, his "Impresa Omnibus" began providing urban public transportation (horse-buses) in 1841 between Genoa and Sampierdarena, a populous industrial area. The following year he began providing the first daily connections between Genoa and Milan with couriers on horseback.

Traditional production, based on a cottage industry and outdated methods of work organization, gradually lost its competitiveness, a situation made even more difficult in the 1840s by the reduction of customs duties. At the same time, new businesses and activities sprang up that

[35] Arese (1953) and Guderzo (1961).

[36] Rollandi (2011).

[37] Doria (1990, 13–64; 2001, 187; 2011), Rollandi (2008, 2010, 2011), Piccione (2010), and Tonizzi (2000, 2010).

brought new life to the local economy, with an inevitable impact on finance and credit: in 1846, Genoa commissioned public lighting to the French "Compagnie d'Eclairage par le Gaz" [Gaslight Company]; the Pezzi and Belleydier foundries in Cogoleto and Sampierdarena, respectively, and the metalworking shops Westermann in Sestri Ponente and Taylor e Prandi in Sampierdarena boosted employment and capital production.

The 1850s were characterized by economic development both in Genoa and internationally. Technological innovation raised GDP both in Europe and in the United States.[38] Growth was further stimulated by the adoption of free-trade policies in numerous countries coupled with a revolution in transportation (rail and steamships) that boosted international commerce. The economic relations between the Kingdom of Sardinia and other countries also expanded, this including ties to the United Kingdom, a leader in trade and engine of economic development in Europe and around the world. A tangible sign of relations with the UK was the influx of English capital into Italy: in 1851, the Hambro bank floated Sardinian securities on the London Stock Exchange; in 1855, the English government lent two million pounds to the Savoy government in exchange for the latter's involvement in the Crimean War; that same year, British capital was invested in the Tuscan and Lombard-Veneto railways. From 1854 to 1860, British exports to Italy doubled (from 2.17 to 4.5 million pounds) while imports from Italy remained stable.[39]

In detail, the Genoese economy benefited in those years not only from the above factors, but also from the policies of the Cavour administration, whose economic mindset developed in the 1840s under liberalist influence.[40] The concrete outcome of Cavour's thinking included public works projects and the implementation of new strategies for regulating trade. The former, aiming to modernize the infrastructure in Italy generally, in Liguria took the form of improved connections between the port of Genoa and the cities of the Po River Valley and with other European trading partners. In terms of trade legislation, starting in 1850 a series

[38] Doria (2008) and Mori (1989).

[39] Bolchini (1969), Allen (2001), Cassis et al. (1995), and Cassis (1997).

[40] Cavour was Minister of Agriculture and Commerce in 1850 with the D'Azeglio government; in 1851 he also assumed leadership of the Ministry of Finance; in 1852 he began his first term as Prime Minister, maintaining this role in four governments until his death in 1861.

of trade treaties were signed with France, England, Belgium, Switzerland, and the Netherlands, containing agreements with clear free-trade inspiration. In keeping with the policy direction of the Cavour government, differential duties, which had made the port of Genoa a rather expensive stop for foreign merchant fleets, were abolished that same year.[41]

The decade maintained a constant upward trend in trade, port traffic, infrastructure (harbor and rail), and industry.[42] The changes introduced by the railway certainly had a major impact. The Turin-Genoa line was completed in 1853 and inaugurated the following year. In 1860, work began on two lines connecting Genoa to the French border to the west and to Tuscany to the southeast.[43] The positive effects of the establishment of these connections are evident if we compare travel times and costs on the routes in question. Freight transport time from Genoa to Turin dropped from 6–7 days to just over 6 hours. Here too, Genoa proved to be the most advantageous transit and exchange point for the Kingdom of Sardinia, reflecting the Kingdom's policy of renewal.

3.4 Credit and Finance During the Cavour Decade

The 1850s marked a phase of great transformation for the world economy, triggered and accelerated by sweeping technological innovations, not least among them the development of railway networks. Other factors had more to do with credit and finance, such as the intensification of international economic relations, greatly facilitated by the telegraph, the new organization of credit to industry, and also the boom in gold production in California and Australia.[44]

This was the context for the development of the credit and finance industry in Genoa. Its principal private bankers maintained relations with some of the main houses in the European *haute banque*. An emblematic case is the Banque Rothschild of Paris, which had dealings over the

[41] Doria (1969, 120–124).

[42] Doria (2008, 233–244).

[43] Guderzo (1961, 2018).

[44] Bachi (1936).

decade with the following Italian banks: Parodi,[45] Pescio,[46] De La Rüe,[47] Ricci,[48] Gastaldi-Spigno,[49] Massone,[50] Cataldi,[51] Dapples et C,[52] and Leonino.[53] In most cases, these dealings involved money lending but there was also some financial activities, especially with Parodi, Gastaldi, and Leonino, with the purchase or sale of public securities on the Genoa stock market (discussed in greater detail in Chapter 4) and trading in shares of companies quoted on the Genoa Stock Exchange. The Genoese maintained relations with the major stock markets in the 1850s, i.e., London and Paris, cities where Duke De Ferrari operated at the highest levels of international finance[54]; in these years he influenced the strategic choices of the most important Parisian banking houses toward investment in innovative sectors, such as the railroads. Thus, during the Cavour decade, merchant bankers conducting traditional banking and commercial activities, with generally modest business volumes, coexisted with more modern private bankers such as the Parodis, involved in the initiatives of international private banking.

The Parodis were among the few Genoese private bankers to establish and invest in new banks in the Ligurian capital, demonstrating their ability to interpret the needs of the new markets, as they had in the previous decade as promoters of the Banca di Genova. The increased opportunities for investing capital boosted their initiative and gave them a leadership position in the modernization of the credit system in the

[45] ANMT, BR, 132 AQ 9 P 096, Parodi (1848–1851), 132 AQ 9 P 097, Parodi (1852–1855) and 132 AQ 9 P 099, Parodi (1860–1863).

[46] ANMT, BR, 132 AQ 9 P 102, Pescio (1843–1855).

[47] ANMT, BR, 132 AQ 9 P 058, De La Rue (1840–1865).

[48] ANMT, BR,132 AQ non coté 160, Ricci (1840–1859).

[49] ANMT, BR,132 AQ 9 P 070, Spigno Gastaldi (1851–1852), 132 AQ 9 P 071, Spigno Gastaldi (1853–1855), 132 AQ 9 P 072, Spigno Gastaldi (1856–1857) and 132 AQ 9 P 073, Spigno Gastaldi (1858–1860).

[50] ANMT, BR, 132 AQ 9 P 090, Massone (1846–1852).

[51] ANMT, BR, 132 AQ non coté 35, Cataldi (1851–1867).

[52] ANMT, BR, 132 AQ non coté 45, Dapples et C. (1858–1867).

[53] ANMT, BR, 132 AQ non coté 112, Leonino (1846–1866).

[54] Regarding Raffaele De Ferrari's financial activities and business and political relations: Doria (1991). Regarding foreign investments in the Italian peninsula and the role of international finance in the modernization of the country: Cameron (1961).

Kingdom of Sardinia and, more generally, all of Italy through the establishment of new, more solidly endowed credit institutes constituted as joint-stock corporations. It is no coincidence that these private bankers traded in government securities in synergy with international players dealing in these first large-scale operations with Piedmont debt. Collaborating with the Rothschilds were Parodi and Gastaldi-Spigno in Genoa, and Bolmida[55] and Mestrezat[56] in Turin.

These relations not only highlight the role of certain private bankers but also their dense network of relations with the principal players in the main European marketplaces: Rothschild, Blanc-Mathieu et C., Hottinguer, Pillet-Will, and Odier in Paris, and Rothschild, Baring, Anderson, and Hambro in London.

Ricci, Bolmida, and Mestrezat invested in the Cassa del Commercio e dell'Industria, established in Turin with notarial deed of December 18, 1852 and authorized by royal decree on January 23, 1853; Parodi, De La Rüe, Cataldi, Ricci, Gastaldi, and Oneto invested in the Cassa Generale, established with notarial deed of June 12, 1856 and authorized by royal decree on July 8, 1856; Ricci invested in the Cassa di Sconto di Genova, established on September 10, 1856 and authorized on October 9, 1856.[57]

All the above-mentioned bankers already owned numerous shares in the Banca Nazionale negli Stati Sardi.[58] Genoese capital also represented a consolidated portion of the Banca Nazionale, growing from 24.72% in 1850 to 53.47% following the increase in share capital in 1852–1853. This dominant role of Genoese capital is explained by the capacity of the Genoese merchant class to accumulate and invest financial resources, attracted by the stability of the bank's stock, thanks to the acumen of its director, Carlo Bombrini, a Genoese. Marco Doria observes that "beyond and more than in the acquisition of shares in the issuing bank, significant portions of savings are invested in government bonds, whose value grew

[55] The correspondence between Rothschild Bank and Bolmida is collected in: ANMT, BR, 132 AQ 9 P 033, Bolmida (1849–1853), 132 AQ 9 P 034, Bolmida (1854–1855), 132 AQ 9 P 035, Bolmida (1857), 132 AQ 9 P 036, Bolmida (1858–1859), 132 AQ 9 P 037, Bolmida (1860–1861) and Banque Rothschild, 132 AQ 9 P 038, Bolmida (1862–1865).

[56] ANMT, BR,132 AQ 9 P 089, Mestrezat (1843–1852).

[57] Da Pozzo and Felloni (1964, 243–258, 259–279, 282–301).

[58] Conte (1990) and Scatamacchia (2008).

nearly ninefold from 130 million lire in 1848 to 1.119 billion lire in 1860. This was possible thanks to increase in income and savings, as witnessed by the increased level of debt—and thus the possibility of investing the capital from savings accounts—in the local banking system".[59]

The Parodis were also among the most enterprising promoters of the establishment of additional joint-stock banks. They were endowed with great ambition, economic competence, and consolidated political ties. An interesting example is the plan to establish a second bank of issue in the Kingdom of Sardinia under the name of Banca Sarda.[60]

The dynamism of the Parodi dynasty continued when Giacomo joined Bartolmeo at the helm; Giacomo was member for many years of the Council of Regency of the Genoa offices of the Banca Nazionale, acting as an important liaison between the bank and the government. One example of his skill as a mediator and the sterling reputation he enjoyed is his appointment to the committee assembled to negotiate with the Ministry of Finance at a crucial juncture in the bank's history. On November 21, 1857, on behalf of the commission composed of Parodi, Bombrini, and Cataldi, he reported to the Council of Regency that he had presented to the Minister of Finance[61]:

> the critical situation of the bank, which prevented it from adequately subsidizing commerce [...] and to have—as a means for alleviating the bank's difficult situation—submitted to him the proposition that the government transfer to the bank eighteen million lire in six-month treasury bonds to offer for discounting to the Rothschild bank in Paris, and to import the equivalent amount in cash.

The successful negotiations with the minister were paralleled by those with the Maison Rothschild. It is important to underscore the active presence of a member of the Parodi family in the management of this particular situation, highlighting the degree to which the personal and professional relations of the family benefited the Banca Nazionale, consolidating the strategic role of the Parodis within it and expanding their influence, which was already significant given their stock portfolio. And

[59] Doria (2008).

[60] Romeo (1977, 503–506). The attempt to establish the Banca Sarda is discussed further in the following section.

[61] Conte (1990, 193).

there was a clear dual positive outcome for the family, both as bankers themselves and as shareholders in the Banca Nazionale.

As we have already seen, the Parodis were also among the founders of the Cassa Generale, established in Genoa in 1856 with share capital of eight million lire in 32,000 shares purchased in unknown proportions by the seven founders: Ditta Bartolomeo Parodi e Figlio, Ditta Bancaria Fratelli Cataldi, Ditta Bancaria Giuseppe Ricci, Ditta Bancaria Leonardo Gastaldi e C., Francesco Oneto, Banca De la Rüe e C., and the merchant Andrea Croce. The business of the bank consisted of the following: discounting bills of exchange and promissory notes with at least two signatories and term of six months or less; extending loans against deposits of government bonds, treasury bonds, company shares, coin, or gold or silver bullion; extending loans against the value of ships; accepting deposits in transactional accounts; and extending credit against appropriate guarantees or in exchange for securities. According to its original bylaws, the bank could acquire government bonds and treasury bonds but not shares in joint-stock companies. In 1861, the original bylaws were revised and the bank was allowed to trade in these shares; with the royal decree of April 7, it was also authorized to extend credit to businesses for the acquisition of capital equipment.[62] It was thus a bank established to meet medium- and long-term credit needs of businesses involved in the industrial sectors that contributed to and participated in the modernization of the country.

In addition to banks, the Parodis were involved in many other financial activities, extending their presence into spheres and enterprises that were often at the cutting edge with regard to the evolution of Italian markets. To better understand the extent to which the Genoese banking world was tempted and predisposed by its nature to tap into the potentials of innovation—both technological and economic—worthy of note is the initiative dating back to 1826 of a group of Genoese entrepreneurs and bankers to build a railroad from Genoa to the Po River Valley.[63] Indeed, it is a significant testament to the ambition and forward thinking of the Ligurians that they were building their first railways at the same time that the British were building the Liverpool-Manchester line, the world's first intercity railroad (1830), which had none of the gradient challenges poses

[62] Da Pozzo and Felloni (1964, 259–279) and Doria (1969, 161–166).

[63] Morabito (1991), Rossi and Nitti (1968, 33), and Doria (1969, 91–93).

by the Apennines. The 1826 plan affirmed the investments in infrastructure development undertaken by the Sardinian state in keeping with the revolution in transportation emerging in that period in other European nations as well. Failing to win approval, the plan was presented again on other occasions, accompanied by reports illustrating its feasibility and utility.[64] A new plan was "submitted to the Royal Throne" in January 1837 by Bartolomeo Parodi, Cesare Cavagnari, and Raffaele Pratolongo for "the construction of a road of iron rails that would extend from Genoa to the Po and the Ticino rivers, and, if advantageous, also to Turin".[65]

As regards the legal status of the enterprise, it is interesting to note that the proponents requested the establishment in Genoa of "a joint-stock company named Società Nazionale della via ferrata Albertina". The associated document described the composition of the corporation, with share capital of 22 million lire divided into 25,000 shares and Parodi as "depositary banker". While not approved, the plan evidences how up-to-date Genoese bankers and merchants were on economic trends and their ability to set up a joint-stock company with a large capital endowment. As for the outcome of the proposed railway, it was not until 1845 that the *Regie Patenti* [royal patents] were published for its construction, which was taken out of the hands of private enterprise and funded by the Piedmont government, which naturally favored the Turin-Genoa line.

Another type of enterprise actively supported by the Parodis was insurance. In the late 1840s and throughout the 1850s, Genoa witnessed a boom in joint-stock corporations, which played an essential role in the economy of a city whose maritime traffic was one of its primary economic resources. The Parodis immediately invested in some of these corporations, also assuming directorial roles (Table 3.1). Bartolomeo Parodi was treasurer in the following corporations: Compagnia dei Generosi Rinnovata; Compagnia dell'Unione; Compagnia Nuova di Assicurazioni; and Compagnia Nuova Generale. Giacomo Parodi was the treasurer for the Compagnia di Assicuratori Nazionali, Prima Rinnovazione.[66]

[64] ADG, FP, 4/40, Progetto d'una strada di ferro fra Genova, il Piemonte, e la Lombardia (1826).

[65] ADG, FP, 5/43, Documenti relativi alla costruzione di una strada ferrata tra Genova e il Po e poi Torino (1837).

[66] ASGe, Fondo Camera di Commercio, 25 and 199.

Table 3.1 Insurance companies for which Bartolomeo and Giacomo Parodi held the position of Treasurer in the 1840s

Company	*Year*	*Capital (lire)*
Compagnia di Assicuratori Nazionali, Prima Rinnovazione	1842	355,000
Compagnia dei Generosi Rinnovata	1846	130,000
Compagnia dell'Unione	1847	1,000,000
Compagnia Nuova di Assicurazioni	1849	250,000
Compagnia Nuova Generale	1849	400,000

Source ASGe, Fondo Camera di Commercio, 25 and 199

Private bankers played a decisive role in this period, especially in virtue of their dual function: promoter of diversified initiatives; mediator between the savings of the Genoese and the financial market.

The Cavour decade thus witnessed a notable change in the industrial context of Genoa, whose social fabric accommodated the growth of a new elite acting as a direct interface with the Piedmont government. The new actors include Bombrini, Rubattino, Nicolay, and Orlando, who envisioned a well-defined model of economic development, based on the total rejection of rivalry between Genoa and Turin. The anti-Piedmont tones in local politics were thus banished along with a municipality-centric vision. Genoa was now cultivating a fully national vision in its industrial aspirations.[67]

3.5 Competition Among Banks and the Institution of a Central Bank

Cavour's initiatives to support the economic and financial development of Piedmont in the early 1850s reflected, on the one hand, the statesman's desire to free the State of its bonds to the Rothschilds and, on the other, the attempt to define and then strengthen the functions of a banking institute that would be able to embody the role of a central bank, in spite of doubts in Piedmont at the time regarding the specific functions of such a bank and its function as currency regulator.[68]

[67] Doria (1969, 120–124) and Gille (1968).

[68] Romeo (1977, 503–506), Gille (1959b), Demarco (1988), and Decugis (1979).

As regards the aspiration to break free of the Rothschilds, an explicit signal was sent out in 1851, precisely when the most important private bankers in the Kingdom of Sardinia were engaged in trade in Piedmont government securities (5% Rendita bond) issued in 1849–1850 via contracts with the Parisian banker family. Cavour made overtures to Hambro of London in search of a new loan. He initially worked through the Genoese banker Emile de la Rüe, a trusted friend, who went to visit Carl Joachim Hambro in London in the summer of 1851 with the goal of convincing him to issue a loan of four million pounds to the Kingdom of Sardinia. The event is ably analyzed by Giuseppe Berta, who points out the various risks involved in the operation.[69] Cavour turned to Hambro following a similar proposal by Vittorio Emanuele II's ambassador to the powerful Barings, who demurred, not wanting to challenge the Rothschilds, the latter having loans with the Grand Duchy of Tuscany, the Kingdom of the Two Sicilies, the Papal State, as well as the Kingdom of Sardinia, in some cases dating back to the end of the Napoleonic era.

Hambro, on the other hand, accepted the challenge and negotiated a loan to the Kingdom of Sardinia with Cavour and the former Minister of Finance, Ottavio Thaon de Revel, to be floated in London. The banker personally underwrote 10% of the loan and issued bonds at 85% of their face value. The investors thus earned a premium of 15% at expiry as well as 5% annual interest. However, the operation was initially a disaster because the Rothschilds promptly blocked placement of Kingdom of Sardinia bonds on the Amsterdam and Brussels stock markets, causing the quotation to fall to 80%. At that point, the London banker assumed the risk and kept a large quantity of "Sardinia-securities" in his portfolio. And indeed, a few months later the bond was quoted at 82%, eventually rising to 87%, exceeding the issue price of 85%.

Cavour's attempt to strengthen the Banca Nazionale, pursuing his model of a central bank, dated to the same year. On May 24, he introduced a bill authorizing the Banca Nazionale to double its capital (from 8 to 16 million lire) to allow its banknotes to be used as legal tender, to open two branches, in Nice and Vercelli, and to allow the institute to assume the functions of "State treasurer". However, Cavour's initiative met with immediate resistance in parliament under the banner of freedom in banking. Cavour sought a middle road, limiting his plan to

[69] Berta (1990) and Conti and Schisani (2011, 155).

allowing the bank to issue legal tender until the end of the year while awaiting negotiations with the Banca Nazionale, but again unsuccessfully. His proposal to institute a bank with authority over the others was based on criteria of greater rationality and modernity in a context where the fiat currency was, as Rosario Romeo observes, "merely a necessary concession to induce the Bank to increase its capital (which would have distributed profits over a larger number of shares and thus reduced the advantages of the current shareholders) and hence to make more extensive resources available to commerce and, if needed, to the State, which would thus emerge strengthened with respect to great financial powers such as the Rothschilds".[70]

Negotiations continued with the Banca Nazionale, leading to the introduction of a new bill in parliament on March 19, 1852: the status of legal tender was now proposed for ten years and the bank was obliged to advance up to 5 million lire to the State, assume the functions of state treasurer, and exchange banknotes in the provincial treasuries. However, at the end of the month of April, a new factor emerged that affected negotiations as well as Cavour's position, prompting him to threaten to withdraw the bill. The change was the initiative of a group of private bankers of Turin and Genoa promoting the establishment of a new bank, the Banca Sarda, with capital of 16 million lire but without the privilege of issuing legal tender. At this point, the Banca Nazionale revised its position and entered negotiations with a new stance. However, the government went into crisis in May, culminating in Cavour's resignation. His successor, Luigi Cibrario, found himself confronted, in early June, with the unexpected withdrawal of the proposal to establish the Banca Sarda by the people originally promoting it, as well as the reversal of position of the Banca Nazionale, which proposed increasing its capital to 32 million, and this time without the privilege of issuing legal tender.[71]

As aptly expressed by Rosario Romeo,[72] the situation is not easily interpreted. However, considered once again from the point of view

[70] Romeo (1977, 505).

[71] Rossi and Nitti (1968) and Romeo (1963).

[72] Romeo (1977, 507–508): "It is difficult to determine whether the Banca Sarda episode was a bluff on Cavour's part to prompt the Banca Nazionale to reduce its demands, as some of his contemporaries suspected, or, as some documents suggest, a genuine attempt to create a competing bank, which was later abandoned and replaced with an agreement between two financial groups, as others supposed. However, it is a

of the dynamics of the banking system, it highlights the cardinal role of private bankers in Genoa and Turin and the extent to which they played an active role in determining the development of the country's economic policies, even in the direction of competition among banks. Although the negotiations were anything but simple, in 1851–1852 relations were strengthened between the Banca Nazionale and the State in a solution that was quite probably advantageous for all parties and allowed private bankers to play a determining role in the operations of the Banca Nazionale.

Documentation from the Banque Rothschild of Paris provides additional information regarding these events, supporting the thesis that private bankers played a determining role in the outcome of the negotiations. In addition to the Parodi correspondence that we will examine in the next chapter, of great interest is the correspondence of the Spigno-Gastaldi bank of Genoa, another Rothschild agent in the Ligurian capital, selling the Piedmont Rendita securities on behalf of the Parisian bank. The documents confirm Rothschild's involvement in the attempt to establish a second issuing bank in the Kingdom of Sardinia, the Banca Sarda. The major banker had clear interests in establishing relations with issuing banks and with their principal shareholders, and in playing a role in negotiating and placing loans.

On March 26, 1852, the price of shares in Banca Nazionale on the Genoa stock exchange ranged from 1825 to 1828 lire and the Parodi and Spigno-Gastaldi banks were the main sellers. Buyers, meanwhile, placed their faith in the passage of the bill introduced in parliament on March 19.[73] In his letter to Rothschild, Gastaldi remarks that the purchase might not be a good choice because discussions were underway among bankers regarding the possible establishment of a new bank. The following day, in another letter, Gastaldi informs Rothschild that the plan for the Banca Sarda seemed to be taking form, having spoken about it with Banca Parodi, which was taking an interest in the affair. The shares in the Banca Nazionale were then quoted at 1830 lire. After the events described above

fact that the economic boom in 1851 and 1852 diminished the importance of the legal tender that the Banca Nazionale had still attributed to it the previous summer".

[73] ANMT, BR, 132 AQ 9 P 070, Spigno Gastaldi (1851–1852).

during the second half of April, Banca Nazionale shares decreased in value to 1645 lire on April 29.[74]

This was also a period of crisis for the "Cavour-Rattazzi connubium", which ensured political stability at the time. Cavour stepped down as Minister of Finance in mid-May and was replaced by Luigi Cibrario on the 22nd.[75] Documents in the Rothschild Archives shed additional light on the events of those days. On May 15, Gastaldi described the ongoing attempt to establish the Banca Sarda to James de Rothschild. Involved in the process were bankers from Turin (Cotta, Barbaroux, Casana, and Calosso) and Genoa (Parodi, Ricci, Oneto, and Spigno-Gastaldi). The bylaws of the *Banque Sarde* had met with the approval of the Minister of Finance (at that time still Cavour) and were at that time being examined by the Council of State, whose decision was expected shortly. Gastaldi said that he was trustful that the initiative would be generally well received, excepting the strong opposition from the Banca Nazionale, which had sent a delegation to Turin to prevent its passage.

On May 17, Gastaldi wrote that a ministerial crisis was underway in Turin but that they had received the best assurances as to progress toward the new bank. At that time, Banca Nazionale shares were selling at 1725–1730 lire. Nevertheless, the letter closes with "We are told that the retirement of the Minister of Finance is final".

The Council of State rejected the Banca Sarda proposal on May 18.[76] The value of Banca Nazionale stock began to oscillate. Based on a letter from the Genoese banker, on May 21 the value fell to 1760 lire from 1800 a few days earlier. On May 22 it was 1710, influenced by the fact that plans for the bank had not been shelved but would be presented to parliament. On May 27, it was 1700. In the following days, the trend was reversed and on June 3, Gastaldi writes that speculators had their attention focused on Banca Nazionale shares, which had reached a value

[74] The available documents do not explicitly explain the reasons for the sale of Banca Nazionale stock by Parodi and Spigno-Gastaldi. While we may interpret the action as a guarantee of impartiality by two bankers who are about to promote another bank that should have similar characteristics and functions to the Banca Nazionale, it might also be a speculative operation, as the Spigno-Gastaldi letter suggests. In any case, the situation developed favorably also for Cavour, who leveraged the proposal for the new bank to influence ongoing negotiations with the Banca Nazionale.

[75] Romeo (1977, 505–506).

[76] Galli (1992, 262).

of 1780 the previous day, then fell to 1750, rose to 1800 and had reached 1830 on June 4.

It is clear that this is a complex affair with many interacting factors. Of most importance to us here is the initiative of the bankers, their networks of relations, and their capacity to penetrate into the political arena. The principal private bankers in the Kingdom of Sardinia attempted an operation that, on the one hand, tended to support the idea of there being competition among banks and, on the other, masked major stock market speculation or a major agreement between the two banks, with the expectation that the Banca Sarda would be successful. Gastaldi's letter also provides other interesting elements in this regard: he recognizes that the opportunity for his bank to be party to the enterprise depends on the benevolence of the Parodis and he underscores the importance of Rothschild perceiving harmony among his main agents in Genoa, here again evidencing relations that are not confined to the Kingdom of Sardinia. Rothschild's involvement in this operation is also suggested by Rosario Romeo, who cites a letter from the Rothschilds to Cavour dated May 7, 1852.

New information on the bankers' choice to withdraw support for the creation of the Banca Sarda, in spite of the fact that the matter was making its way toward discussion in parliament, is provided in a letter from Spigno Gastaldi to Rothschild dated June 7, 1852.[77] The Genoese banker writes that shares in Banca Nazionale are selling for 1790 lire despite the fact that the proposal for the Banca Sarda had just been abandoned/withdrawn because its promotors rejected the conditions demanded by the government: "a commitment from the new bank to establish two discount houses"; to advance up to 15 million lire to the Treasury (the bankers only wanted to advance 5 million); and to sell half of the shares on the open market.

The letter also states that Rothschild was aware of these operations and that Gastaldi had unsuccessfully tried to involve him in the initiative. However, after describing the situation, Gastaldi made another attempt to draw in the Parisian banker.[78]

[77] ANMT, BR, 132 AQ 9 P 070, Spigno Gastaldi (1851–1852).

[78] ANMT, BR, 132 AQ 9 P 070, Spigno Gastaldi (1851–1852): "We made all due haste, Gentlemen, to share this project with you to see if you wanted to join us. You will have had your good reasons for declining it, and we can only respect your decision to abstain. We now believe, Gentlemen, that the Turin promoters were of the opinion

It was the Genoese bankers who torpedoed the operation. Whose game were they playing? It was the Parodis who buried it. Gastaldi, initially full of gratitude toward them, immediately changed his tune and attempted once again to convince Rothschild to enter the affair.

Further information on the proposal to establish the Banca Sarda, negotiations with the government, and the decision of the proponents themselves to withdraw from the initiative is found in the record of the parliamentary proceedings of June 23–24, 1852.[79] The debate revolved around the prerogatives that might be attributed to the Banca Nazionale and, more generally, competition among banks and the role of the central bank. The words of Minister Cibrario reveal that the sponsors of the Banca Sarda have withdrawn the plan because they did not accept the proposals advanced by the Ministry of Finance in response to those from the private bankers proposing the establishment of the new corporation. Specifically, the proponent bankers requested that two conditions be met,[80] as Cibrario writes:

> that all the shares be at the disposal [of the Banca Sarda], and that the Banca Nazionale is not granted advantageous conditions with respect to it; they wanted to bind the government both now and in the future never to grant any favors. I could not allow this second condition because I did not feel it was prudent to put conditions on the future, and having opened an account at the Banca Nazionale, I could not be obliged a priori also

to accept the Ministry's conditions, which at the same time has undertaken to treat the [Banca] Nazionale and the Banca Sarda on the same footing. You might consider taking the place of the three promoters of Genoa, who have decided to withdraw. The fourth promoter, ourselves, has withdrawn in deference to our neighbors, but would ask nothing more than to have the honor of following you, without any pretensions as to the number of shares allocated to us, which we leave to you to decide. We believe the affair merits your consideration".

[79] Parliamentary records for the June 23 and 24, 1852 sessions may be found at the following links: https://storia.camera.it/regno/lavori/leg04/sed508.pdf, https://storia.camera.it/regno/lavori/leg04/sed509.pdf.

[80] A few lines below, the Minister declares his inclination to apply the principle of competition while also admitting his hesitation, shared by others, of a speculative action: "If I had just kept in mind the esteem I professed for each of the founders, I would not have doubted their loyalty or the desire to establish a principle of competition that I highly approved; but given the nature of the affair, I wanted to prevent it from ever transforming into a stock market game, and that with all these shares in hand it could have an influence on the Banca Nazionale and perhaps obtain conditions, as a result of which the promoters of the new bank could have withdrawn".

> to open one at the Banca Sarda. As regards the other point, regarding the availability of all the stock, in line with the opinion of the Commission, I felt it was more prudent to direct a portion to the open market, and I had proposed one half. Some of the founders of the Banca Sarda were not against accepting this.

Bartolomeo Parodi played a prominent role in this operation. He was probably the most active Genoese promoter of the Banca Sarda, and he drew other bankers, such as Gastaldi, into the initiative. He was also among those who decided to withdraw from the proposal, whereas the bankers from Turin were more given to pursuing the initial objective. After the Genoese bankers pulled out, Gastaldi actually made entreaties to Rothschild to convince the Parisian bankers to pick up their share.

Many questions regarding the undertaking to establish the Banca Sarda are revealed in the speech of the moderate, liberal member of parliament Paolo Farina on June 24, 1852, hinting at well defined speculative interests and relations among bankers, with an outline agreement ready in the event that the Banca Sarda was actually established[81]:

> Thus, without wanting to rebuke the underwriters of the Banca Sarda, as would be natural, they wanted to engage in speculation, and consequently advanced conditions to favor this speculation. At any rate, I cannot deny that there was one person among the underwriters of that new bank who was director of the Banca Nazionale, which arouses serious suspicions that he wanted nothing other than to favor a coalitions between the old bank and the new one, as a means to destroy any competition.

These affairs make it clear that Genoese private bankers in the 1850s were engaged in an effort to modernize the banking sector, which was in a process of opening to international relations and dialogue with the political arena, searching for new opportunities for growth, without neglecting opportunities for profit. Based on the statements of some (Farina), the bankers were acting like wheeler-dealers and speculators. Based on others (speech of Minister Cibrario), they were entrepreneurs believing in competition and dialectic in the banking sector, in which the Banca Nazionale was emerging as the bank of reference for the State. This

[81] Parliamentary records for the June 23 and 24, 1852 sessions may be found at the following links: https://storia.camera.it/regno/lavori/leg04/sed508.pdf, https://storia.camera.it/regno/lavori/leg04/sed509.pdf.

is all set against the background of the complex set of relations among the financier groups of Genoa and Turin.

It is also essential to note that, a few weeks later, the Law of July 11, 1852 concluded negotiations with the Banca Nazionale, which was then on its way to becoming the country's central, regulated bank. The bank's capital was increased from 8 to 32 million lire, divided into 32,000 shares. This recapitalization, as we observed earlier, favored the Genoese in terms of both number of shareholders and number of shares owned.[82] After the recapitalization, among shareholders generally holding few or a few dozen shares, standing out are the Parodis with 1641 shares and the newly founded Cassa di Commercio e di Industria (bank established after the July law and led by a group that included some of the preeminent bankers in Turin and Genoa) with, combining the Turin and Genoa branches, 953 + 2812 = 3765 shares.

Other Genoese capitalists and bankers owned a large number of shares in 1853, immediately following recapitalization. Many of these shareholders were closely linked to the Parodis and had joined them in the ownership structure of many companies: Banca Cataldi (253); Banca De la Rue (580); Leonino frères (274); Banca Quartara (205); Ravasco (204); Rocca (378); the Riccis (519).

A final point of interest relates to the shares in the recapitalized Banca Nazionale owned by the promoters of the Banca Sarda, which highlight the different interests of the Turinese and the Genoese. As regards the former: Cotta (247); Barbaroux (11); Casana (70); and Calosso (23). As regards the latter: Parodi (1641); the Riccis (519); Spigno-Gastaldi (160); and Oneto (75) for a total of some 2400 shares. This additional information makes it clear that the complex business of the promotion of the Banca Sarda had clear political implications, as was aptly observed by Romeo, but also economic implications. We note the network of relations between national and international bankers and the many competencies brought to bear to influence the market and achieve control of the modern banking system that was taking shape, control both of the central bank and of commerce and industry banks.

[82] For information on shares and shareholders, see Scatamacchia (2008, 68–102).

Bibliography

Archives

Archivio di Stato di Genova (ASGe).
Fondo Camera di Commercio, 25, Corrispondenza e contratti a stampa.
Fondo Camera di Commercio, 199, Quadro delle compagnie di Assicurazioni Marittime in Genova (1850).
Archivio Doria di Genova (ADG).
FP, 4/40, Progetto d'una strada di ferro fra Genova, il Piemonte, e la Lombardia (1826).
FP, 5/43, Documenti relativi alla costruzione di una strada ferrata tra Genova e il Po e poi Torino (1837).
Archives Nationales du Monde du Travail – Banque Rothschild (ANMT, BR).
BR, 132 AQ 9 P 033, Bolmida (1849–1853).
BR, 132 AQ 9 P 034, Bolmida (1854–1855).
BR, 132 AQ 9 P 035, Bolmida (1857).
BR, 132 AQ 9 P 036, Bolmida (1858–1859).
BR, 132 AQ 9 P 037, Bolmida (1860–1861).
BR, 132 AQ 9 P 038, Bolmida (1862–1865).
BR, 132 AQ 9 P 058, De La Rue (1840–1865).
BR, 132 AQ 9 P 070, Spigno Gastaldi (1851–1852).
BR, 132 AQ 9 P 071, Spigno Gastaldi (1853–1855).
BR, 132 AQ 9 P 072, Spigno Gastaldi (1856–1857).
BR, 132 AQ 9 P 073, Spigno Gastaldi (1858–1860).
BR, 132 AQ 9 P 089, Mestrezat (1843–1852).
BR, 132 AQ 9 P 090, Massone (1846–1852).
BR, 132 AQ 9 P 096, Parodi (1848–1851).
BR, 132 AQ 9 P 097, Parodi (1852–1855).
BR, 132 AQ 9 P 099, Parodi (1860–1863).
BR, 132 AQ 9 P 102, Pescio (1843–1855).
BR, 132 AQ non coté 160, Ricci (1840–1859).
BR, 132 AQ non coté 35, Cataldi (1851–1867).
BR, 132 AQ non coté 45, Dapples et C. (1858–1867).
BR, 132 AQ non coté 112, Leonino (1846–1866).

Printed Contemporary and Near Contemporary Sources

Aycard, Maurice. 1867. *Histoire du Crédit Mobilier.* Paris: Librairie Internationale.

Bailleux de Marisy, Alexis. 1872. "Les sociétés de crédit en France et à l'étranger." *Revue des deux mondes* 102, no. November–Dicember: 410–31.

Bertolotti, Davide. 1834. *Viaggio nella Liguria marittima*. Torino: Tipogradi Eredi Botta.
Bonnet, Victor. 1864. *La liberté des banques d'èmission et le taux de l'intérêt*. Paris: Guillaumin et Cie.
Cevasco, Giacomo. 1838. *Statistique de la ville de Gênes*. Genova: Imprimerie Ferrando.
Cibrario, Luigi. 1852. *Cenni sulle condizioni delle finanze dal 1847 al 1852*. Torino: Dalla Stamperia Reale.
Codice di Commercio per gli Stati di S. M. il Re di Sardegna. 1842. Torino: Stamperia Reale.
Coquelin, Charles. 1848. *Du crédit et des Banques*. Paris: Guillaumin et Cie.
Pereire, Isaac. 1866. *Enquêt sur la Banque de France*. Paris: P. Dupont.
Quaglia, Luigi Z. 1846. *Prospetto per ordine alfabetico dell'attuale industria fabbrile e manifattrice genovese*. Torino: Dalla tipografia di Giuseppe Fodratti.
Sieveking, Heinrich. 1906. *Studio Sulle Finanze Genovesi nel Medioevo e in particolare sulla casa di S. Giorgio*. Genoa: Tipografia della Gioventù.
Virgilio, Jacopo. 1869. *Il commercio indo-europeo e la marina mercantile italiana a vela ed a vapore*. Genova: Tipografia Sociale.

Secondary Sources

Abrate, Mario. 1961. *L'industria siderurgica e meccanica in Piemonte dal 1831 al 1861*. Torino: Museo Nazionale del Risorgimento.
Allen, Larry. 2001. *The Global Financial System*, 1750–2000. London: Reaktion Books.
Angeli, Stefano. 1982. *Proprietari, commercianti e filandieri a Milano nel primo Ottocento*. Milano: FrancoAngeli.
Arese, Franco. 1953. *Cavour e le strade ferrate*. Milano: Amici Museo del Risorgimento.
Avallone, Paola. 2014. *Alle origini del credito agrario. I monti frumentari nel Regno di Napoli e le riforme di fine '700*. Napoli: CNR Edizioni.
Bachi, Riccardo. 1936. "La crisi economica del 1853–54 nel Regno di Sardegna." *Rivista di storia economica* 1: 119–42.
Bergier, Jean François. 1985. "Le dynamisme de la banque privé, XVII-XIX siécles." In *Credito, banche e investimenti, sec. XIII-XX*, edited by A. Vannini Marx, 257–67. Firenze: Le Monnier.
Bernardello, Adolfo. 2002. "'Iniziative economiche, accumulazione e investimenti di capitale (1830–1866)." In *Storia di Venezia. L'Ottocento e il Novecento*, edited by M. Isnenghi and S. Woolf, 567–601. Roma: Treccani.
Berta, Giuseppe. 1990. *Capitali in gioco: cultura economica e vita finanziaria nella City dell'Ottocento*. Venezia: Marsilio.

Bertini, Fabio. 1994. *Michele Giuntini. La carriera di un banchiere privato nella Toscana dell'Ottocento (1777–1845)*. Firenze: L. S. Olschki.

Bolchini, Piero. 1969. "La Gran Bretagna e la formazione del mercato italiano (1861–1883)." *Miscellanea Storica Ligure* 1, no. 2: 1–264.

Bouvier, Jean. 1961. *Le Crédit lyonnais*. Paris: Sevpen.

Cafaro, Pietro. 1990. "Finanziamento e ruolo della banca. Il sistema tradizionale in evoluzione (1860–1878)." In *Storia dell'industria lombarda, 2, Alla guida della prima industrializzazione italiana*, edited by S. Zaninelli, 159–259. Milano: Edizioni Il Polifilo.

Cafaro, Pietro. 2000. "Alle origini del sistema bancario lombardo: casse di risparmio e banchieri privati (1860–1880)." In *Banche e reti di banche nell'Italia postunitaria, 2*, edited by G. Conti and S. La Francesca, 437–502. Bologna: il Mulino.

Calzavarini, Mirella. 1969. "Carlo Bombrini." In *Dizionario Biografico degli Italiani 11*, 391–95. Roma: Treccani.

Cameron, Rondo. 1953. "The Credit Mobilier and the Economic Development of Europe." *The Journal of Political Economy* 61, no. 6: 461–88.

Cameron, Rondo. 1961. *France and economic development of Europe (1800–1914)*. Princeton: Princeton University Press.

Cassis, Youssef. 1984. *Les banquiers de la City à l'époque édouardienne*. Genève: Droz.

Cassis, Youssef. 1997. *Big Business. The european Experience in the Twentieth Century*. Oxford: Oxford University Press.

Cassis, Youssef. 2006. *Capitals of Capitals. The Rise and Fall of International Financial Center 1780–2009*. Cambridge: Cambridge University Press.

Cassis, Youssef, Gerald D. Feldman, and Ulf Olssun. 1995. *The Evolution of Financial Institutions and Markets in Twentieth Century Europe*. Aldershot: Scolar Press.

Cassis, Youssef, and Philip Cottrell, eds. 2009. *The World of Private Banking*. Farnham-Burlington: Ashgate.

Castronovo, Valerio. 1965. *L'industria cotoniera in Piemonte nel secolo XIX*. Torino: ILTE.

Cipolla, Carlo M. 1953. "Agli inizi della rivoluzione industriale nell'economia ligure." In *Genova. Uomini e fortune*, 3–24. Genova: Levante, Società di Assicurazioni e Riassicurazioni.

Conte, Leandro. 1990. *La Banca Nazionale. Formazione e attività di una banca di emissione (1843–1861)*. Napoli: Edizioni Scientifiche Italiane.

Conti, Giuseppe, and Maria Carmela Schisani. 2011. "I banchieri italiani e la *haute banque* nel Risorgimento e dopo l'Unità." *Società e storia* 131, no. 1: 133–70.

Coppini, Romano P. 1994. "Carlo Bombrini finanziere e imprenditore." In *Storia dell'Ansaldo, 1, Le Origini (1853–1882)*, edited by V. Castronovo, 51–75. Roma-Bari: Laterza.

Cova, Aalberto, and Anna Maria Galli, eds. 1991. *Finanza e sviluppo economico-sociale. La Cassa di Risparmio delle Provincie Lombarde dalla fondazione al 1940.* 4 vols. Milano-Roma-Bari: Cariplo-Laterza.

Da Pozzo, Mario, and Giuseppe Felloni. 1964. *La borsa valori di Genova nel secolo XIX.* Torino: ILTE.

De Bonis, Riccardo, Farabullini Fabio, Rocchelli Miria, and Alessandra Salvio. 2012. *A Quantitative Look at the Italian Banking System: Evidence from a New Dataset since 1861.* Roma: Department of the Treasury, Ministry of the Economy and of Finance.

De Luca, Giuseppe. 2003. "La storiografia più recente sulla finanza italiana dell'età moderna: gli studi sulla moneta, i banchi e i banchieri." *Rivista di storia finanziaria* 10: 11–31.

De Luca, Giuseppe. 2007. "Tra reti e istituzioni. Per una lettura del sistema creditizio milanese nei primi anni dell'Ottocento." *Storia in Lombardia* 27, no. 2: 5–33.

De Luca, Giuseppe. 2013a. "Credito informale versus credito bancario a Milano nella prima metà dell'Ottocento." In *Studi in ricordo di Tommaso Fanfani*, edited by M. Berti, A. Bianchi, G. Conti, D. Manetti, M. Merger and V. Pinchera, 269–79. Pisa: Pacini.

De Luca, Giuseppe. 2013b. "Informal Credit and Economic Modernization in Milan (1802–1840)." *The Journal of European Economic History* 42, no. 1: 211–34.

De Luca, Giuseppe, and Angelo Moioli. 2008. "Il potere del credito. Reti e istituzioni in Italia centro-settentrionale fra età moderna e decenni preunitari." In *Storia d'Italia, Annali 23, La Banca*, edited by C. Bermond, A. Cova, A. Moioli and S. La Francesca, 212–55. Torino: Einaudi.

De Rosa, Luigi. 2004. "L'Archivio del Banco di Napoli e l'Attività dei Banchi pubblici Napoletani." *De Computis: Revista Española de Historia de la Contabilidad* 1: 54–66.

De Simone, Ennio. 1993. *Alle origini del sistema bancario italiano (1815–1840).* Napoli: Edizioni Scientifiche Italiane.

Decugis, Carlo. 1979. *Banca e credito nel decennio cavouriano.* Milano: UNICOPLI.

Demarco, Domenico. 1988. "Banca e credito nel Risorgimento." In *Credito e sviluppo economico in Italia del Medio Evo all'Età contemporanea*, 335–85. Verona: SISE.

Doria, Giorgio. 1969. *Investimenti e sviluppo economico a Genova alla vigilia della Prima Guerra Mondiale (1815–1882).* Milano: A. Giuffrè Editore.

Doria, Giorgio. 1990. *Debiti e navi. La compagnia del Rubattino 1839–1881.* Genova: Marietti.

Doria, Giorgio. 1991. "La strategia degli investimenti finanziari di Raffaele De Ferrari dal 1828 al 1876." In *I duchi di Galliera. Alta finanza, arte e filantropia tra Genova e l'Europa nell'Ottocento, 1,* edited by G. Assereto, G. Doria, P. Massa Piergiovanni, L. Saginati and L. Tagliaferro, 449–510. Genova: Marietti.

Doria, Marco. 2001. "Un'economia in trasformazione tra progetti e realtà. Genova nella prima metà del XIX secolo." *Atti della Società Ligure di Storia Patria* 41, no. 2: 171–92.

Doria, Marco. 2008. "Economia e investimenti finanziari a Genova nell'età cavouriana." *Atti della Società Ligure di Storia Patria* 48, no. 1: 225–51.

Doria, Marco. 2011. "Industria e finanza a Genova in età cavouriana." In *Cavour e Genova. Economia e politica*, edited by M.E. Tonizzi, 39–60. Genova: De Ferrari.

Felisini Daniela. 2016. *Alessandro Torlonia. The Pope's Banker.* London: Palgrave Macmillan.

Felloni, Giuseppe. 1956. *Monete e zecche negli stati sabaudi dal 1816 al 1860.* Torino: ILTE.

Felloni, Giuseppe. 1961. *Popolazione e sviluppo economico della Liguria nel secolo XIX.* Torino: ILTE.

Felloni, Giuseppe, ed. 1997. *Moneta, credito e banche in Europa: un millennio di storia.* Genova: Brigati.

Felloni, Giuseppe. 2008. "Dall'Italia all'Europa: il primato della finanza italiana dal Medioevo alla prima età moderna." In *Storia d'Italia, Annali 23, La Banca*, edited by C. Bermond, A. Cova, A. Moioli and S. La Francesca, 93–149. Torino: Einaudi.

Felloni, Giuseppe. 2010. "A Profile of Genoa's 'Casa di San Giorgio' (1407–1805): A Turning Point in the History of Credit." *Rivista di storia economica* 26, no. 3: 335–46.

Fratianni, Michele. 2006. "Government debt, reputation and creditors' protections: the tale of San Giorgio." *Review of Finance* 10, no. 4: 497–501.

Fratianni, Michele. 2010. "The Evolutionary Chain of International Financial Centers." In *The Changing Geography of Banking and Finance*, edited by P. Alessandrini, M. Fratianni and A. Zazzaro, 251–76. New York: Springer.

Fratianni, Michele, and Franco Spinelli. 1997. *A Monetary History of Italy.* Cambridge: Cambridge University Press.

Galli, Anna Maria, ed. 1992. *La formazione e lo sviluppo del sistema bancario in Europa e in Italia: letture scelte.* Milano: Vita e Pensiero.

Giacchero, Giulio. 1980. *Genova e Liguria nell'età contemporanea.* Genova: Sagep.

Gille, Bertrand. 1959a. *La banque et le crédit en France de 1815 à 1848*. Paris: Presses Universitaires de France.

Gille, Bertrand. 1959b. "Les capitaux français en Piémont (1849–1859)." *Histoire des Entreprises* 3: 4–88.

Gille, Bertrand. 1968. *Les investissements français en Italie (1815–1914)*. Torino: ILTE.

Goodhart, Charles A. E. 1988. *The Evolution of Central Banks*. Cambridge: MIT press.

Graziani, Ersilia. 1995. "La Banca romana (1834–1870)." In *Gli archivi degli istituti e delle aziende di credito e le fonti d'archivio per la storia delle banche. Tutela, gestione, valorizzazione*, 462–92. Roma: Ministero per i Beni Culturali e Ambientali – Ufficio Centrale per i Beni Archivistici.

Grendi, Edoardo. 1964. "Genova nel Quarantotto." *Nuova Rivista Storica* 48, nos. 3–4: 307–49.

Guderzo, Giulio. 1961. *Vie e mezzi di comunicazione in Piemonte dal 1831 al 1861*. Torino: Museo Nazionale del Risorgimento.

Guderzo, Giulio. 2018. *Ferrovie nel Piemonte preunitario: storia e immagini*. Milano: Hoepli.

Guglielmino, Enrico. 1940. *Genova dal 1814 al 1849. Gli sviluppi economici e l'opinione pubblica*. Genova: Regia Deputazione di Storia Patria per la Liguria.

Hawtrey, Ralph G. 1932. *The Art of Central Banking*. London: Frank Cass and Co.

Landes, David S. 1956. "Vieille banque et banque nouvelle." *Revue d'histoire moderne et contemporaire* 3, no. 3: 202–22.

Levati, Stefano. 1997. *La nobiltà del lavoro. Negozianti e banchieri a Milano tra Ancien Régime e Restaurazione*. Milano: FrancoAngeli.

Licini, Stefania. 1997. "Banca e credito a Milano, nella prima fase dell'industrializzazione (1840–1880)." In *Antonio Allievi: dalle "scienze civili" alla pratica del credito*, edited by E. Decleva, 527–59. Roma-Bari: Laterza.

Marchese, Ugo. 1957a. *L'industria armatoriale ligure dal 1816 al 1859*. Torino: ILTE.

Marchese, Ugo. 1957b. *L'industria ligure delle costruzioni navali dal 1816 al 1859*. Torino: ILTE.

Marchese, Ugo. 1959. *Il porto di Genova dal 1815 al 1891*. Torino: ILTE.

Marongiu, Gianni. 2011. "Libertà, consenso e rinnovamento nel Regno di Sardegna." In *Cavour e Genova. Economia e politica*, edited by M. E. Tonizzi, 15–37. Genova: De Ferrari.

Montale, Bianca. 1999. *Mito e realtà di Genova nel Risorgimento*. Milano: FrancoAngeli.

Morabito, Leo. 1991. "Raffaele De Ferrari e la società promotrice di una ferrovia da Genova al Piemonte." In *I duchi di Galliera. Alta finanza, arte e filantropia tra Genova e l'Europa nell'Ottocento, 1*, edited by G. Assereto, G.

Doria, P. Massa Piergiovanni, L. Saginati and L. Tagliaferro, 511–31. Genova: De Ferrari.

Mori, Giorgio. 1989. "Industrie senza industrializzazione. La penisola italiana dalla fine della dominazione francese all'Unità nazionale (1815–1861)." *Studi Storici* 30, no. 3: 603–36.

Piccione, Paolo. 2010. "L'età del vapore. Raffaele Rubattino armatore." In *Raffaele Rubattino. Un armatore genovese e l'Unità d'Italia*, 17–37. Cinisello Balsamo: Silvana Editoriale.

Piluso, Giandomenico. 1999. *L'arte dei banchieri. Moneta e credito a Milano da Napoleone all'Unità*. Milano: FrancoAngeli.

Piluso, Giandomenico. 2000. "Il mercato del credito a Milano dopo l'Unità: strutture e dinamiche evolutive." In *Banche e reti di banche nell'Italia postunitaria, 2,* edited by G. Conti and S. La Francesca, 503–56. Bologna: Il Mulino.

Piluso, Giandomenico. 2002. "Regole, istituzioni, mercati: modelli e innovazioni istituzionali a Milano dalla Restaurazione all'Unità." In *Regole e mercati: fiducia, concorrenza e innovazioni finanziarie nella storia creditizia italiana*, edited by G. Conti and T. Fanfani, 67–86. Pisa: Plus.

Pinchera, Sergio. 1961. *Le spese effettive e il bilancio dello Stato Pontificio dal 1827 al 1867.* Torino. ILTE.

Plessis, Alain. 1982. *La Banque de France et ses deux cent actionaires.* Genève: Droz.

Plessis, Alain. 1985. *La politique de la Banque de France de 1851 a 1870.* Genève: Droz.

Podestà, Gian Luca. 2004. "L'evoluzione del sistema creditizio dalla Restaurazione alla legge bancaria del 1936." In *Attori e strumenti del credito in Liguria. Dal mercante banchiere alla banca universale*, edited by P. Massa, 143–73. Genova: Fondazione Carige.

Polsi, Alessandro. 1993. *Alle origini del capitalismo italiano. Stato, banche e banchieri dopo l'Unità 1861–1981.* Torino: Einaudi.

Rollandi, Maria S. 1991. "La filanda di Voltaggio e i Duchi di Galliera: dislocazione industriale e intervento padronale." In *I duchi di Galliera. Alta finanza, arte e filantropia tra Genova e l'Europa nell'Ottocento*, 2, edited by G. Assereto, G. Doria, P. Massa Piergiovanni, L. Saginati and L. Tagliaferro, 617–46. Genova: De Ferrari.

Rollandi, Maria S. 2008. "Il porto di Genova e il problema del trasferimento della base navale." *Atti della Società Ligure di Storia Patria* 48, no. 1: 253–84.

Rollandi, Maria S. 2010. "Tra rischi d'impresa e azzardo. Le strategie di un armatore genovese nelle relazioni internazionali dell'Ottocento." In *Raffaele Rubattino. Un armatore genovese e l'Unità d'Italia*, 77–89. Cinisello Balsamo: Silvana Editoriale.

Rollandi, Maria S. 2011. "Navigazione e porto. Progetti e realizzazioni della politica cavouriana." In *Cavour e Genova. Economia e politica*, edited by M. E. Tonizzi, 61–74. Genova: De Ferrari.

Romeo, Rosario. 1963. *Dal Piemonte sabaudo all'Italia liberale*. Torino: Einaudi.

Romeo, Rosario. 1975. *Gli scambi degli Stati Sardi con l'estero nelle più importanti voci della bilancia commerciale (1818–59)*. Torino: Centro Studi Piemontesi.

Romeo, Rosario. 1977. *Cavour e il suo tempo (1842–1854)*, 2. Roma-Bari: Laterza.

Rosselli, Nello. 1954. *Inghilterra e Regno di Sardegna dal 1815 al 1847*. Torino: Einaudi.

Rossi, Ernesto, and Gian Paolo Nitti, eds. 1968. *Banche, Governo e Parlamento negli Stati Sardi, Fonti documentarie (1843–1861)*. Torino: Fondazione Luigi Einaudi.

Scatamacchia, Rosanna. 2008. *Azioni e azionisti. Il lungo Ottocento della Banca d'Italia*. Roma-Bari: Laterza.

Strangio, Donatella. 2001. *Il debito pubblico pontificio. Cambiamento e continuità nella finanza pontificia dal periodo francese alla restaurazione romana 1798–1820*. Padova: CEDAM.

Strangio, Donatella. 2006. "«Facilitare al governo il mezzo di conoscere e di soddisfare i veri bisogni del commercio e delle arti » . La disciplina della borsa di Roma nella prima metà del XIX secolo." *Studi storici Luigi Simeoni* 56: 387–402.

Strangio, Donatella. 2013. "Public Debt in the Papal States, Sixteenth to Eighteenth Century." *The Journal of Interdisciplinary History* 43, no. 4: 511–37.

Toniolo, Gianni. 1995. "Sull'arte del banchiere centrale in Italia: fatti stilizzati e congetture (1861–1947)." *Banca d' Italia, Temi di discussione del servizio studi* 255: 9–65.

Tonizzi, Elisabetta. 2000. *Merci, strutture e lavoro nel porto di Genova tra '800 e '900*. Milano: FrancoAngeli.

Tonizzi, Elisabetta. 2010. "«Amico degli amici » . Rubattino e le reti sociali dell'élite genovese dal Regno di Sardegna all'Unità d'Italia." In *Raffaele Rubattino. Un armatore genovese e l'Unità d'Italia*, 39–47. Cinisello Balsamo: Silvana Editoriale.

Ugolini, Stefano. 2017. *The Evolution of Central Banking: Theory and History*. London: Palgrave Macmillan.

CHAPTER 4

Financial Intermediation: The Rothschilds and the Private Bankers in the Kingdom of Sardinia

4.1 Genoese Credit and Financial Operators and the Placement of National and International Government Loans

The propensity for saving money and accumulating capital, an element consistently characteristic of the people of Genoa, was mainly expressed via investment of monetary resources in credit and finance operations involving national and international government loans: this tradition, which involved flotation of government loans during the *Ancien Regime*, continued also after the upheaval of the Napoleonic period, a time during when new financial players in the city stepped to the fore.[1]

This explains why the big players in the *haute banque* sought information on what was happening in the Genoa financial market through their network of agents, presumably to judge what prospects it held for them. In fact, the international *haute banque* is the only institution capable of guaranteeing ever more substantial resources, either directly with its own capital or indirectly through its placement in the markets. At the same

[1] Regarding the socioeconomic context in Genoa in this economic period: Rollandi (2012), Felloni (2016, 71–79), Massa (1991), and Piccinno (2013, 43–44).

L. Maffi, *Private Bankers in the Italian 19th Century*, Palgrave Studies in Economic History,
https://doi.org/10.1007/978-3-030-63361-5_4

time, public securities in their various forms become the most traded products within the exchanges, attracting all types of investors.[2]

Documents regarding the Rothschild bank of London and its economic relations with the principal stock exchanges in northern Italy—Turin, Milan, Trieste, and, of course, Genoa—reveal an emblematic case. In chronological order, the London bankers conducted relations with the Bansa-Ulrich-Bandeuf bank during period of the Congress of Vienna, then with Bandeuf (1822–1828) and later Bandeuf's son-in-law Pescio (1829–1847), and finally, starting in 1847, with Leonino frères.[3]

The Rothschilds were very interested in the Genoa stock market and the ongoing relationship with Jean Bandeuf highlights a long-established dialogue which had certainly become more effective over the years.

The London bank's strategy of penetration, involving the collection of detailed, specific information, is evident particularly in Bandeuf's request for records of loans taken out by the King of Denmark in Genoa in the 1780s. In a letter dated July 1, 1826, Jean Bandeuf provides detailed information regarding two loans taken out by the Danish king in Genoa in 1786 and 1788, of which part had been repaid and another part later restructured. Denmark's debt to the Genoese was reduced to 5 million lire *fuori banco* (Lfb, the old Genoese lire, replaced by the Piedmont lire *nuove* in the 1850s) that the Danish government repaid periodically and annually from 1827 to 1832; interest was paid regularly at a rate of 4% per year and per half-year in June and December.[4] Bandeuf complained of great difficulty in obtaining this information because of the resistance of the Genoese players directly involved in this financial operation, who refused to provide details that might benefit competitors in the acquisition of portions of the Danish debt. In spite of this, the Genoese merchant

[2] Concerning the role and the relations between private bankers in the most important european market in nineteenth century: Cassis and Cottrell (2009), Cassis (2006, 7–40), Berta (1990), and Chapman (1984, 9–15, 34–38). Regarding Italian context: Conti and Schisani (2011). Ugolini (2018), Ferguson (1998), Bouvier (1961, 224–233; 1968), Gille (1965), and Landes (1956). Concerning Italy: Felisini (1990a, 2016), Scatamacchia (2013, 793–800), Barbagallo (2000), and Guderzo (1970, 567–670; 1973).

[3] RAL, XI/38/40, Ulrich – Bansa & Baudeuf (1823–1828), XI/38/203a, Pescio (1829–1835), XI/38/203b, Pescio (1836–1847) and Letter copy books 148/109 (March 20–July 31, 1849).

[4] RAL, XI/38/40, Ulrich – Bansa & Baudeuf (1823–1828). Regarding Genoese loans to the Kingdom of Denmark in the eighteenth and nineteenth centuries, see: Felloni (1971).

banker displayed his skill and an excellent network of relations, eventually stating he was able to acquire at that time up to 300,000 lire *fuori banco* at a price of 82–84% of their nominal value.

This first case study, tracing its origins to the eighteenth century, clearly reveals the importance of inter-bank and political relations combined with specific competence in financial brokerage. Documents regarding Bandeuf's successor, his son-in-law Stefano Pescio, show that Genoese bankers had the necessary qualities to play an active role both in negotiations on loans by the Kingdom of Sardinia and in the placement of those loans on the market. The competencies and relations of the Genoese were leveraged a few years later (1831) during negotiations for a large government loan between representatives of the Kingdom of Sardinia and national and international financial players.

One of these international players was the Rothschilds, who played a leading role in the earliest Sardinian financial operations through their network of agents. An edict issued on May 30, 1831 authorized the Savoy government to contract a loan that would be floated on the international market. The loan was necessary to pay large military expenses and amounted to 20 million lire, with the government expecting to sell it at 90% of nominal value. Negotiations took place with Turinese bankers, who only offered 87%. Unsuccessful in their attempt to secure a loan that could be floated within the Kingdom, the representatives of the Sardinian government turned to certain Parisian bankers,[5] failing here as well. Attributed to a Parisian banker at the time, the following statement succinctly sums up the situation: "I spoke to certain capitalists of the advantages of the loans, but without much success".[6] The Sardinian ambassador dispatched a rather pessimistic report to Turin stating that the Piedmont securities were too expensive with respect to their French counterparts or other foreign funds usually traded on the Paris stock exchange. Furthermore, the Piedmont securities had never been quoted in Paris and their novel character was not an advantage in this situation. To resolve the impasse, the proposal was advanced to establish a solid bank in Piedmont backed by important French shareholders in order to be able to place the loan under the aegis of a large banking house.

[5] Gille (1965, 229–231). Regarding the credit system in France: Gille (1959).

[6] Gille (1965, 229–230).

The length of negotiations gives us ample material to analyze the way Ligurian bankers leveraged their connections with the Rothschilds. It is also important to point out that the Genoese, based on currently available information, were not directly involved in organizing and placing the loan; this took place, as explained above, through the agency of the Turinese and the Parisians. To understand how the Genoese got involved in this financial opportunity, we must meticulously review the legislative timeline of the loan, comparing it with the information gleaned from the correspondence between Stefano Pescio[7] and the London Rothschilds. Their exchange highlights the quality of information sharing, showing that quite often bankers communicate intentions and opportunities regarding money-lending operations in step with the enactment of legislation, if not several days in advance. While it might seem obvious that operators at this level have well-honed tools for anticipating the outcome of national processes, we must also recognize that their network of relations and multi-level dialogue, both in international finance and political spheres, evidences clearsightedness and discernment that allowed them to rightfully be an integral part of a new financial mechanism for the Kingdom of Sardinia.

Examining the chronology of events, the royal edict of May 31, 1831 instituted a 5% bond that was recorded in a general ledger divided into two sections, one containing nominative certificates (the bonds being extracts) and the other bearer certificates (detached from a counterfoil registry).[8] On August 31, the Royal Secretary of Finance issued instructions explaining how to obtain a voluntary loan through a redeemable security that was sold for 90% of face value and yielded 5 lire for every 90 lire invested.[9] Lastly, on September 22, additional *regie patenti* [royal patents] were issued providing further indications as regards the conditions of the placement of the loan.[10]

On May 19, shortly before the publication of the royal edict authorizing the loan (issued on May 31), Pescio informed the Rothschilds that the late king of Sardinia, Carlo Felice di Savoia (d. April 27, 1831), had

[7] Stefano Pescio is mentioned among the bankers operating in Genoa in: *L'indicatore* (1834, 1840).

[8] Mancardi (1874, 132–133).

[9] *Raccolta degli Atti del Governo* (1847, 272–274).

[10] *Raccolta degli Atti del Governo* (1847, 287–290).

requested a loan of 15 million lire *nuove* the previous December. This is precious information revealing that the idea for the loan originated with Carlo Felice, who was not successful in his negotiations with the bankers, mainly because of the difficulty in placing it within national boundaries. Pescio brokered negotiations at Banque Rothschild in Paris in December 1830. Rothschild, however, did not find the proposal attractive because of the king's exorbitant demands.[11] Negotiations continued during the following months, but the bankers' offers were excessively onerous for the Kingdom's finances, and the new king, Carlo Alberto, initially refused to authorize the loan, changing his mind shortly thereafter.

Pescio's approach in this circumstance, as well as in others documented in the archives, is emblematic of Genoese bankers, who were accustomed to acting as intermediaries and, in general, to weaving relations with financial agents without missing any opportunities. They wielded broad-ranging competencies. Grounded in solidly established relationships within the commercial arena and the credit systems of the Ligurian city, and ramified at different levels, these competencies ensured they kept their finger on the pulse, benefiting from first-hand news and information from critical financial arenas. Pescio reiterated that the loan in question represented an advantageous opportunity for the Rothschilds and offered his services for negotiations, information gathering, and developing the best offer. He argued his position by highlighting the advantages of the operation and the favorable financial framework of the Kingdom: "Piedmont does not have a large government debt. Prior to the French Revolution it was at 109% and 110%, and unless another war breaks out, we believe it will not begin to grow again".[12] Thus, a reciprocal and complementary relationship was developing between the Genoese bankers and the Rothschilds. Initially via Bandeuf and Pescio and later the Parodis, Spigno-Gastaldi, and the Leonino brothers, the Rothschilds gained a foothold in a structured regional financial system and discerned viable opportunities to float government debt securities and to perform other financial operations.

The documentation we have consulted leads precisely in this direction. On May 26, a date close to the issue of the royal edict, Pescio again wrote

[11] RAL, XI/38/203a, Pescio (1829–1835).

[12] RAL, XI/38/203a, Pescio (1829–1835).

to the London bankers,[13] informing them that he would be going to Turin to negotiate the loan and act as an intermediary with the Piedmont government, being authorized also by Banque Rothschild of Paris. In the loan negotiations, he thus found himself at the center of the network of relations established by the French bankers, who had branches in all the main European financial marketplaces: Paris, London, Vienna, Frankfurt, and Naples.[14] Some of these were already handling the government debt of the pre-unification states in those years through the banks of Paris, London, and Naples. The Kingdom of Sardinia, which had not hitherto been involved in financial operations with the Rothschilds, now entered their sphere of interest.

On September 1, the day after the issue of the royal patents with information regarding the placement of the loan, Pescio informed his interlocutors in London that he knew that Casa Rothschild of Naples was in contact with them for the Sardinian loan and that for several months now he himself had been negotiating in Turin on behalf of the Parisian Maison. The chosen stock exchange for the bulk of the placement of the Piedmont government debt securities was Paris, Baron James de Rothschild's home territory.[15] Negotiations with the bankers were very slow and the Sardinian government, which had yet to conclude a contract, eventually took out a loan for ten million. It was a voluntary underwriting at 90% of face value, to be placed within the State. The king "invited" all people holding public office to contribute, instructing his administrators to do the same with their employees.

Another 15 million lire were to be placed on commission, and the bankers wanted them at a price of 84 or 85%. A fundamental passage in the correspondence of the Ligurian banker evidences the strong potential for placing the debt on the Genoa and Turin markets, where the banker found many willing to buy, especially at 84% of nominal value.[16]

The voluntary loan was successful and on September 10 two out of ten million lire had already been placed in Turin. This induced Pescio to play for time. He knew that the Genoese investors were interested and

[13] RAL, XI/38/203a, Pescio (1829–1835).

[14] RAL, XI/38/203a, Pescio (1829–1835).

[15] Operations relating to the Neapolitan public debt are studied in: Schisani (2010). Per quanto riguarda lo Stato Pontificio: Felisini (1990a, b).

[16] RAL, XI/38/203a, Pescio (1829–1835).

had the necessary resources and felt he could get better terms for the remaining 15 million.[17] The public administrators and their employees who had been constrained to buy into the voluntary loan at 90% of face value resold it at 87 or 86, or even as low as 85 or 84. Many of these unwilling investors were forced to borrow money to buy the securities and thus had to resell them immediately at whatever price they could get to pay back their debt. This had a dual advantage for the bankers: it put them in a favorable position to negotiate the remaining portion of the loan on commission; it gave them the opportunity to repurchase the debt securities at a lower price.

A lot happened in the second half of September regarding the Kingdom of Sardinia loan. By September 17, approximately 4 out of 10 million had already been floated in Turin and Genoa at 90% but were being resold everywhere at 85%.[18] As for negotiations for the remaining 15 million, Jonas Hagerman of Paris (previously a banker in Genoa) was in Turin in that period to negotiate with the government. Pescio also made several trips to the capital to negotiate directly with the minister of finance, who was in favor of proceeding on commission, also expressing the desire to privilege the Rothschilds in the affair.

By September 24, some 6 out of 10 million of the Sardinian voluntary loan had already been placed, but were resold for 86 or 85%. Hagerman had not secured a deal and left Turin. There was still the possibility that the Rothschilds might initiate negotiations for the remaining 15 million on advantageous terms.[19] The correspondence provides important information on the attitude of the buyers in the Kingdom of Sardinia. In Pescio's opinion, the Genoa stock exchange, where a part of the voluntary loan had been sold, might be very receptive to the purchase of the part that the Rothschilds could take on commission. This would ensure the success of the operation and allow the Rothschilds to sell the securities in Paris and London. This makes it clear that there was capital in Genoa and a willingness to invest it, in addition to well developed brokerage capabilities for organizing and placing loans. This assessment is somewhat at

[17] RAL, XI/38/203a, Pescio (1829–1835).

[18] RAL, XI/38/203a, Pescio (1829–1835).

[19] RAL, XI/38/203a, Pescio (1829–1835).

odds with descriptions of the Genoese economy frequently found in the literature.[20]

In spite of Pescio's intermediation skills and efforts, and in spite of the advanced stage of the negotiations, the Rothschilds did not reach an agreement with the Piedmont government. Nevertheless, 1831 was a crucial year for the Sardinian kingdom as it began to assume a more central role in the affairs of the Italian peninsula and witnessed the first participation of foreign investors. In the period that followed, some banks in the Parisian *haute banque* (André & Cottier, Fould & Oppenheim, Blanc, Collin & C., Odier & C., Wells & C., Hagermann) formed a consortium to organize the placement of the part on commission on the other side of the Alps. On this occasion, they excluded the Rothschilds, who immediately took revenge by driving down the price of the securities in the first half of 1832.

4.2 The Parodis' Brokerage Capabilities

In the 1840s, the Parodis made great strides in their international financial operations. The family consolidated their business and network of relations, particularly their connections with the Papal State via the Torlonia family. The Banca Parodi had already shared business with Giovanni Torlonia in the late eighteenth century, expanding it with his son. Daniela Felisini writes: "Parodi was one of the Italian banks with whom also Alessandro did a great deal of business, even sharing issues from the Roman treasury".[21] The Parodis were listed as Banco Torlonia agents in both 1830 and 1847. Their credit in the latter year, 355,000 scudi, is particularly relevant.[22]

An important joint financial operation with this family of Roman princes was the issue in 1846 negotiated by the Papal State with the Torlonia bankers.[23] The loan had a nominal value of 2 million Roman

[20] Cipolla (1953) and Grendi (1964).

[21] Felisini (2004, 104; 2016, 69–70, 120–121).

[22] Felisini (2004).

[23] Tobone (1872, 273–274); Tobone writes: "The securities representing this debt are distinguished by bond names; they have a face value of one thousand lire, or 185 and 10/54 Roman *piastre*, each. The extinction is accomplished by purchase at quoted value by the Parodi bank of Genoa and in the measure of 1% of the face value of the loan increased by the interest on redeemed bonds".

piastre, the equivalent of 10,800,000 lire at a fixed rate of 5% (in a procedure similar to modern-day bank-guaranteed loans).[24] It was thus not sold publicly via bank brokerage, instead the bankers were the direct creditors of the Papal State and handled its flotation.

Alessandro Torlonia initially sought out the Rothschilds as a partner in this affair. They were accustomed to handling government loans on the international level and had specific experience with the Papal State.[25] On January 24, a few days after the negotiation, Torlonia wrote directly to James de Rothschild, explaining that he himself had negotiated a loan with the Papal State and had discretionality over it both as regards issue of securities and payment of interest.[26] He also told him that he had communicated this to Baron Charles de Rothschild, a banker in Naples. On February 20, probably not yet having received a definitive reply from the Paris and Naples Rothschilds, Torlonia again wrote to James to tell him that he would be meeting the Treasurer of the Papal State the following day to sign the agreement "and halt determination of securities".[27] The following day, Torlonia informed James that he had failed to reach a satisfying agreement with the barons Charles and Adophe, but hoped that they might consolidate their relations in other affairs.

To find a marketplace to float his Roman bonds, Torlonia turned to the Parodis, who represented the alternative "foreign" bankers with recognized competence, connections, and ability to float securities.[28] And even

[24] Manzitti (2003, 179). Details on this loan are found in the documents kept in: ASR, Camerale II, Debito pubblico, 14. The loan is issued per contract signed on January 20, 1846 between the Papal government and Messrs Torlonia. In addition to his "high and sovereign guarantee", the Pope "assigns as general collateral all the assets and income of the Roman State, and nominally the product of the customs office, the joint salt and tobacco administration, and all products of land taxes". Lastly, the following are assured: "all guarantees and all privileges that can be attributed to the *rendita* recorded in the Gran Libro of the Roman State". The interest to be paid on the Genoa market implies a semiannual disbursement of 324,000 francs, or 648,000 francs annually. The interest on amortized bonds will not be accrued but go into the amortization fund, until the total extinction of the loan (in other words, the annual payment does not vary with progressing amortization of the loan).

[25] Felisini (1990a).

[26] ANMT, BR, 132 AQ 9 P 110 Torlonia di Roma (1845–1846).

[27] ANMT, BR, 132 AQ 9 P 110 Torlonia di Roma (1845–1846).

[28] The ties to the Torlonias were later strengthened with the acquisition by the same of the Villa on Lago di Traiano: in 1852, with the banker Parodi intermediating, Prince Alessandro Torlonia began negotiations with the marchesi Pallavicino of Genoa

after national unification, the categories of redeemable debt included the "Parodi loan", and it is significant that the only loan bearing the name of an Italian bank among those to pre-unity states recorded in the Kingdom of Italy's *Gran Libro* of government debt is this one, on a par with Blount and Rothschild.[29] During discussions on pre-unity state loans in the Chamber of Deputies on December 21, 1868, the Minister of Finance Luigi Guglielmo Cambray-Digny stated: "There is the Parodi loan, [...] this too fully borne by the Italian treasury and paid in Genoa via the Parodi bank".[30]

Another area of activity where the Parodis were associated with the *haute banque* was their contribution to the establishment of new banking institutes taking the form of joint-stock companies, similarly to other European banking families. David S. Landes points out that, alongside the new way of banking taking hold in the middle decades of the nineteenth century, activities characteristic of the "old bank" endured. However, the customers and partners are different, as are the banks' objectives.[31] The Parodis took part in initiatives of this sort as far back as the 1840s, contributing to the establishment of banks in Genoa. Their participation

to purchase the Porto Estate, but the latter asked too high a price. Negotiations resumed in the following years and concluded with the notarial deed of May 26, 1856, with notary Filippo Bacchetti, via whom the Pallavicinos sell the villa to the Torlonias for the price of 1.5 million francs. See: Lugli and Filibeck (1935, 204–205).

[29] Manzitti (2003, 179).

[30] *Rendiconti del Parlamento* (1869, 8661). The importance of the Banca Parodi in the post-unification period is also affirmed by the estimation of a foreign observer. Isidore Sachs includes this bank among those with which the Treasury of the newly born state maintains relations. Only a few Italian and foreign banks and bankers were included. Those outside of Italy were the Banque Rothschild frères of Paris; Société de Crédit Industriel et Commercial; Société Générélle pour favouriser le développement du Commerce et de l'Industrie en France; N. M. Rothschild and Sons Bank of London; C. J. Hambro and Sons of London; Baring Brothers and Co. of London; and A. de Rothschild und Söhne of Frankfurt. In Italy: Banca Bartolomeo Parodi e Fratelli in Genoa; Cassa Generale; Società Generale di Credito Mobiliare e la Società per la vendita dei beni demaniali. See: Sachs (1885, 546–548).

[31] Landes (1956, 204–222). Regarding the activities of the *vieille banque* Landes writes: "Their principal instrument was the letter of exchange, the concrete expression of short-term credit. They discounted the results of trade, they issued loan payments, they accepted and banked customer banknotes, at the same time advancing the funds necessary to support their correspondents from the beginning of transactions to the obtainment of benefits. In a word, the merchant bankers performed all the functions necessary to make commerce possible between separate places" (p. 208).

in the creation of the Banca di Genova in 1844[32] was of great relevance in the economy of the Italian peninsula. With its banking institutes, the Ligurian capital became one of the modernizing hubs of the economic structures of the Sardinian state.

Further evidence of the financial acumen of the Parodis and direct testimony of Bartolomeo's idea of economic development and the banking sector are provided in his speeches as president at the first three general stockholders meetings: May 13, 1845; July 14, 1846; and July 13, 1847. Regarding the usefulness of discount banks, he observed in 1845 that banks play a fundamental role in economic and mercantile development because "they have the great advantage of relieving the country of the obligation of having general wealth circulate as metal specie, a form that is often inconvenient and not always immune to risk [...]. We thus have in banknotes a representation of money, much more convenient and secure as currency, and for the facility of transactions, because the representation can be converted into coin upon simple request of the bearer".[33] He also pushed for the expansion of commercial transactions with France, England, countries on the Black Sea, and countries in South America that could be intermediated by the Banca di Genova, and also for growth in the national economy through development of infrastructure and manufacturing.

In the Report of 1847, in addition to expressing his satisfaction with the general progress of the institute, which was rapid, he underscored that this type of banking agency was advantageous for the development of the local and State economy because it was able to supply capital to commerce and businesses during an international crisis caused mainly by increases in food costs.[34] As Parodi stated: "In this manner, the bank accustomed merchants to rely on its support, and with imports exceeding

[32] Conte (1990), Scatamacchia (2008), and Doria (1969, 82–85). When it was established, the bank had share capital of 4 million lire divided into 4,000 shares.

[33] Parodi (1845). Regarding the activities of Bartolomeo Parodi at the Banca di Genova, see also: Cerioni (2016).

[34] Parodi (1847). At the end of his speech, Bartolomeo Parodi says this of the bank of which he is president: "Favored by trade, protected by the Prince, sustained by public trust, it begins to replace the great mass of currency in circulation with its banknotes, it attends to the needs of the banker's discount, keeping the interest on the market within moderate limits, it removes the scarcity of cash and thus prevents crises; it provides capitalists with a safe and profitable investment when buying its shares; it attracts large industrial operations to our marketplace".

cash outlays, it was in a position where it did not have to reduce its issue of credit, which would have harmed commerce, but to increase it and reap significant profits".

However, Cavour was not entirely impressed by the management of the bank. In an article in *Il Risorgimento* on January 29, 1848, he accused the directors of "timidity", i.e., excessive prudence that translated into the issue of less credit than would have been possible and lower returns for the shareholders. At the same time, however, Cavour admitted that the "timid" management of the bank gave it solidity and liquidity, which pleased him within the current political climate, probably imagining how that money could be spent. In the fall of 1848, during the First Italian War of Independence, the Ministry of Finance requested a loan of 20 million lire from the bank, which was issued to the treasury as a 2% mortgage.

In the period under consideration, the Banca Parodi stood out within the national panorama for its history, solidity, reputation, and mutual relations with other private banks. Furthermore, as mentioned above, the bank handled major financial operations, from loans to governments to investments in joint-stock companies such as banks, railroads, mines, and maritime transport. Their business volume was less than that of other families such as the Rothschilds, Pereires, or Hambros, but they carried out the same type of activity using similar methods.[35]

4.3 Financial Intermediation in the Years Prior to the First War of Independence

The Banca Parodi played a prominent role during the years 1848–1849, which were marked by political and economic difficulties for the Kingdom of Sardinia. They helped shape the government's financial policies, especially while Vincenzo Ricci was Minister of Finance.[36] The Parodis played a dual role in that period: they were private bankers but also active participants in the management of the Banca di Genova. The Kingdom of Sardinia was at war at the time and the situation was very complicated both politically and economically. Vincenzo Ricci served as Minister of

[35] Stoskopf (2002). On the role and wealth of the elites operating in the finance and credit sector: Stanworth and Giddens (1974), Daumard (1973), Bergeron (1978a), Cassis (1993), Cameron (1994), Volpi (1997), Tilman (2006), Bonin (2000), and Berta (2013).

[36] Guderzo (1970, 642). For the events of 1848 in Genoa: Montale (1967a).

Finance for three different administrations during that delicate period: those of Gabrio Casati, Vincenzo Gioberti, and Chiodo-Rattazzi.[37] A member of the Genoese economic elite, he preferred to do business with his fellow townsfolk. The conflict between the Ligurians and the Piedmontese, arising with the annexation of the Republic to the Kingdom of Sardinia at the Congress of Vienna, had its repercussions also in the government's economic strategies. Here, in 1848–1849, Ricci found Cavour to be an implacable adversary who judged him mediocre. The dislike was mutual, Ricci defining the Piedmontese statesman a "political adventurer".[38]

The Ricci correspondence[39] evidences the role to which the Parodis and Carlo Bombrini were summoned in support of state finances, a role that contrasted strongly with the famously cautious nature of the former. In the early phase, it was Bombrini who was sent abroad to meet with representatives of some of the major banks in London and Paris and work out agreements for the issue of loans to the Piedmont government. The plan was to develop a negotiation process between December 1848 and March 1849 that would lead to the first major international loan for the Kingdom of Sardinia. Bombrini negotiated with representatives of the following Parisian banks: Pillet Will, Snider Pellegrini & C, Hottinguer, A. Fould & Fould Oppenheim, Gabriel Odier & C., M. Mathieu & C., Mallet Frères, and Ardoin (practically speaking, the French *haute banque*). In London, he met with the Rothschilds, the Barings, and the Andersons. In the meantime, Ricci was seeking to obtain a loan both via the agency of the Banca di Genova and with certain Genoese bankers and capitalists whose reputation would be an incentive for foreign bankers. However, the business community was skeptical about the operation: while bankers would be favored by such financial initiatives and the issue of banknotes by the Banca di Genova,[40] businesses would be penalized.

[37] Montale (1999, 2016) and Guderzo (1970, 577, 597–98).

[38] Guderzo (1970, 597). Regarding Vincenzo Ricci and context: Montale (1967b, 1971) and Treves (1938).

[39] The correspondence is kept in the Archivio dell'Istituto Mazziniano at the Museo del Risorgimento in Genoa. Guderzo (1970).

[40] Guderzo (1970, 635): in an anonymous letter to Ricci dated March 1, we read "The city is now at the eve of great and new upheavals due to the monopoly of certain bankers (Parodi at the lead) on Banca di Genova bonds".

Cavour, on the one hand, was trying to get the preeminent Turinese bankers involved in the economic and financial development of the Kingdom of Sardinia in that period and saw a foreign loan as an opportunity to tap into international finance[41]; on the other, he supported the merger between the Banca di Genova and the Banca di Torino.

Returning to the role of the Parodis in the Kingdom of Sardinia's credit and finance system, it is evident that they acted in a mixed manner, showing prudence in the face of uncertainties and unscrupulousness when success appeared guaranteed. As private bankers, they were hesitant, for example, to support Ricci's request to lend money to the Kingdom of Sardinia, as is evident from the words of Tommaso Spinola, royal inspector at the Banca di Genova and governmental intermediary, in March 1849[42]:

> Mr. Parodi is of the opinion that such a loan will not be difficult to negotiate in Paris, and so a first attempt might be made there, but he resists my earnest entreaties to take the initiative and the onus, drawing in other Genoese capitalists so as to establish a base of lenders here.

The attitude of the Genoese financier, like that of his fellow bankers, diminished the likelihood that other private bankers in foreign markets would grant loans to the Sardinian state. The Niçois banker Enrico Avigdor, who mobilized his network in favor of the Piedmont loan, felt that there would be no point in looking for lenders abroad if the bankers of Genoa could not be enticed into the affair.[43]

In this specific circumstance, the Parodis leveraged their advantageous position, initially within the Banca di Genova and subsequently in the Banca Nazionale, institutes benefiting from government backing in which they had invested large amounts of money and where they enjoyed the support of Bombrini.

In effect, the governmental bank entailed fewer risks and offered the Parodis numerous opportunities, both as investors and as private bankers. As a director in the Banca di Genova, Bartolomeo, for example, was

[41] Gulì (1932), Marchetti (1952), Norsa (1959), Rendi (1960), Luzzatto (1961, 1–12), Pautassi (1961), Mori (1962), Di Gianfrancesco (1974), Bracco (1988), Luraghi (1967), and Felloni (1956, 1959).

[42] Guderzo (1970, 635).

[43] Guderzo (1970, 648–651) and Maffi and Romani (2019).

hostile to investment in government funds, observing that many stockholders view money invested in such a manner as lost. However, at the same time, as a private banker, he readily operated in that sector. In the guise of a money lender, he also enjoyed advantages from the issue of banknotes by the bank, profiting, as we read in the *Corriere Mercantile*, "rather handsomely from currency trading, bills of exchange, and even from bank drafts following the loss on banknotes".[44] The Banca di Genova presented relatively low risks for private banker-investors, having to guarantee a margin of safety for the issued banknotes and not competing with their own lines of credit. Among other things, the private banks' possibility of rediscounting allowed the development of conditions favorable to the expansion of financial operations generally.

The result of these events revolving around the financial policy of the Kingdom of Sardinia was, as we have said, the establishment in 1849 of the Banca Nazionale, with later modifications to banking policies based on the new economic policy orientation promoted by Cavour in the early 1850s.[45] In effect, Cavour changed his position regarding the Genoese market over time. In an article, he wrote in 1850 for *Il Risorgimento*, supporting a nascent Genoese corporation for trade with the Far East, we read[46]:

> We do not doubt that this worthy project will soon be brought to fruition, both because we believe in the wisdom and resources of its promoters, Messrs. Giacomo Millo, Paolo Sconnio, and Giuseppe Gamba, and because we know that they have already obtained the support of the principal names in Genoese commerce, Messrs. Parodi, Bombrini, Grendy, Penco, and others.

4.4 The Beginnings of the 5% Sardinian Loan (1849–1850)

The wartime economy provided the occasion for a financial turning point. The Savoy state abandoned the traditional Albertine autarchy and turned to the Parisian and London houses of issue, whose intervention was all the

[44] Guderzo (1970, 636).

[45] Conte (1990, 100).

[46] Doria (1969, 108).

more necessary because of the lack of an "Italian" intermediary with credibility beyond the local sphere, able to mobilize internal resources.[47] The large international banks and their networks could ensure the extension of a loan, but floating the securities was not automatically guaranteed. The support of local brokers was also necessary. Having their finger on the pulse of the local securities market, they could support the quotation of bonds circulating on the secondary market and create a propitious climate for profitable placement of the newly issued securities on the primary market, rather than calling in securities initially sold abroad. In the case of the Piedmont loan, these local resources were identified in Genoa and Turin both by the Rothschilds and by the men in government, an essential condition for the success of the operation. These aspects still remain partially unexplored in current historiography, partly because of limited access to sources.

In 1848, government debt became structural in the pre-unification states. Unlike in previous decades, it was now the Kingdom of Sardinia bearing the greatest debt.[48] After the war of 1849, the Kingdom had to pay indemnity of 75 million lire to Austria, at a time when its revenues only amounted to 60 million. The Rothschilds were the main source of lending to aid the Sardinian state. Data from their archives allow us to make an initial assessment of capital markets in the Kingdom of Sardinia and of the mechanisms regulating financial operators in the years 1849–1851. New strategies were implemented in 1851 that further complicated an already complex panorama when Cavour initiated negotiations with London and the Hambro bank.[49] The first Rothschild loans to the Kingdom, which had emerged victorious from the unification process, have been analyzed by scholars who examine events either from the Rothschilds' point of view[50] or in the light of Italian politics and institutions.[51]

The 5% Rendita bond was the most important security traded on the Genoa stock exchange and other Italian securities markets. Stock market investments were the least risky and thus the most frequently practiced

[47] Della Torre (2007) and De Cecco (1990).

[48] Conti and Schisani (2011).

[49] Berta (1990).

[50] Gille (1965), Bouvier (1968), and Ferguson (1998).

[51] Guderzo (1970, 1973), Berta (1990), and Rossi and Nitti (1968).

by savers and capitalists. The issues in 1849–1850 already made it clear that the local peninsular markets were not large enough to absorb all the government debt. It was thus advantageous, via foreign bankers, to float these bonds on the major European markets.[52]

Three loans were authorized in the space of one year (5% Sardinian loan) and registered in the Rothschild books as follows[53]:

- Loan 1: October 4, 1849—nominal capital L. 45,726,000
- Loan 2: February 3, 1850—nominal capital L. 80,000,000
- Loan 3: October 2, 1850—nominal capital L. 120,000,000

Nominal capital amounted to a total of 245,726,000 lire, but the document reports that two million lire of Rendita were held by the government and not put on the market, not even for public flotation. The sum of the three loans was thus L. 205,726,000 of nominal capital or L. 10,286,000 of Rendita (annuity). These financial operations, authorized by the Subalpine Parliament and managed specially by the Minister of Finance Vincenzo Nigra, were complex and provided that a part of the yield would go to the Rothschilds as a lump sum, that a part would be sold on commission by the Rothschilds, and that a third portion would be sold via public flotation. Specifically, on October 4, 1849, a loan contract was signed between the Rothschild bank and the Sardinian government for 2,286,300 lire of annuity, corresponding to nominal capital of 45,726,000 lire. On this occasion, the Rothschilds took 937,000 lire as a lump sum and reserved an option for an additional 312,500 lire; a further 1,036,300 lire were earmarked for public flotation.[54]

This contract did not meet with unanimous approval in Piedmont; Cavour, in particular, was very critical of it, insisting that the bankers of Turin and Genoa should be involved in a different manner, not leaving the entire affair in the hands of the Rothschilds, who would have mainly floated the Rendita bonds on foreign markets. As he saw it, the entire amount should be floated within the State, without the intervention of

[52] Da Pozzo and Felloni (1964).

[53] ANMT, BR, 132 AQ 56, Emprunt piémontais (1849–1860).

[54] ANMT, BR, 132 AQ 56, Emprunt piémontais (1849–1860). Gille (1967, 78–79). The loan was authorized by the Laws of June 12 and 16, and October 3, 1849. See also: Guderzo (1973).

the French bank. However, Cavour never got his way, even on loans issued during his term in office.

In truth, the financial elite of the Kingdom of Sardinia was ready for this international turn of events and even campaigned for it on several occasions as far back as 1848 through their European contacts. Well organized and endowed with sufficiently competent players, the State opened to European finance. The competence and international stature of the Genoa bankers were beyond question; the Turin bankers, in turn, were specialized in credit operations in the silk business, which was mainly oriented to exports.[55]

As regards the 1849 loan, Banque Rothschild was in complete agreement with other Parisian banks, to whom it paid an interest of one-fourth of the operation: Blanc-Mathieu et C., Hottinguer, Pillet-Will, and Gabriel Odier.[56] On October 27, 1849, the bankers paid James de Rothschild the sum of 3,600,000 francs (900,000 per bank) which amounted approximately to the sum necessary for the operation. The banks also requested to receive the Rendita bonds due them as soon as possible.[57] At the beginning of December 1849, a new agreement was signed between Gustave Landauer, "plenipotentiary" of the Rothschilds in Turin, and the Minister of Finance regarding the sale on commission of Rendita bonds worth 586,300 Italian lire.[58] Specifically, the Rothschild bank committed to selling these bonds on a fixed 1% commission. It is interesting to observe that these financial operations regarding the Kingdom of Sardinia continued to involve, via Rothschild, other members of the French *haute banque*. In two letters dated December 10, 1849, representatives of the four Parisian banks (Blanc-Mathieu et C., Hottinguer, Pillet-Will, Gabriel Odier) ask to be informed of the status of ongoing and future operations.[59]

On February 3, 1850, the Piedmont government was authorized to issue Rendita bonds at a face value of 80 million lire, undertaking to pay a yield of 4 million lire. The Rothschild bank negotiated and signed

[55] Guderzo (1973, 247).

[56] Gille (1967, 79).

[57] ANMT, BR, 132 AQ 9 P 033, Bolmida (1849–1853).

[58] ANMT, BR, 132 AQ 56, Emprunt piémontais (1849–1860), agreement between the government of Sardinia and the Rothschild bank.

[59] ANMT, BR, 132 AQ 56, Emprunt piémontais (1849–1860).

a contract for 750,000 lire in yield and a option for another 500,000 at a price of 87.5%; one million lire was allocated for public flotation.[60] However, Gille observes in his analysis that, with this contract, 1,250,000 lire in yield were taken as a lump sum by the Rothschilds, 1,316,000 lire were sold on commission, and 1,433,000 lire were floated publicly.[61]

On October 2, 1850, another contract was signed between the Rothschilds and the Piedmont government for 6 million lire of Rendita, corresponding to 120 million lire of nominal capital.[62] The Rothschild bank took 500,000 lire of Rendita as a lump sum at a price of 85%, with an option for an equal amount at 87%. Another 2 million lire of Rendita remained with the government, which intended to satisfy the requests within the Kingdom, but this amount was never floated. In April 1851, Cavour replaced Nigra at the Finance Ministry, bringing new prospects for foreign loans and a search for new partners and financial markets (Hambro in London).

[60] ANMT, BR, 132 AQ 56, Emprunt piémontais (1849–1860). Gille (1967, 82). The issue of the new loan was authorized by Law no. 982 of February 1, 1850. The loan was authorized by Law no. 1056 of July 12, 1850. The loan was structured as follows:

Total nominal capital: 80,000,000
Rendita: 4,000,0
Public flotation: 28,679,000 nominal capital or 1,433,950 of rendita
Rothschild: 51,321,000 nominal capital or 2,566,050 of rendita. Of this, 41,721,000 nominal capital or 2,086,050 of rendita as lump sum. Commission, 9,600,000 nominal capital or 480,000 of rendita.

[61] Gille (1967, 82).

[62] ANMT, BR, 132 AQ 56, Emprunt piémontais (1849–1860). Gille (1967, 84). The loan was structured as follows:

Total nominal capital: 80,000,000
Rendita: 4,000,000
Rothschild: 80,000,000 nominal capital or 4,000,000 of rendita. Of this, 10,000,000 nominal capital, or 500,000 of rendita as a lump sum. Commission, 70,000,000 nominal capital or 3,500,000 of rendita.
In the event that sales on commission did not take place in a timely manner, the Rothschild bank had pledged to advance up to 10 million in 4 months to the Savoy Treasury. But in 1851, Nigra, in the hope of finding better prices, probably suspended sales, obtaining other advances which had risen to 25 million.

4.5 The Affairs of Private Bankers

In opposing Nigra's agreement with the Rothschilds, on October 5, 1849 Cavour wrote to De la Rüe regarding finding financing to indemnify Austria and float bonds[63]:

> I have every reason to believe that Nigra has allowed himself to be hoodwinked by that sly old fox Rothschild. We had agreed that Rothschild would leave a sum to the markets of Turin and Genoa corresponding to the means they currently possess. I had spoken of 12 million, telling Nigra to transfer 2 million and keep 10. This way everyone would have been satisfied. We would have had 600,000 francs, and Parodi and Leonino a million each.

In his opinion, the entire amount could be floated in the country without the intercession of the private French bank. On the other hand, the Rothschilds, once they had the contract in hand, had all the interest in strengthening their relations with the bankers in the Kingdom of Sardinia and in Genoa and Turin. Management of the operation was entrusted to Gustave Landauer, who had lived in Trieste in previous years and mainly dealt with colonial affairs, moving west to help the Rothschilds develop their business, living in Turin in the years 1849–1851.[64] In addition to maintaining relations with the Ministry of Finance, Landauer had a network of relations with the principal Genoese and Turinese bankers. Rothschild's intent was thus to capture the interests of the bankers in the Kingdom of Sardinia in his operation on the 5% Rendita. In a letter dated October 17, 1849 (the loan was from October 4), James de Rothschild made 50,000 francs (one Piedmont lire was worth one franc) of Rendita available to Landauer, corresponding to a million francs of nominal capital, so that it could be distributed "among the banks here".[65] The price was fixed at 81% and the bankers would have paid by November 25. In the space of a few days, Landauer placed 44,500 francs of Rendita, corresponding to 890,000 francs of nominal capital. As

[63] Cavour (1889, 344–345), Gille (1967, 77–79), and von Mülinen (1875).

[64] The nearly daily letters by Gustave Landauer in these years are kept in London: RAL, XI/38/163, Gustave Landauer (1844–1849) and ANMT, BR, 132 AQ 6293, 132 AQ 6294, 132 AQ 6295. For information on Landauer and his ties to the Rothschild family: Lòpez-Morell (2013).

[65] ANMT, BR 132 AQ 9 P 033, Bolmida (1849–1853).

Table 4.1 Bankers and businessmen directly involved by Rothschild in Turin

Rendita in francs	*Nominal capital in francs*	*Name*
7,500	150,000	Bolmida
5,000	100,000	Conte di Cavour
5,000	100,000	Fratelli Nigra
3,000	60,000	Mestrezat
3,000	60,000	Conte de Fernex
3,000	60,000	Barbaroux
3,000	60,000	Dupré
3,000	60,000	Cesana
3,000	60,000	Piaggio
3,000	60,000	Donina
3,000	60,000	Long
3,000	60,000	Todros
44,500	890,000	Total

Source ANMT, BR, 132 AQ 9 P 033, Bolmida (1849–1853)

illustrated in Table 4.1, the preeminent bankers and businessmen in Turin were involved, including Cavour.

Giulio Guderzo focused on the trend in Rendita quotations and Rothschild's business acumen, observing that the first loan was successfully floated in the markets of Paris, Lyon, Geneva, Frankfurt, Genoa, and Turin.[66]

Furthermore, Gustave Landauer handled relations with the bankers to whom Rothschild entrusted his credit operations in the Kingdom of Sardinia, especially Bolmida[67] in Turin and Parodi in Genoa. The relations between Rothschild and the Parodis in Genoa were very long-lived, stretching from the 1820s to the early 1900s.

The interest of Genoese agents in this type of financial operation was solid and they had years of consolidated experience. They had been entrusted in 1846 with the placement of a loan to the Papal State, negotiated by the Torlonias, on the Genoa market.[68] Furthermore, thanks to their involvement in the Banca Nazionale and their relations with Carlo

[66] Guderzo (1973, 280–296).

[67] Although he was the minister who supported this operation, Nigra preferred that his brother bankers were not the agents of the Rothschilds' operations in Turin. He dissuaded them and it was they who gave him the name of Bolmida. See: Guderzo (1973, 280–296).

[68] Felisini (2016).

Bombrini, the Parodis were kept informed of financial policy discussions in that period.[69] Bombrini saw his prestige and the recognition of the value of his contribution to the business of the Banca Nazionale and financial policy increase precisely in those years both nationally and internationally. Like the most important private bankers in the Kingdom, on October 18, 1849, Rothschild offered him a share of 5000 francs of Rendita at the same price and conditions as listed in the contract. This was a move that not only represented a gesture of high esteem, but also highlighted the privileged treatment by Rothschild enjoyed by the director of the Banca Nazionale.[70] It is worth highlighting that precisely in his letter to Bombrini, Rothschild expressly insisted on the twofold importance of this financial operation: in addition to establishing a solid basis for trust in the nation by external observers as regarded the economic and political affairs of the Kingdom of Sardinia, the involvement of the eminent Rothschild would make the Piedmontese securities more familiar and trustworthy in the eyes of foreign investors.

Already in the first weeks following the first Rothschild loan, the Parodis performed a number of major bank transactions for the Parisian bank: following instructions from G. Landauer, on October 24, they remitted the sum of 500,000 Piedmont lire *nuove* to the Minister of Finance in Turin "in banknotes from our bank".[71] On November 13, Parodi wrote to Rothschild that he had met with Ignace Bauer, at the time Rothschild's other man in northern Italy, later one of the main players in finance in Madrid,[72] "to further deepen our relations". In November and December, Rothschild performed transactions for nearly one million lire in favor of Landauer and Bauer[73] via Banca Parodi. Parodi also informed Rothschild repeatedly of the good price for the 5% Rendita on the Genoa market.

[69] Sul ruolo dei Parodi nella Banca di Genova/Banca Nazionale: Conte (1988, 1990) and Scatamacchia (2008).

[70] ANMT, BR, 132 AQ 9 P 033, Bolmida (1849–1853).

[71] ANMT, BR, 132 AQ 9 P 096, Parodi (1848–1851). Regarding transactions between Parodi and Landauer and more generally, Landauer's activities in the months following the loan, see Guderzo (1973, 290–300).

[72] Lòpez-Morell (2013).

[73] ANMT, BR, 132 AQ 9 P 096, Parodi (1848–1851).

On January 19, 1850, Bartolomeo Parodi wrote directly to James de Rothschild regarding a loan that would soon be signed on February 3.[74] He wanted to be included in the deal. In the letter, we read:

> Well supposing that the new Loan of our Government of 4 million in rendita can be concluded, as I would like to take part in it, I am writing to inform you confidentially that a company of bankers and traders has come to me to propose a project, namely to take part in a subscription between 20 and 25 million, and to sent a Delegate to Turin to make a submission to our Government.

Parodi later stated that he was little inclined to commit to this "essentially public" affair and preferred to take a share in Rothschild's operation, partly so as not to interfere or compete in ongoing negotiations between the baron and the Piedmont government. The Genoese banker had already spoken with Ignace Bauer and received a letter from Gustave Landauer informing him that Rothschild would have given him serious consideration if the loan went through. He thus asked for 140,000 lire of Rendita (approximately 2.4 million nominal capital) from the part that Rothschild would take for himself and on the same terms and conditions. On February 3, 1850, Rothschild took 1,250,000 lire of Rendita as a lump sum, then discovered that Parodi's share was part of this.

Unfortunately, the documents in the Parodi archive do not allow us to reconstruct the placement on the Genoa market of the Rendita owned directly by the Genoese bank. It is possible, on the other hand, to reconstruct the operations carried out by the Parodis on behalf of the Rothschilds in this marketplace in the years 1851 and 1852, both as regards the placement/sale of the 5% Rendita (1851) and as regards the purchase of the same (1852).

A review and analysis of the commercial correspondence of 1851 reveal that the Parodis floated 235,750 lire *nuove* of Rendita on the Genoa market for the Rothschilds of Paris with a value of nearly 3.9 million lire of nominal capital[75] (Table 4.2).

The fact that the private bankers of the Kingdom were sought after as key players in financial operations associated with Rothschild loans in the years 1849–1850 has already been observed by Giulio Guderzo,

[74] ANMT, BR, 132 AQ 9 P 096, Parodi (1848–1851).

[75] ANMT, BR, 132 AQ 9 P 096, Parodi (1848–1851).

Table 4.2 Placement of Rendita at 5% on the Genoa market by Banca Parodi on behalf of the Banque Rothschild of Paris in 1851

Date	*Rendita (nominal capital) nominale in £*	*Sale in £*	*Course of sale of 100 £ of Rendita 5%*
February 1	12,800	215,040	From 84 to 87
February 13	17,300	257,405	From 84 to 84 and 1/2
February 21	4,500	76,140	To 84 and 5/8
February 25	22,000	369,600	From 84 and 1/2 to 84 and 5/8.
March 7	10,000	169,000	From 83 and 1/2 to 83 and 2/5
April 1	15,500	262,012.50	From 84 and 1/2 to 84 and 5/8
April 29	21,750	367,875	From 84 and 1/2 to 84 and 7/8
June 28	30,000	490,925.60	FROM 81 and 1/2 to 83 and 7/8
September 1	16,000	260,950	81 and 5/8
September 4	14,600	237,099.25	81 and 3/10
October 2	51,000	826,337.50	From 80 and 9/10 to 81 and 3/8
December 31	20,300	348,626.55	From 85 and 1/2 to 89 and 3/4
	235,750	3,881,011.40	

Source ANMT, BR, 132 AQ 9 P 096, Parodi (1848–1851)

while more recent historiography has placed more attention on the fact that the Kingdom of Sardinia, by means of loans from Rothschild and Hambro, turned to the major European marketplaces of London and Paris to float their securities.[76] Both positions are correct because if the economic dimension of these initiatives did not allow—as Cavour initially wished—placement wholly within the State, there was a clear possibility of allocating part of the Rendita to the markets of Genoa and Turin, and Rothschild was an informed promoter through the energetic work of Gustave Landauer and Ignace Bauer.

This type of operation once again features certain bankers in the Kingdom whose competency and networks made them more capable than

[76] Conti and Schisani (2011), Berta (1990), Cassis (2006), and Cassis and Cottrell (2009).

others at earning the trust of the marketplaces in which they worked and channeling investments into related operations.

The relations between Parodi and Rothschild in 1850 also regarded the Parodi-Torlonia loan to the Papal State in 1846. The turbulent situation characterizing the State of the Church in that period was such that the Minister of Finance of the government of Rome communicated to Parodi on November 29 that he had engaged Rothschild to bring the Genoese banker 324,000 lire *nuove* to pay for the 6-month interest due on the Obbligazioni Romane.[77]

The two-year period 1851–1852 represents an emblematic case study for analyzing the financial intermediation involved in the placement of the Sardinian loan, underscoring the role of the internal market, which was more receptive to securities trading than has hitherto been revealed by historiographers. Data obtained from weekly written transmissions between Banque Rothschild and the Genoese banks Parodi and Spigno-Gastaldi allow us to highlight not only the financial strategies, but especially the amount of capital invested in these transactions. Specifically, 1851 was a year when the two Geonese bankers floated some 7.9 million lire of Sardinian Rendita issued in 1849–1850.[78] The following year, on the other hand, consisted of acquisitions by the two bankers on behalf of Rothschild: Banca Parodi purchased a total of roughly 2 million lire in Sardinian 5% Rendita (Table 4.3); the only two sales recorded for the year 1852 were dated January 31 for 9000 lire of 5% Rendita, corresponding to nominal capital of 156,886 lire and, on December 1, with a certificate for 3400 pounds of the Anglo-Sardinian loan with a value of 86,000 lire.[79]

[77] ANMT, BR, 132 AQ 9 P 096, Parodi (1848–1851). For the economic and financial situation of the Papal State in that period: Felisini (1990a, 2016).

[78] The figure of 8.3 million lire is the sum of the securities floated on the Genoa market by Spigno-Gastaldi and Parodi alone. As regards Banca Parodi, 3.9 million lire were sold on behalf of the Rothschild bank, while the remaining 2.4 million lire would represent the portion obtained by Banca Parodi directly for itself under the same conditions as in the Rothschild contract with the government. This total amount is roughly 3.4% of the total nominal capital of the three loans contracted during the two-year period.

[79] The information is re-elaborated in the business letters from the year 1852: ANMT, BR 132 AQ 9 P 097, Parodi (1852–1855); as well as in "*Rothschild conto loro secondo semestre 1852*" [Rothschild account, second half 1852]: ANMT, BR, 132 AQ non coté 145, Parodi (1852–1868).

Table 4.3 Purchases of 5% Rendita in the Genoa marketplace by Banca Parodi on behalf of Banque Rothschild of Paris in 1852

Date	*Type*	*Value (lire)*
January 2	coup. Rend 5%	57,132.50
January 5	coup. Rend 5%	26,285.96
January 9	coup. Rend 5%	19,426.20
January 15	coup. Rend 5%	12,312.00
January 21	£n 4900 Rendita 5%	90,783.50
January 29	£n 7900 Rendita 5%	136,530.45
January 31	£n 500 Rendita 5%	9,261.55
March 10	£n 2400 Rendita 5%	44,037.05
March 16	£n 3000 Rendita 5%	55,419.20
March 16	£n 2950 Rendita 5%	55,583.65
March 20	£n 2800 Rendita 5%	53,406.65
March 23	£n 2900 Rendita 5%	55,459.25
March 24	£n 3500 Rendita 5%	66,933.55
March 29	£n 26,300 Rendita 5%	494,642.50
April 5	£n 2800 Rendita 5%	53,546.85
April 15	£n 4400 Rendita 5%	84,783.35
April 30	£n 18,000 Rendita 5%	354,138.10
June 30	coup. Rend 5%	55,674.40
July 7	coup. Rend 5%	48,546.21
July 10	coup. Rend 5%	40,234.80
July 17	coup. Rend 5%	8,617.00
July 20	coup. Rend 5%	7,151.00
July 24	coup. Rend 5%	9,577.00
July 27	coup. Rend 5%	8,626.00
August 9	coup. Rend 5%	3,500.00
November 29	£n 5000 rendita 5%	100,375.30
December 1	£n 2000 rendita %	40,150.10
December 31	coup. Rend 5%	16,958.65
Total		2,009,092.77

Source ANMT, BR 132 AQ 9 P 097, Parodi (1852–1855) and ANMT, BR, 132 AQ non coté 145, Parodi (1852–1868). Rendita prices ranged from 91 to 96% of face value that year

The name Spigno-Gastaldi alongside that of the Parodis is pertinent in this analysis of the two-year period in that the names were found in association a significant number of times in the documents available from the Rothschild Archive. Furthermore, a comparison of accounting data found in business correspondence from that period reveals analogies and agreements that allow us to map out a clear trend line. In the first half of 1851, Spigno-Gastaldi sold a total of some 2 million lire of Piedmont Rendita (Table 4.4). The following year they purchased 750,000 lire of

Table 4.4 Sales of 5% Rendita on the Genoa market by the Banca Spigno-Gastaldi on behalf of the Banque Rothschild of Paris in 1851

Date	*Quantity of Rendita of sale for Rothschild (lire)*	*Nominal capital*	*Price of 100 lire of Rendita*
1851-April 11	5,000	82,439.70	82.75
1851-April 11	3,000	82,788.40	83 and 1/10
1851-April 11	2,000		83 and 1/10
1851-April 16	5,000	83,286.50	83.6
1851-April 30	2,000	32,800	82
1851-April 30	1,000	16,387.50	81 and 15/16
1851-April 30	2,000	32,750	81 and 7/8
1851-April 30	2,000	32,950	82 and 3/8
1851-April 30	3,000	49,350	82 and 1/4
1851-May 6	5,000	243,495.95	81 and 1/2
1851-May 6	1,000		81 and 1/2
1851-May 6	1,000		81 and 1/2
1851-May 6	2,000		81 and 1/2
1851-May 6	2,500		81 and 1/2
1851-May 6	3,500		81 and 3/8
1851-May 6	1,000	309,011.85	81 and 5/8
1851-May 6	2,000		81 and 5/8
1851-May 6	500		81 and 5/8
1851-May 6	4,500		81 and 5/8
1851-May 6	3,000		81 and 5/8
1851-May 6	2,000		81 and 5/8
1851-May 6	2,000		81 and 5/8
1851-May 6	1,000		81 and 5/8
1851-May 6	1,000		81 and 5/8
1851-May 6	2,000		81 and 5/8
1851-May 7	2,000	65,114.90	81.7
1851-May 7	2,000		81.7
1851-June 16	2,000	99,300	82.75
1851-June 16	1,000		82.75
1851-June 16	3,000		82.75
1851-June 16	1,000	596,255.63	83 and 1/8
1851-June 16	2,000		83 and 1/8
1851-June 16	5,000		83 and 1/8
1851-June 16	5,000		83 and 1/8
1851-June 16	4,000		83 and 1/8

(continued)

Table 4.4 (continued)

Date	*Quantity of Rendita of sale for Rothschild (lire)*	*Nominal capital*	*Price of 100 lire of Rendita*
1851-June 16	2,000		83 and 1/8
1851-June 16	12,000		83 and 1/8
1851-June 16	5,000		83 and 1/8
1851-June 17	1,200	19,821.40	82.9
1851-June 28	200	3,317.40	83 and 1/4
1851-June 28	3,000	49,822.50	83 and 7/20
1851-June 29	3,500	202,985.90	81 and 1/2
1851-June 29	3,000		81 and 1/2
1851-June 29	6,000		81 and 1/2
Total	121,900	2,001,877.63	

Source ANMT, BR, 132 AQ 9 P 070, Spigno Gastaldi (1851–1852)

Rendita on behalf of the Rothschilds and sold a portion for 138,000 lire.

We may ask why there was a change in strategy from selling in 1851 to purchasing in 1852. In 1851, the Banque Rothschild's sale of Sardinian bonds issued in the previous two years was one of the objectives for the success of the loan. However, in the first three months of 1852, it began buying Rendita bonds (Table 4.5). There are two plausible reasons for this: they may be able to resell securities purchased on the Genoa market in the price range of 88.75–98.375 francs for prices ranging from 89 to 100.75 francs on the Paris market,[80] giving a non-negligible speculative edge to these bankers who deal in large sums and who have mastery, if not control, over the rules of the *haute banque*; after Hambro of London's loan to Sardinia, the Rothschilds pursued their strategy of playing a leading role as financial intermediaries in new opportunities for loans to the Kingdom of Sardinia taking shape in those months.[81] It is thus reasonable to hypothesize that the purchase of the securities in question on the Genoa market was part of a far-sighted strategy of preparing the market for floating securities from new loans. Indeed, after having purchased the Rendita security at prices ranging between 80 and 89, the city capitalists have the opportunity to sell them the following year at a

[80] Courtois (1862).

[81] For the chronology of the principal loans issued in the Kingdom of Sardinia, see: Conti and Schisani (2011, 151–153).

Table 4.5 Purchases of 5% Rendita on the Genoa market by the Banca Spigno-Gastaldi on behalf of the Banque Rothschild of Paris in 1852

Date	*Quantity of Rendita of purchase for Rothschild (lire)*	*Nominal capital (lire)*	*Price of 100 lire of Rendita*
1852-February 13	1,200	21,300	88 and 3/4
1852-February 13	2,000	35,600	89
1852-February 13	1,000	17,800	89
1852-February 13	800	14,280	89 and 1/4
1852-February 21	2,000	35,744.63	89 and 1/4
1852-February 21	1,000		89 and 1/4
1852-February 21	1,000	35,722.32	89 and 1/4
1852-February 21	1,000	17,859	89 and 3/4
1852-February 24	5,000	88,950	88.95
1852-February 27	3,000		88 and 3/4
1852-February 27	1,000		88 and 3/4
1852-February 27	1,000		88 and 3/4
1852-February 27	500		88 and 3/4
1852-February 27	2,500	178,000	88 and 3/4
1852-March 3	1,500		89
1852-March 3	3,500	89,000	89
1852-March 21	1,000		95 and 1/2
1852-March 21	1,000		95 and 1/2
1852-March 21	570		95 and 1/2
1852-March 21	600		95 and 1/2
1852-March 21	300		95 and 1/2
1852-March 21	500		95 and 1/2
1852-March 21	1,250		95 and 1/2
1852-March 21	2,100		95 and 1/2
1852-March 21	4,000	216,212	95 and 1/2
Total		750,467.95	

Source ANMT, BR, 132 AQ 9 P 070, Spigno Gastaldi (1851–1852)

higher price, making a clear profit. This clearly inspires them to reinvest and thus to be receptive to the new proposals that the Parisian bankers would soon have presented to the market.

The Genoa financial market thus proved to be extremely receptive to the purchase of public loan securities, whether foreign (e.g., from the Papal State) or national (5% Sardinian loan). In the decades prior to Italian unification, there was thus a process of accumulation of capital and investment of savings, two key factors in the industrial growth of the city after unification, in addition, naturally, to the presence of bankers who find opportunities to leverage their competency and networks of relations.

4.6 Financial Networks and the Exchange of Information

The success of financial operations, as regards the negotiation of the first loans of the Kingdom of Sardinia and their listing on national and international stock exchanges, is closely linked to the exchange of information in the world of finance.[82]

The various networks which connected emblematic members of the political and financial elite are a key element in events which took place at the beginning of the First Italian War of Independence and in the early 1850s. In order to analyze these networks and the exchange of information, it is useful to further inspect what emerged in the previous paragraphs thanks to news preserved in the Rothschild bankers' documents, which allows us to construe networks on various levels.

The Rothschild family, in fact, hold a legendary role in this field and the extension and efficiency of the networks of information which they use mean they have high-quality data available to analyze earlier and more quickly than their competitors and, at times, even governments. Thus, they have a formidable competitive advantage due to the information they receive from their correspondents and the investors who join them over the years. The Rothschild family's power to influence the primary market, indirectly affecting the secondary market, derives, among other things, from the quantity of bonds traded (representative of States' debts), and from information provided by well-nurtured political contacts.[83]

Between 1848 and 1851, networks develop which see the most important private bankers and political figures of the Kingdom of Sardinia involved with the international *haute banque*.

[82] Networks between the banking and financial elite are the object of attention of historians internationally, with various methodological approaches: Bergeron (1978b), Levy-Leboyer (1979), Scott (1982), Plessis (1982), Lisle-Williams (1984), Mosse (1985), Charle (1987), Bruguiere (1988, 101–120), Bottomore (1993), Kaelble (1993, 1996), Cassis (1996, 369–383), Banti (1996), Mension-Rigau (1997), Piluso (1998), Kurgan-Van Hentenryk (1999), Plessis (2000), and Bussière and Dumoulin (1998).

[83] Gille (1967, 75–91). Reference Texts on the Rothschild bankers are: Ferguson (1998) and Bouvier (1968).

I have identified two networks connected to the negotiation phase of loans:

- The bankers-politicians network which tries to arrange a loan in 1848/1849. It includes: Vincenzo Ricci (finance minister of Genoese origin, bitterly opposed by Cavour); a group of Genoese bankers; Carlo Bombrini, manager of *Banca Nazionale*; the banker Henry Avigdor; and some members of the international *haute banque*.
- The bankers-politicians network which organizes the 1849 loan. It includes: the King of Sardinia; Giovanni Nigra, finance minister; some private bankers from Turin; Carlo Bombrini, who has strong connections with Genoese private bankers; Gustave Landauer; and James de Rothschild.

Two other networks regard bond listings:

- The network which deals with listings, made up of: James de Rothschild, on the Paris Stock Exchange; Gustave Landauer, who coordinates the network in the north of Italy; the banker Bolmida, whom Nigra wanted as a representative in Turin; the bankers Parodi and Spigno-Gastaldi in Genoa; and the Ulrich-Brot bankers in Milan.
- The network which is not explicitly involved in the listings, made up of: Genevan bankers operating in the Kindom of Sardina, namely De La Rüe in Genoa and the bankers De Fernex and Mastrezat in Turin. Each of them, through personal and business relations with Cavour, tries to participate in the listing, but they are not directly involved by the Rothschilds.

The first of these four networks, dealt with in paragraph 4.3, is particularly important, as it launches the Kingdom of Sardinia's season of international loan negotiations.

As I have already observed, the initiative is unsuccessful because the group of Genoese bankers does not support it fully enough, instead guaranteeing the government a loan through the Bank of Genoa.

The success of the second network, with the active and favorable participation of James de Rothschild, benefits from the important role played by Giovanni Nigra in 1849.[84] The Nigra family's bank has worked in credit and the silk trade since the 1700s, but it is through Giovanni (1798–1865) that both their relationship with the monarchy[85] and their work in finance operations are consolidated. Despite his involvement in the Turin city administration, Giovanni, who has run the bank since 1833, invests in finance operations from the 1840s, in particular in the fields of railway companies, banks (*Banca di Torino*), and insurance (*Compagnia di Assicurazioni contro gli incendi di Torino* – today's *Toro Assicurazioni*).[86]

Furthermore, since the 1830s the "Nigra brothers" company has also worked in credit and finance operations with the Rothschilds, drafting, making payments, and sending letters of credit for the nobility and the Piedmontese bourgeoisie. This relationship grows in the 1840s to such a degree that in February 1843, Nigra brothers propose a deal to the Paris and Naples Rothschilds on behalf of the intendant of the private assets of His Majesty the King of Sardinia. They want to negotiate a loan of 1,500,000 francs for the King, against 4,000,000 francs' worth of property belonging to the Crown, not to the state. The intendant's proposal sees repayment of the capital with annual payments of 100,000 francs[87]; however, the negotiation is unsuccessful.

The role of this bank in economic policies in the first few years of the First Italian War of Independence is evident when Giovanni Nigra, finance minister from March 27, 1849 to April 19, 1851, stipulates Piedmontese loans with the Rothschilds.

In the company's correspondence in 1849, interests in the Kingdom's economic policies and interests in the listing of the loan on the Turin market are mixed. From April, the letters of the "Nigra fratelli" are full of references to the political situation and the negotiation of the loan led by Carlo Bombrini.[88] In October, they express satisfaction with the

[84] In Turin, the bankers with whom the Rothschilds have the greatest business relationships are: Bolmida, De Fernex, Mestrezat and Nigra.

[85] ANMT, BR, 132 AQ 9 P 092, Nigra (1838–1847) and 132 AQ 9 P 093 Nigra (1848–1851).

[86] Roccia (2013).

[87] ANMT, BR, 132 AQ 9 P 092, Nigra (1838–1847). Letter dated 4 February 1843.

[88] ANMT, BR, 132 AQ 9 P 093 Nigra (1848–1851). The letter of April 4, 1849 mentions military operations. Nigra writes that the situation is rapidly moving towards peace and mentions the armistice with Austria. "Our government is favourable to the

result of the negotiation of the first loan between the Rothschilds and the Kingdom of Sardinia: Nigra is evidently satisfied on two fronts, both as the government minister who achieved this result and as a prominent banker, highlighting the fact that it is the first successful operation in their collaboration.[89] The involvement of the Nigra bank in the operations regarding the listing is of great significance and in fact, on December 8, 1849, Nigra himself congratulated James de Rothschild on the general good progress of the listing, thanking him for having involved the "Nigra fratelli" through Landauer.[90] In this phase, however, Rothschild needs somebody on the Turin market who can manage his affairs in a bolder way; thus, following Nigra's advice, he turns to Vicenzo Bolmida, who becomes his Turin correspondent. This handover reveals the incompatibility of the strategies requested by Rothschild with the public role held by Nigra, as well as the special relationship which ties him to the Crown; so strong a tie that in 1856 King Vittorio Emanuele II names him "Minister of the Royal House", making him a sort of *éminence gris* with absolute power on the "public and private purse of the sovereign".[91]

Thus from the end of the 1840s, Bolmida is the correspondent for banking and financial operations and for all activities related to the listing of the Piedmontese loans on the Turin market.

This takes us back to the formation of the first network regarding listing which sees the Genoese private bankers taking on a central role again. In the period 1849–1851, Gustave Landauer manages his credit operations in the Kingdom of Sardinia through Bolmida in Turin[92] and Parodi and Spigno-Gastaldi in Genoa. Luigi Bolmida (1811–1856) and

loan" which would in part be for war costs and in part for the continuation of the railway line between Genoa and Turin, for which another 34–40 million lire are required. He maintains that negotiations will regard a total sum of 80–100 million. Nigra offers to work as an intermediary in the negotiations. He also mentions the fact that the minister, with the authorization of Parliament, has issued a 4% voluntary loan (for 30 million, it seems).

[89] ANMT, BR, 132 AQ 9 P 093 Nigra (1848–1851). Letter dated 28 October 1849.

[90] ANMT, BR, 132 AQ 9 P 093 Nigra (1848–1851). Letter dated 8 December 1849.

[91] Roccia (2013).

[92] Despite being the minister who supported this operation, Nigra preferred his brothers not to be the executors of the Rotschilds' operations in Turin. He dissuaded them from this opportunity and they recommended Bolmida. See: Guderzo (1973, 280–296). The corrispondence between the Rotschilds' Paris bank and Bolmida can be found in: ANMT, BR, 132 AQ 9 P 033, Bolmida (1849–1853), 132 AQ 9 P 034, Bolmida (1854–1855),

his brother Vincenzo are the owners of “Bolmida e C.”, which unites credit activities and the silk trade. The rise of Bolmida starts in the mid-1840s, partly thanks to his tie with Cavour through some shared finance operations.[93] In 1847, he promotes the foundation of the Bank of Turin “thus standing out from the group of private bankers, who, to protect privileged sectorial interests, placed obstacles before the implementation of Cavour’s plan of credit modernization”.[94] During the First Italian War of Independence, Bolmida stands out thanks to his economic-financial abilities and, on being elected deputy in the 4th and 5th legislatures, he proves to be influential in economic and financial policies.

Counterbalancing this network, which is responsible for managing listings, another network emerges, which has benefitted less from the listing operations. It is made up of bankers from Geneva, operating in the Kingdom of Sardinia, who are close to Cavour. This network’s protagonist on the Genoa market is Emile De la Rüe, who will benefit from his closeness to Cavour when the count becomes a minister in 1851, taking part firstly in the negotiation of the loan organized with Hambro and then, after its agreement, in the bond listing.[95]

In opposing Nigra’s agreement with the Rothschilds, Cavour writes to De la Rüe on October 5, 1849, as mentioned before.[96]

132 AQ 9 P 035, Bolmida (1857), 132 AQ 9 P 036, Bolmida (1858–1859), 132 AQ 9 P 037, Bolmida (1860–1861) and 132 AQ 9 P 038, Bolmida (1862–1865).

[93] The tie between Cavour and Bolmida is documented by the personal correspondence between them; see: Cavour (1895, 1883–1887).

[94] Sirugo (1969).

[95] This important bank had been founded by Gèdéon de La Rue. He was succeeded by his sons Emile, Hippolyte and David, under the name of de La Rue Freres; after Hippolyte left the bank (and took on a small farm in Piedmont) and David went back to Geneva, Emile was left alone. The company became de La Rue & Co.. Emile, more than his brothers, had a constant friendship with Cavour; for the whole time Cavour didn’t take on ministerial responsibilities, they collaborated in all manner of speculations. Cavour availed himself of Emile in 1851 for the negotiation of the loan known as the “Anglo-Sardian” loan. On supranational networks and the context of private bankers in Switzerland, see: Burkhardt (1914).

[96] Cavour (1889, 344–345) and Gille (1967, 77–79).

The Genevan bankers Guglielmo Mestrazat[97] (active in the Bank of Turin and the insurance sector) and Charles De Fernex operate in Turin. The latter has contacts with Rothschild and, besides credit operations, he deals with financial aspects, in particular as regards the building of railways—both in the Kingdom of Sardinia and abroad—and state loans.

In February 1845, De Fernex tells Rothschild that the Piedmontese government has decided to take on the laying of some railways lines in the Kingdom of Sardinia: from Genoa to Lake Maggiore and the two branch lines—one for Turin and the other for the border with Milan. In order to pay for this, the government feels the need to take out a loan of 100 million. De Fernex presents himself as an interlocutor: "If, therefore, you are of the idea of opening credit lines with our government regarding this, a proposal which we would happily join, I would be honoured to present it to the minister, to support it to the best of my ability and follow negotiations".[98]

However, the initiatives related to economic growth which are promoted by the government in this period do not find the best solution in foreign loans.

From July 1848, references to negotiations regarding the Kindom of Sardinia's loans begin to appear in the correspondence between De Fernex and Rothschild, reporting the government's intention to present the houses with a financing project. It is a loan of 40 to 50 million, which they wish to take out against the property of The Order of Saints Maurice and Lazarus, along with other state properties, worth approximately 50 million. On this occasion too, De Fernex carries out his role of interlocutor contributing to the exchange of information which is so useful in the field of finance, informing Rothschild of a business opportunity which has come to his attention.[99] De Fernex's interlocutary approach seems to place him among Rothschild's favorites for handling future bond listings, but he dies before this can take place, in April 1849. Once negotiations

[97] Romeo (1977, 358): "The native Genevan Guglielmo Mestrezat was, at the time, one of the bankers that Cavour most esteemed in Turin"; he was active in the Bank of Turin and in the insurance sector.

[98] ANMT, BR, 132 AQ 9 P 069 Fernex di Torino (1838–1862), letter dated 6 February 1845.

[99] ANMT, BR, 132 AQ 9 P 069 Fernex di Torino (1838–1862), letter dated 15 July 1848.

are completed, correspondence in the second half of that year recognizes the role played by the bank he managed, which, however, no longer enjoys the privileged relationship with the Paris bank, as Rothschild's trust is now placed in another interlocutor.

The change in the reciprocal trust between two private banks, as on Charles De Fernex's death, brings our attention back to an exchange of information which travels in preferential and exclusive channels; it is the fruit of confidential, direct exchanges of both sensitive and general news, with more or less evident financial implications of great interest. In the networks of relations at the root of the credit-finance market, therefore, purely social connections act by taking advantage of links with friends and family, or economic, political or geographical links. This consideration implies an increase in the value of the concept of financial information, focusing on the worth of the more "informal" and "emotional" content, which is richer and fuller than the cold, stylized transmission of information purely connected to the trend in prices.

For example, correspondence between bankers in a crucial period, such as 1848–1849, explicitly expresses all of these aspects, showing how correspondence which transmits information regarding credit and finance operations is also the preferred channel for passing on information which is so precious because the recipient will know how best to use it.

A large amount of political and military news of 1848–1849 can be found in the letters of the Avigdors of Nice, correspondents of the Rothschilds of Paris.[100] In the spring and summer of 1848, updates are constantly sent on the state of the conflict and there is insistence on the opportunity of keeping business on Italian soil or transferring it to safer markets, such as Marseille, depending on how events unfold. On August 9, 1848, on the same day as the Salasco armistice, which ratifies the Austrians' victory, Avigdor does not hide his fear that they may decide to go further in their future ambitions for conquest. During 1849, fresh conflict makes the Avigdors confirm their advice not to make remittances in Italy.[101]

It is clear to see how events in Italy interest the Rothschilds, not only due to an obvious preoccupation regarding business already active there, but also due to an express desire to maintain their privileged,

[100] XI/38/9b, Avigdor l'Aine et fils (1844–1849).

[101] XI/38/9b, Avigdor l'Aine et fils (1844–1849).

influential position on a potential, rising market. Explicit confirmation of this strategy can be found in a letter dated March 31, 1849, in which the Rothschilds' London bank informs its Havana agent of the King of Sardinia's signing of the armistice of Vignale (March 24), assuring him that positive conditions for transactions will return "in Italy".[102] This information holds a sign of activation on a global level, starting with commercial interests which are brought into question by the recent conflicts (especially as regards tobacco imports through Trieste and Genoa). It is also useful for preparing foreign investments in a financing project, which is still at an initial phase, regarding the future listing of public debt. It is no coincidence that four days later, on April 4, Baron Anselm Salomon von Rothschild of Vienna explains to his cousin in London that a loan from Piedmont, under guarantee of England and France would be very useful. In this case, the family network within the Rothschild banks uses an exchange of information which is codified in shared strategies and can presumably be traced to objectives on a European level, in which the roles and spheres of influence are shared out according to common agreement and are not explicitly declared.

Moving on to the correspondence between the Rothschilds in Paris and the Milanese correspondent Charles Brot, from Ulrich and Brot, we have the testimony of another network between private bankers involved in the events of these two years.[103]

In this correspondence too, along with data regarding financing and credit, concise reports regarding the events unfolding from March to June 1848 appear, written by Brot himself. They are rich in detail of military operations, accounts of market stagnation, and passionate reflections on the city of Milan, accompanied by observations of a political-risorgimento air. Such enunciations are also a way of externalizing and sharing a widespread desire for the creation of a unitary state, which englobes

[102] RAL, Letter copy books 148/109 (20 March–31 July 1849).

[103] The Ulrich and Brot bank is founded in Milan in 1847 and closes in 1857. Regarding this Swiss banker's activity, see: Martignone (2001, 14, 24, 28, 46–47). On the Swiss in Italy, see: Bonnant et al. (1972). Charles Brot's civic engagement was particularly intense in that period. In fact, in June, the Austrians damage the railway line between Milan, Brescia and Peschiera del Garda as they retreat. However, the line is quickly repaired and reopened for the transport of people, materials, and munitions. This outcome is thanks to the interest of Brot, who, at the time, is the only member of the board of directors of "Chemins de fer lombard-vénitiens" in Milan, Dunant (2009, 93). Regarding the Milanese credit and finance context, see: Fiocca (1984).

Lombardy-Venetia and the Kingdom of Sardinia. This desire is proven by the results of a referendum on June 8, 1848: "561,000 votes to 680 in favor of immediate union".[104] Brot does not limit himself to this account, but offers his interlocutor a macroeconomic reflection regarding the opportunity such a union would present: "If Venetia does the same, which is to be hoped because the provinces of the mainland have already expressed themselves in this sense, this constitutional realm of the *haute Italie*, with its 10½ million inhabitants, a budget which will have to exceed 200 million francs and public debt which is today below 16 million *rente*, has a bright future and, without credit, it will be solid".[105] Again, what at first appears to be a correspondent's personal update on his situation as a banker and as a citizen at a time of conflict, shows itself to be a clear example of one of the most far-sighted exchanges of information at the limit of officially professional correspondence. Brot proves that he fully understands the Rothschilds' level of interest in the fate of the Italian risorgimento affair and, therefore, the mutual benefits that this relationship brings.

Brot reappears in a financial network which gravitates around the Rothschilds and the listing of Piedmontese debt three years later, in an exchange of letters between the Rothschilds' Paris bank correspondents on the markets of Genoa, Turin, and Milan: Parodi, Bolmida, and Ulrich and Brot, respectively. The recurring reciprocal use of the words *ami* or *amis*, in referring to one another, confirms the close relationship of trust between the members of a *haute banque* network which works on solid personal/friendly relationships.

An exemplary case of good use of the constant exchange of information, via the networks surrounding the Rothschilds, is the letter sent to Gustave Landauer from Baron James.

Dated August 7, 1850, it is a consultation offered following the repeated request for financial opinions regarding the feasibility of a new financing of the Kingdom of Sardinia. The capital is needed for its modernization and for war compensation owed to Austria.[106] The Paris banker expresses his conviction that such sums must come from capitalists who are active on the main stock exchanges, despite the fact that they

[104] BR, 132 AQ 9 P 117, Ulrich & C. (1847–1850).

[105] BR, 132 AQ 9 P 117, Ulrich & C. (1847–1850).

[106] BR, 132 AQ 820, Copie d'affaires italiennes (30 juillet 1850–3 février 1851).

have already received requests for investment in numerous loans that the states (Austria and Prussia) are negotiating.

Working on a hypothesis of a loan of 6 million lire of profit on 120 million lire of capital, Rothschild emphasizes that August is not the best month in which to attract capitalists and speculators and outlines three opportunities to define the terms of the new issue to the finance minister of the House of Savoy: the opening of a lottery in Turin; "an adjudication of the loan"; or the favored option of continuation of the negotiation of a third loan with the Rothschilds. As regards the impracticability of the first option, he reminds Landauer that during the last lottery, the public involved lost "*de l'argent*" (some money) due to a lack of cash and the refusal of the National Bank to issue investment loans. For this reason, a fresh lottery in Piedmont would find only a frail echo: "*chat brulé craint le feu*!" (a burnt cat fears the fire); the same reasons invalidate the hypothesis of a public adjudication. The option of the Rothschilds' intervention remains the only feasible one. The Baron suggests two scenarios: the first with a bipartition of the loan, in true Rosthchild style, one part with a fixed price and the other on commission, with the guarantee that they themselves will take part in a lottery on the Turin market: "We do not doubt that the public will come toward us because they know full well that we will provide the funds the very same day of the issue and they trust the way we manage business".[107]

However, knowing that the market is currently in stagnation means that a delay in the operation is taken into account, awaiting more favorable circumstances. This leads the Baron to propose the only plausible solution with which he intends to persuade the minister of the House of Savoy: the urgency on the government's part to immediately have a sum between 8 and 10 million lire provides the conditions for Rothschild to offer to anticipate the sum on the condition that he could take on the loan and sell between 35 and 40 million lire on commission on the same conditions stipulated in the first contract between them in October 1849. "This, dear Landauer, appears to be the best solution at present. It has the double advantage of ensuring the Minister receives the sum he requires

[107] BR, 132 AQ 820, Copie d'affaires italiennes (30 juillet 1850–3 février 1851).

by the end of October and it enables him to wait for a more favorable moment for an issue".[108]

In this important letter, it is possible to see the effects of a network of contacts on various levels, which is active in the entire area of interest, and the use of the exchange of information which it provides: the abundance of options and suggestions, the foreseeing of scenarios which could otherwise not be imagined, the operational proposals according to the needs of the other party and the awareness of one's own central role on the stock exchanges, as well as the channel of direct communication with governmental institutions. All this enables the private banker to solidify his professional, social and personal credibility in company profit strategies, in which the exchange of information is a tool and a resource.

Bibliography

Archives

Rothschild Archive London (RAL).
XI/38/9b, Avigdor l'Aine et fils (1844–1849).
XI/38/40, Ulrich—Bansa & Baudeuf (1823–1828).
XI/38/163, Gustave Landauer (1844–1849).
XI/38/203a, Pescio (1829–1835).
XI/38/203b, Pescio (1836–1847).
Letter copy books 148/109 (20 March–31 July 1849).
Archives Nationales du Monde du Travail – Banque Rothschild (ANMT, BR).
BR, 132 AQ 56, Emprunt piémontais (1849–1860).
BR, 132 AQ 820, Copie d'affaires italiennes (30 juillet 1850-3 février 1851).
BR, 132 AQ 6293, Lettres de Gustave Landauer, Lettres envoyées de Vienne, Milan, Turin, Trieste, Venise (1848–1849).
BR, 132 AQ 6294, Lettres de Gustave Landauer, Lettres envoyées de Turin (1850).
BR, 132 AQ 6295, Lettres de Gustave Landauer, Lettres envoyées de Turin (1851).
BR, 132 AQ 9 P 033, Bolmida (1849–1853).
BR, 132 AQ 9 P 034, Bolmida (1854–1855).
BR, 132 AQ 9 P 035, Bolmida (1857).
BR, 132 AQ 9 P 036, Bolmida (1858–1859).
BR, 132 AQ 9 P 037, Bolmida (1860–1861).
BR, 132 AQ 9 P 038, Bolmida (1862–1865).

[108] BR, 132 AQ 820, Copie d'affaires italiennes (30 juillet 1850–3 février 1851).

BR, 132 AQ 9 P 069, De Fernex (1838–1862).
BR, 132 AQ 9 P 092, Nigra (1838–1847).
BR, 132 AQ 9 P 093 Nigra (1848–1851).
BR, 132 AQ 9 P 096, Parodi (1848–1851).
BR, 132 AQ 9 P 097, Parodi (1852–1855).
BR, 132 AQ non coté 145, Parodi (1852–1868).
BR, 132 AQ 9 P 110 Torlonia di Roma (1845–1846).
BR, 132 AQ 9 P 117, Ulrich & C. (1847–1850).
Archivio di Stato di Roma.
Camerale II, Debito pubblico, 14.

Printed Contemporary and Near Contemporary Sources

Cavour, Camillo. 1883–1887. *Lettere edite e inedite*, edited by Luigi Chiala, 7 vols. Torino: L. Roux et C.

Cavour, Camillo. 1889. *Nouvelles lettres inédites*, edited by Amédée Bert. Torino: L. Roux et C.

Cavour, Camillo. 1895. *Nuove lettere inedite*. Torino: L. Roux et C.

Courtois, Alphonse. 1862. *Tableaux des cours des principales valeurs négociées et cotées aux bourses des effets publics de Paris, Lyon et Marseille du 17 janvier 1797 à nos jours*. Paris: Garnier Frères – Gouillaumin et Cie.

L'indicatore ossia Guida per la Città e Ducato di Genova, anno secondo 1834. 1834. Genova: Stamperia Casamara.

L'indicatore, ossia guida per la città e ducato. 1840. Genova: Stamperia Casamara.

Mancardi, Francesco. 1874. *Cenni storici sull'amministrazione del debito pubblico del Regno d'Italia e sulle amministrazioni annesse offerti al Parlamento nazionale*, vol. 1. Roma: Stamperia Reale.

Parodi, Bartolomeo. 1845. *Discorso detto alla prima adunanza generale degli azionisti della Banca di Genova il 13 maggio 1845*. Genova.

Parodi, Bartolomeo. 1847. *Rendiconto presentato a nome del Consiglio di Reggenza all'adunanza generale degli azionisti della Banca di Genova il 13 luglio 1847*. Genova.

Raccolta degli Atti del Governo di s. m. il Re di Sardegna dall'anno 1814 a tutto il 1852, volume XXI (1. gennaio a 31 dicembre 1831) (n. 2567 al 2470.). 1847. Torino: Stamperia Ferrero, Vertamy e comp.

Rendiconti del Parlamento Italiano - Discussioni della Camera dei Deputati, X Legislatura - Sessione 1867 (24/11/1868 - 02/02/1869), Volume (VIII) Prima della legislatura dal 24/11/1868 al 02/02/1869. 1869. Firenze: Tipografia Eredi Botta.

Sachs, Isidore. 1885. *L'Italie, ses finances et son développement èconomique depuis l'unification du royame, 1859–1884*. Paris: Guillaumin.

Tobone, Giovanni. 1872. *Guida pratica per le operazioni sulle varie rendite iscritte nel gran libro del debito pubblico del Regno d'Italia*. Torino: Tipografia Eredi Botta.

Von Mülinen, Friedrich R. 1875. *Les finances de l'Austriche*. Paris: Guillaumin.

Secondary Sources

Banti, Alberto M. 1996. *Storia della borghesia italiana. L'Italia liberale. (1861–1922)*. Roma: Donzelli.

Barbagallo, Francesco. 2000. "The Rothschilds in Naples." *Journal of Modern Italian Studies* 5, no. 3: 294–309.

Bergeron, Louis. 1978a. *Banquiers, négociants et manufacturiers parisiens du Directoire à l'Empire*. Paris: École des Hautes Études en Sciences Sociales.

Bergeron, Louis. 1978b. *Les capitalistes en France (1780–1914)*. Paris: Gallimard-Julliard.

Berta, Giuseppe. 1990. *Capitali in gioco: cultura economica e vita finanziaria nella City dell'Ottocento*. Venezia: Marsilio.

Berta, Giuseppe. 2013. *L'ascesa della finanza internazionale*. Milano: Giacomo Feltrinelli Editore.

Bonin, Hubert. 2000. *Le monde de banquiers français au XXe siècle*. Bruxelles: Editions Complexe.

Bonnant, Georges, Schutz, Hermann, and Emilio Steffen. 1972. *Svizzeri in Italia (1848–1972)*. Milano: Collegamento Svizzero in Italia – Camera di Commercio Svizzera in Italia.

Bottomore, Tom. 1993. *Élite and Society*. London-New York: Routledge.

Bouvier, Jean. 1961. "Les interventions bancaires françaises dans quelches grandes affaires de l'Unité italienne." *Annali Feltrinelli* 4: 224–33.

Bouvier, Jean. 1968. *I Rothschild*. Bari: Laterza.

Bracco, Giuseppe. 1988. *Commercio, finanza e politica a Torino da C. Cavour a Quintino Sella*. Torino: Centro Studi Piemontesi.

Bruguiere, Michel. 1988. "L'aristocratique descendance des affairistes de la Révolution." In *Les noblesses européennes au XIXe siècle*, 101–20. Rome: École Française de Rome.

Brussiere, Éric., and Michel Dumoulin, eds. 1998. *Milieux économiques et intégration européenne en Europe occidentale au XXe siècle*. Arras: Artois Presses Université NON C'è NEL TESTO Cercare di aggiungerlo nel cap. 5 o 6.

Burkhardt, Carl Felix. 1914. *Zur Geschichte der Privatbankiers in der Schweiz*. Zürich: Art. Institut Orell Füssli.

Cameron, Rondo. 1994. "Bankers as Entrepreneurs." In *Entrepreneurship and Transformation of the Economy (10th-20th centuries), Essay in Honour of Herman Van der Wee*, edited by P. Klep and E. Van Cauwenberghe, 411–18. Leuven: Leuven Univerisity Press.

Cassis, Youssef. 1993. "Businessmen and the Bourgeoisie in Western Europe." In *Bourgeois Society in Nineteenth-Century Europe*, edited by J. Kocka and A. Mitchell, 103–24. Oxford-Providence: Berg.

Cassis, Youssef. 1996. "Monde des affaires et bourgeoisie en Europe de l'Ouest." In *Les bourgeoisies européennes au XIXe siècle*, edited by J. Kocka, 369–83. Paris: Belin.

Cassis, Youssef. 2006. *Capitals of Capitals. The Rise and Fall of International Financial Center 1780–2009*. Cambridge: Cambridge University Press.

Cassis, Youssef, and Philip Cottrell, eds. 2009. *The World of Private Banking*. Farnham-Burlington: Ashgate.

Cerioni, Isabella. 2016. *Dalle banche di Genova e di Torino alla Banca Nazionale. Inventario delle carte degli istituti progenitori della Banca Nazionale*. Roma: Banca d'Italia.

Chapman, Stanley D. 1984. *The Rise of Merchant Banking*. London: Allen & Unwin.

Charle, Christophe. 1987. *Les élites de la République (1880–1900)*. Paris: Fayard.

Cipolla, Carlo M. 1953. "Agli inizi della rivoluzione industriale nell'economia ligure." In *Genova. Uomini e fortune*, 3–24. Genova: Levante, Società di Assicurazioni e Riassicurazioni.

Conte, Leandro. 1988. "La Banca Nazionale nel sistema del credito degli Stati Sardi." In *Credito e sviluppo economico in Italia dal medioevo all'età contemporanea*, 583–611. Verona: Sise.

Conte, Leandro. 1990. *La Banca Nazionale. Formazione e attività di una banca di emissione (1843–1861)*. Napoli: Edizioni Scientifiche Italiane.

Conti, Giuseppe, and Maria Carmela Schisani. 2011. "I banchieri italiani e la *haute banque* nel Risorgimento e dopo l'Unità." *Società e storia* 131, no. 1: 133–70.

Da Pozzo, Mario, and Giuseppe Felloni. 1964. *La borsa valori di Genova nel secolo XIX*. Torino: ILTE.

Daumard, Adeline, ed. 1973. *Les fortunes françaises au XIXe siècle*. Paris-La Haye: Mouton.

De Cecco, Marcello, ed. 1990. *L'Italia e il sistema finanziario internazionale 1861–1914*. Bari: Laterza.

Della Torre, Giuseppe, 2007. "Collocamento del debito pubblico e sistema creditizio in Italia (1861–1914)." In *Debito pubblico e mercati finanziari in Italia. Secoli XIII-XX*, edited by G. De Luca and A. Moioli, 451–75. Milano: FrancoAngeli.

Di Gianfrancesco, Mario. 1974. "La politica commerciale degli Stati Sardi dal 1814 al 1859." *Rassegna storica del Risorgimento* 61, no. 1: 3–36.

Doria, Giorgio. 1969. *Investimenti e sviluppo economico a Genova alla vigilia della Prima Guerra Mondiale* (1815–1882). Milano: A. Giuffrè Editore.

Dunant, Henry J. 2009. *Un souvenir de Solferino*, edited by Costantino Cipolla and Paolo Vanni. Milano: FrancoAngeli.

Felisini Daniela. 1990a. *Le finanze pontificie e i Rothschild. 1830–1870*. Napoli: Edizioni Scientifiche Italiane.

Felisini Daniela. 1990b. "La banca di emissione nello Stato Pontificio nel corso dell'Ottocento: le iniziative e il dibattito." *Rassegna economica* 54, no. 2: 281–316.

Felisini Daniela. 2004. *Quel capitalista per ricchezza principalissimo: Alessandro Torlonia principe, banchiere, imprenditore nell'Ottocento romano*. Soveria Mannelli: Rubbettino.

Felisini Daniela. 2016. *Alessandro Torlonia. The Pope's Banker*. London: Palgrave Macmillan.

Felloni, Giuseppe. 1956. *Le entrate degli Stati Sabaudi dal 1825 al 1860*. Torino: ILTE.

Felloni, Giuseppe. 1959. *Le spese effettive e il bilancio degli Stati Sardi dal 1825 al 1860*. Torino: ILTE.

Felloni, Giuseppe. 1971. *Gli investimenti finanziari genovesi in Europa tra il 1600 e la Restaurazione*. Milano: A. Giuffrè.

Felloni, Giuseppe. 2016. "Genova e il capitalismo finanziario dalle origini all'apogeo (secc. X-XVIII)." *Atti della società ligure di storia patria* 56: 71–9.

Ferguson, Niall. 1998. *The world's banker. The history of the House of Rothschild*. London: Weidenfeld & Nicolson.

Fiocca, Giorgio, ed. 1984. *Borghesi e imprenditori a Milano dall'Unità alla prima guerra mondiale*. Roma-Bari: Laterza.

Gille, Bertrand. 1959. *La banque et le crédit en France de 1815 à 1848*. Paris: Presses Universitaires de France.

Gille, Bertrand. 1965. *Histoire de la Maison Rothschild, 1, Des origines a 1848*. Genève: Droz.

Gille, Bertrand. 1967. *Histoire de la Maison Rothschild, 2, (1848–1870)*. Genève: Droz.

Grendi, Edoardo. 1964. "Genova nel Quarantotto." *Nuova Rivista Storica* 48, nos. 3–4: 307–49.

Guderzo, Giulio. 1970. "Il Piemonte e le grandi Banche europee nel 1848–49." In *Ricerche di storia economica in memoria di Corrado Barbagallo*, edited by L. De Rosa, 567–670. Napoli: Edizioni Scientifiche Italiane.

Guderzo, Giulio. 1973. *Finanza e politica in Piemonte alle soglie del decennio cavouriano*. Santena: Fondazione Camillo Cavour.

Gulì, Vincenzo. 1932. *Il Piemonte e la politica economica del Cavour*. Napoli: ITEA.

Kaelble, Hartmut. 1993. *Bourgeois Society in Nineteenth-Century Europe*. Oxford-Providence: Berg.

Kaelble, Hartmut. 1996. "Bourgeoisies françaises et allemandes au XIXe siècle." In *Les bourgeoisies européennes au XIXe siècle*, edited by J. Kocka, 247–81. Paris: Belin.

Kurgan-Van Hentenryk, Ginette. 1999. "Finance and Society. Social and Personal Aspects of Financial Networks." In *Finance and the Making of the Modern Capitalist world*, edited by C. E. Núñez, 71–80. Sevilla: Fundación Fomento de la Historia Económica.

Landes, David S. 1956. "Vieille banque et banque nouvelle." *Revue d'histoire moderne et contemporaire* 3, no. 3: 202–22.

Levy-Leboyer, Maurice, ed. 1979. *Le patronat de la seconde industrialisation*. Paris: Editions Ouvrieres.

Lisle-Williams, Michael. 1984. "Merchant Banking Dynasties in the English Class Structure: Ownership, Solidarity and Kinship in the City of London, 1850–1960." *The British Journal of Sociology* 35, no. 3: 333–62.

Lòpez-Morell, Miguel Ángel. 2013. *The House of Rothschild in Spain, 1812–1941*. Farnham: Ashgate.

Lugli, Giuseppe, and Goffredo Filibeck. 1935. *Il Porto di Roma imperiale e l'Agro Portuense*. Roma: Istituto Italiano Arti Grafiche.

Luraghi, Raimondo. 1967. *Agricoltura, industria e commercio in Piemonte dal 1848 al 1861*. Torino: Comitato Torinese dell'Istituto per la Storia del Risorgimento.

Luzzatto, Gino. 1961. "L'economia degli stati sardi nel decennio cavouriano." *Annali, Università degli Studi di Napoli* 2: 1–12.

Maffi, Luciano, and Marina Romani. 2019. "Banche private in Italia nel XIX secolo. Il network 'ebraico' dei Parodi di Genova." *Materia giudaica* 24: 91–100.

Manzitti, Beppe. 2003. "Un intraprendente banchiere belga e le sue operazioni finanziarie in Italia: il conte André Legrand-Dumonceau (1826–1900)." *Atti della Accademia ligure di scienze e lettere* 6: 153–80.

Marchetti, Leopoldo. 1952. *Cavour e la Banca di Torino*. Milano: Edizioni Amici del Museo del RIsorgimento.

Martignone, Cinzia. 2001. *Imprenditori protestanti a Milano (1850–1900)*. Milano: FrancoAngeli.

Massa, Paola. 1991. "Eredità, acquisti e rendite: genesi e gestione del patrimonio dei duchi di Galliera (1828–1888)." In *I duchi di Galliera. Alta finanza, arte e filantropia tra Genova e l'Europa nell'Ottocento, 1,* edited by G. Assereto, G. Doria, P. Massa Piergiovanni, L. Saginati and L. Tagliaferro, 391-448. Genova: Marietti.

Mension-Rigau, Eric. 1997. *Aristocrates et grans bourgeois. Éducation, traditions, valeurs*. Paris: Perrin.

Montale, Bianca. 1967a. "'Il 48 a Genova." *Rivista Storica Italiana* 79, no. 1: 195–205.

Montale, Bianca. 1967b. "Per un profilo del moderatismo genovese (1849–54)." In *Miscellanea in onore di A. Codignola*, 219–47. Genova: Istituto per la Storia del Risorgimento Italiano.

Montale, Bianca. 1971. "Per la storia della classe dirigente subalpina: Vincenzo Ricci ministro degl'Interni (marzo-luglio 1848)." *Bollettino Storico-Bibliografico Subalpino* 69, nos. 1–2: 176–220.

Montale, Bianca. 1999. *Mito e realtà di Genova nel Risorgimento*. Milano: FrancoAngeli.

Montale, Bianca. 2016. "Vincenzo Ricci'." In *Dizionario biografico degli italiani* 87. Roma: Treccani.

Mori, Giorgio. 1962. "Sul libero scambismo dei moderati nel Risorgimento." In *Problemi dell'Unità d'Italia*, 703–17. Roma: Editori Riuniti.

Mosse, Werner. 1985. *Jews in the German Economy. The German-Jewish Economic Elite 1820–1935*. Oxford: Clarendon.

Norsa, Paolo. 1959. *Finanziamenti stranieri nel periodo del risorgimento e dell'Unità d'Italia (1832–1863)*. Milano: Banca Commerciale Italiana.

Pautassi, Vincenzo. 1961. *Gli istituti di credito e assicurativi e la borsa in Piemonte dal 1831 al 1861*. Torino: Museo Nazionale del Risorgimento.

Piccinno, Luisa. 2013. *I trasporti in Liguria all'inizio dell'Ottocento. Nuove dimensioni e modelli operativi*. Milano: FrancoAngeli.

Piluso, Giandomenico. 1998. "Per una storia della cultura economica dei banchieri 'milanesi': formazione, culture e istruzioni (1890–1914)." In *Milano e la cultura economica. Gli anni 1890–1920*, edited by P. I. Porta, 425–63. Milano: FrancoAngeli.

Plessis, Alain. 1982. *La Banque de France et ses deux cent actionaires*. Genève: Droz.

Plessis, Alain. 2000. "Une maison de la haute banque parisienne, les Mirabaud, et le financement des enterprises de la fin du XIXe siècle à la seconde guerre mondiale." In *Banques et enterprises industrielles en Europe de l'ouest, XIXe–XXe siècles: aspects nationaux et régionaux*, edited by P. Marguerat, L. Tissat and Y. Froidevaux, 239–50. Genève: Droz.

Rendi, Giuliano. 1960. "La politica bancaria di Cavour." *Moneta e credito* 13, no. 51: 373–84.

Roccia, Rosanna. 2013. "Giovanni Nigra." In *Dizionario Biografico degli Italiani, 78*, 563–65. Roma: Treccani.

Rollandi, Maria S. 2012. "Patrimoni e spese della nobiltà genovese nella Restaurazione." In *Gio. Carlo di Negro (1769–1857). Magnificenza, mecenatismo, munificenza*, edited by S. Verdino, 9–28. Genova: Accademia Ligure di Scienze e Lettere.

Romeo, Rosario. 1977. *Cavour e il suo tempo (1842–1854)*, 2. Roma-Bari: Laterza.

Rossi, Ernesto, and Gian Paolo Nitti, eds. 1968. *Banche, Governo e Parlamento negli Stati Sardi, Fonti documentarie (1843–1861)*. Torino: Fondazione Luigi Einaudi.

Scatamacchia, Rosanna. 2008. *Azioni e azionisti. Il lungo Ottocento della Banca d'Italia*. Roma-Bari: Laterza.

Scatamacchia, Rosanna. 2013. "I banchieri questi sconosciuti. Appunti di ricerca (XIX–XX secolo)." In *Studi in ricordo di Tommaso Fanfani*, edited by M. Berti, A. Bianchi, G. Conti, D. Manetti, M. Merger and V. Pinchera, 793–800. Pisa: Pacini.

Schisani, Maria Carmela. 2010. "How to Make a Potentially Defaulting Country Credible: Karl Rothschild, the Neapolitan Debt and Financial Diplomacy (1821–26)." *Rivista di Storia Economica* 26, no. 2: 233–77.

Scott, John. 1982. *The Upper Classes. Property and Privilege in Britain*. London: Macmillan.

Sirugo, Francesco. 1969. "Luigi Bolmida." In *Dizionario Biografico degli Italiani*, 11. Roma: Treccani.

Stanworth, Philip, and Anthony Giddens, eds. 1974. *Elites and Power in British Society*. Cambridge: Cambridge University Press.

Stoskopf, Nicolas. 2002. De la banque privée à la banque par actions dans la France de la seconde moitié du XIXe siècle. In *Proceedings from the 6th Annual Congress of the European Business History Association (EBHA)*. Helsinki-Finlande: EBHA.

Tilman, Samuel. 2006. *Les grand banquiers belges (1830–1935). Portrait collectif d'une élite*. Bruxelles: Accademie Royale de Belgique.

Treves, Piero G. 1938. "Finanza straordinaria piemontese del 1848." *Rivista italiana di scienze economiche* 10, no. 4: 243–63.

Ugolini, Stefano. 2018. "The origins of Swiss Wealth Management? Genevan Private Banking, 1800–1840." *Financial History Review* 25, no. 2: 161–82.

Volpi, Alessandro. 1997. *Banchieri e mercato finanziario in Toscana (1801–1860)*. Firenze: Olschki.

CHAPTER 5

Private Bankers in the Economic and Political System of Unified Italy

5.1 The Economic and Political Context in the Decades Following the Unification of Italy

In the period following the unification of Italy, the banking and finance sector was characterized by different and conflicting development models that hampered Italy's progress with respect to other European nations in the early industrialization phase.[1] The banking sector suffered from underdevelopment of the legislative and regulatory framework, with consequences becoming evident in the decades immediately following unification (1861). It is true that instruments were in place to regulate the market and banking and financial operations, starting with the

[1] There is a great deal of literature and lively historiographic debate on economic development in Italy in the post-unification period: Ciccarelli and Fenoaltea (2007), Ciocca and Cotula (1994), Clementi et al. (2015), Cohen and Federico (2001), Delli Gatti et al. (2005), Federico (1986), Fenoaltea (1982), and Artoni and Biancini (2003), Baffigi (2011), Castronovo (1969), and Luzzatto (1957).

L. Maffi, *Private Bankers in the Italian 19th Century*, Palgrave Studies in Economic History,
https://doi.org/10.1007/978-3-030-63361-5_5

Minghetti Law (1874), which allowed the government to actively regulate the activities of banks of issue.[2] At that time, there were six banks that enjoyed this opportunity; among them, the Banca Nazionale nel Regno d'Italia (Banca Nazionale) played a prominent role.[3] The lack of rationalization in the system was the result of a complicated interweave of politics and a tendency toward parochialism. The Banca Nazionale itself encountered strong hostility, to that point where parties in many cities, even in northern Italy, preferred to do their banking with the Banco di Napoli or the Banco di Sicilia.

The banking sector is closely bound to the performance of the national and the international economies. As early as 1866, there was a direct demonstration of this when Italy had to cope with a recession caused by an international financial crisis. Following the Civil War (1861–1865), the United States called in debts extended to numerous countries, with repercussions on financial markets, which witnessed a drop in value of all securities, including the relatively safe government bonds.[4] The Italian government, needing capital not only to cope with the crisis but also to meet current and military expenditures, undertook legislative action to improve the rules regulating commercial companies and instituted fiat money (*corso forzoso*). This measure put the issuing banks in an advantageous position, especially the Banca Nazionale, whose capital and operations increased thanks to the opening of new branches throughout the Kingdom of Italy.[5] Given the paucity of bank deposits, the principal source of credit in those years was the issue of banknotes: the

[2] Gigliobianco and Giordano (2010, 13–17). Regarding banking and finance in the early decades after unification: Cardarelli (1990), Bartoletto and Garofalo (2014), Belli (2008), Brambilla (2011), and Cameron (1985).

[3] Conte (1990), Bonelli (1991), Pani (2017, 9), Canovai (1912), Alberti and Cornaro (1929), Di Nardi (1953), Demarco (1956), De Mattia (1990a, c), Gigliobianco (1990), Tuccimei (1990), De Rosa (1964, 1989), La Francesca (2004), and Giannini (2004). Regarding debate among economists about banks in this period: Realfonzo and Ricci (2000). Regarding books written in the 19th century and the lively discussion of this topic in those years: Benvenuti (1856), Boccardo (1879, 1863), Papa (1866), Pallavicino (1863, 1864), Bertolotto (1863, 1867), Amici (1867), De Cesare (1874, 1867–1869), Giulio (1853), Musso (1864), Garelli (1869), and Martello and Montanari (1874).

[4] Felloni (1997, 185, 194–196).

[5] Felloni (1997, 187): "At the end of 1865, the bank already had paid-up capital of 46.2 million lire compared to a total of 35 million of all the other issuing banks, and its position was further strengthened by the decree of May 1, 1866, which stipulated that the State would receive from Banca Nazionale a loan of 250 million lire in a transactional account

modernization of the Italian monetary system was thus decisively favored by banks financing production and investment through the issue of banknotes. Furthermore, the increase of banknotes in circulation allowed the Banca Nazionale to support banks in difficulty via advances and deferrals allowing them to meet demand for withdrawal of deposits.[6]

In spite of the enactment of new legislation, the relative weakness of Italian industry and business community—still struggling after the defeat at Lissa and, more markedly, the industrial inquest of the 1870s—induced the more enlightened governmental representatives to consider the option of revising the Cavourian agricultural-commercial development model.[7] Further pressure in this regard built in the late 1870s, when the deflationary impact of a crisis affecting farming, finance, and also industry contributed to a change in economic ideology. In a nation with few natural resources and substantially lacking strategic industries, the abandonment of liberal dogma forced the government to take a front-line role in boosting the economy, a factor that inevitably led to a meshing of politics and the banking and finance industry.

The fiat currency was legally abolished by the Law of April 7, 1881, which restored the faith of foreign capitalists—mainly Belgian, Swiss, English, and German—in Italian investments, albeit without modifying the essential features of the Italian financial system. While the Italian financial markets did not initially appear to benefit from the return to convertibility, signs of change began to be seen in 1884, when the German Reichsbank accepted Italian *Rendita* securities as worthy of investment, triggering an increase in exportation of these securities.[8] Foreign investment in the ten-year period 1881–1890 amounted to some 2.5 billion lire, of which 800 million was invested in the private sector and the rest in government bonds.[9]

In spite of these developments, the structural fragility of the Italian economy persisted into the 1880s: the national budget, which had run a

while also relieving it of the obligation to redeem its banknotes in cash on demand". See also: Scatamacchia (2008), Gigliobianco and Giordano (2010), and Ottolino (2005).

[6] Gregorini and Cafaro (2018), Fratianni and Spinelli (1997), Pittaluga (1994), Fumi (1993), Roccas (1990), Sannucci (1990), Ferraris (1879), and Busacca (1870).

[7] Concerning social and economical situation refear: Zamagni (1998, 2007) and Toniolo (1990).

[8] Felloni (1997, 185, 194–196).

[9] De Bernardi and Ganapini (1996).

surplus since 1876, closed with a deficit again in 1882, initially masked by accounting tricks and only becoming evident starting in 1885–1886; there also remained a large quantity of government bonds burdening Italian financial markets and only partially absorbed by foreign investment. Indeed, in spite of Italy's membership in the Triple Alliance (it joined in 1882) and the continuing application of protectionist foreign trade policies, French capitalists remained the principal foreign holders of the *Rendita* and Italy's main foreign investors. It would only be after 1890 that French primacy was superseded by the Germans.

The premises thus developed in the 1880s for Schumpeterian creative destruction, renewing Italy's credit structure. The country witnessed a credit boom from the influx of foreign capital invested in companies operating in Italy, the placement of bonds and other securities, and the discounting of promissory notes or bills of exchange, fueling speculation in the real estate market. However, Marco Pani points out that this influx of capital neither supported nor provided incentives for significant growth since the still embryonic industrial development limited opportunities for investment.[10] At the same time, there was an increase in foreign debt, which reached 1.6 billion lire during the decade, compounded by the proportional increase in servicing costs.[11] Nevertheless, the number of banks extending credit in the real estate market increased, as did the number of loans, only some of which went to the industrial sector, the bulk going to inflate the speculative bubble in big-city real estate, particularly in Rome, Naples, Turin, and Genoa.[12]

Italian economics and finance in the 1880s were characterized by an interweave of negative factors compounding the complex status of the newly unified nation. The customs agreements with France had not produced the desired effects and, as noted by Gino Luzzatto, these negative consequences worsened an already difficult situation in the agricultural system, leading to the prices of some products falling by as much as 20–40%.[13] Paolo Frascani, noting that this crisis has received little attention in recent studies, underscores the fact that Italy's principal agricultural products—wine, silk, rice, wheat, livestock, dairy

[10] Pani (2017, 11–16).

[11] Hertner (1984).

[12] Regarding the Esquilino and the real estate sector, see Doria (1973).

[13] Luzzatto (1963, 175–178).

products—all suffered, especially in regions practicing monocultures, such as winegrowing in Apulia.[14]

The historiography evidences governmental weakness in implementing banking legislation and regulation. The problem of poor management of this sector is thus closely linked to the actions and strategies of governmental economic policy, which in those years did not manifest any strong will to resolve the problems extending throughout the country's entire monetary system.[15] The perception of the crisis as being a phase in the economic cycle, in spite of the fact that foreign capital had begun to pull out and the first signs of a crisis in the real estate market had begun to appear,[16] prompted both the eighth Depretis administration and the first Crispi administration at the end of the decade to continue the strategy of government borrowing coupled with an increase in taxes on direct consumption. Furthermore, while recognizing the fragility of the Italian banking system and the need for new regulations to be legislated, they were aware that such a reorganization would introduce significant conflict and be difficult to implement.[17]

Financial thermometer readings provide important indicators of those years, during which fees increased and the price of the Italian *Rendita* decreased on the Paris market. In 1888, the government asked Bismarck to intercede so that certain important German bankers, including Bleichröder, would support investment in the *Rendita*,[18] providing evidence of the growing relevance of the new financial partner north of the Alps. The positive response from a number of German bankers, as well as Hambro and Barings of London and several important Italian banks, made it possible to slow the decline in value of Italian consolidated debt.[19] When Italy again requested the Chancellor's help in 1889 after the resumption of downward speculation, Bismarck expressed some concern about the Italian budget deficit. This concern was echoed among

[14] Frascani (2012, 21–36).

[15] Concerning monetary policy: Cerrito (1999), Toniolo, Conte, and Vecchi (2003), and Alberti and Cornaro (1929).

[16] Confalonieri (1979–1980) and Carocci (1956).

[17] Pecorari (1994, 90–117).

[18] Hertner (1984) and Pecorari (1994).

[19] Luzzatto (1963, 185–187) and Corbino (1934, 297–304).

potential German investors, who nevertheless continued to pump money into the country.[20]

Continuing recourse to foreign financial support, which did not resolve the problem, illustrates the fact that Italian economic players and policy-makers failed to perceive that the rise in fees and the depreciation of the *Rendita* securities were the direct effects of a deteriorating situation. At the start of the new decade, international markets also suffered the repercussions of instability originating outside of continental Europe: Barings Bank of London was the source of the crisis, known as the Panic of 1890, generated by an insufficiency of funds to support Argentine bonds (already in the second half of the 1880s), leading to serious problems of overexposure of the private English bank to South American debt. Thanks to the acumen of William Lidderdale, governor of the Bank of England, who organized a consortium of banks, it was possible to save the Barings Bank, preventing the acute recession from engulfing the entire financial system. However, the bank was never able to recover the trust and prestige that had always been associated with its name.[21]

On the national level, the critical situation in the first half of the 1890s derived partially from the dynamics of production shifts already underway during the Unification years (1850s–1860s). However, according to Stefano Fenoaltea, a longer-term analysis (1861–1918) shows expansion and modernization of the Italian economy, improvement in the Italian standard of living, and significant infrastructure development.[22] One example is the industrial production index, which was stagnant in the years from 1888 to 1896 but then grew rapidly from 1897 to 1908, partially due to revisions to the banking system.

As regards the Italian financial system (credit and insurance), in 1890 it amounted to less than 1% of GDP, and its principal component, the public banking system, comprised just under 1100 institutes: 153 credit unions,

[20] On Italy's role in the Triple Alliance see: Sciarrone (2014).

[21] Körnert (2003), Miles (2002), and Austin (2007, 191–193). For further information on the international financial context, see Hautcoeur (2003).

[22] Fenoaltea (2011, 3–5). See also: Biscaini Cotula and Ciocca (1979), Bonelli (1978), Cafagna (1962), Conti (1999), De Mattia (1990b), Gallegati and Stanca (1998), Hertner (1990), Masi (1989), Nardozzi and Piluso (2010), Parravicini (1958), Marongiu (1995), Pecorari (1995), and Are (1974).

216 savings banks, and some 700 cooperative banks.[23] These banks were more developed and numerous in northern Italy than elsewhere on the peninsula, especially in Lombardy, Piedmont, and Liguria, where industrialization was already underway, and were complemented by private banks in all major Italian cities.

In 1893, Italy experienced a banking crisis highlighting the significant weaknesses of its financial system, which had already become evident in the 1870s, and accelerating efforts at reform. National and international historiography has studied the causes of this shock, its consequences, and the economic policies implemented to remedy the defects in the system.[24] H. James and K. H. O'Rourke give an idea of the immediate impacts of this situation: "for most of the period after the re-establishment of the gold standard, the lira-sterling exchange rate was very close to parity, but after June 1893 the exchange rate fell sharply. The depreciation of the lira reached as much as 13 percent".[25]

Economic historians dedicated particular attention to the collapse of Banca Romana and its fraudulent management, including issue of banknotes without a corresponding increase in gold or currency reserves and violation of its own charter and Italian law. Two other important banks also failed: Società Generale di Credito Mobiliare Italiano and Banca Generale.[26]

The analysis of the dynamics and repercussions of this instability reveals a clean break with the previous period thanks to the reform of the banking system, the creation of Banca d'Italia, and the institution of new mixed or universal banks, copied from the German model and financed by international, mainly German, capital.[27]

The much needed reform moved in the direction of reorganization of banks of issue and rationalization and control of monetary policy, addressing, for example, the maximum allowable circulation and how

[23] Pani (2017). Regarding the Italian banking and financial system in the second half of the nineteenth century, see also Natoli et al. (2016, 47–48) and Piluso (1995).

[24] Toniolo (1990, 2013, 13–16), Bonelli (1991), Di Nardi (1953), and Frascani (1988, 2012).

[25] James and H. O'Rourke (2013, 52).

[26] Regarding the factors that led to the failure of these two major banks: Pantaleoni (1936), Luzzatto (1963, 193–206), Corbino (1934, 359–367), Da Pozzo and Felloni (1964, 259–279, 303–325), and Galli (1997).

[27] James and O'Rourke (2013, 52–54).

to enforce it. It is accepted that regulation plays a crucial role in determining the viability of a banking and finance system, affecting allocational effectiveness, which is key to the performance of key bank and capital market functions, i.e., regulation is crucial "to mobilize saving, to evaluate investment projects and allocate resources, to exert corporate control, to facilitate liquidity and risk management".[28] The reform of 1893 is considered the first of the three principal reforms of the Italian banking system—the others occurring in 1926 and 1936—and is a direct response to a serious crisis. "The new legislation strictly regulated, merged, and reorganized the banks of issue (reduced in number from six to three) by giving prominence to the newly founded Bank of Italy, and set the stage for modern central banking and universal, German-style banking".[29]

As mentioned above, the rationalization of the banking system enabled the development of a number of institutes of credit that were established or reestablished after the crash, often with foreign capital.[30] Among them are Credito Italiano, Banca Commerciale Italiana, and Banco di Roma, all three of which soon assumed a leading role in supporting and financing industrial development. This period also witnessed an increase in deposits at savings banks, cooperative banks, and rural banks, which also began to extend credit, thus supporting commerce, industry, and farming.[31]

5.2 Private Bankers in the Post-unification Period

The activities of private bankers in Italy in the first decades after unification have not received extensive attention from current historians. As we have seen, since the Concert of Europe period (beginning in 1814), some of these operators developed increasingly specific areas of specialization in the "new model of private banking",[32] i.e., in financial activities involving

[28] Battilossi et al. (2013).

[29] Battilossi et al. (2013, 489).

[30] Hertner (1984).

[31] Corbino (1934, 388–389).

[32] The definition is advanced in Ugolini (2018, 161–182). Regarding the development of this type of banking operations in the cited cities, see: Levy-Leboyer (1964), Gille (1965), Hoffman et al. (2000), Chapman (1984), Kindleberger (1984), and Landes (1990). See also Cassis and Cottrell (2009). Case studies on individual private banking families: Bouvier (1968), and Schisani and Caiazzo (2018).

placement of government bonds, loans to businesses, and stock trading. And it is quite understandable that the industrial development that took place only further consolidated this operating model.

Starting in the 1860s, in addition to foreign capital flowing into Italy, private bankers invested large sums in the banks themselves and in businesses, especially the railroad. As a result, they fell victim—sometimes in a dramatic manner—to the negative repercussions of the crises they helped generate. These bankers were thus active participants in the banking and real estate boom, providing expertise and carrying out operations which, while initially having the merit of initiating a growth phase in Italy, also promoted the establishment of mixed banking on the German model. Toward the end of the century, they involuntarily found themselves as the principal actors in the crisis, feeding the speculative bubble.

Italian historiographers, while constantly emphasizing the need to study the activities of private bankers, complain of difficulties in finding documentary resources, much of which ended up in private family archives and were rarely preserved.[33]

However, thanks to a well-endowed and surviving archive, the Banca Parodi of Genoa—which was strongly invested in financial operations, holding stock in banks and railroad companies—represents an opportunity for in-depth study and new interpretation. This bank played a prominent role in Italy starting in the decades prior to unification in terms of business volume and types of operations and also for its active relations with the local and international political and financial establishments.

To develop our analysis of the Parodi family and their bank, it is necessary to review the context of their banking activities and examine the characteristics of the economic, banking, and financial development taking place in Genoa in the period immediately preceding Italian unification and, even more importantly, in the decades immediately following it, when the Ligurian capital witnessed significant growth in its financial market with the establishment of joint-stock and limited liability companies.[34]

[33]A discussion of the role of private bankers in Italy prior to national unification is found in Conti and Schisani (2011). Regarding the need for further studies of private bankers in the nineteenth century: Segreto (2001), Scatamacchia (2013), Balbo (2000), Cafaro (2000), and Romani (2011). Per il tipo di operazioni creditizie svolte dai banchieri privati in quel periodo: Palumbo (1921).

[34]Doria (1969, 160).

Returning briefly to those years, Giorgio Doria estimates that the Genoese invested 80–85 million lire of savings in the financial market, stimulated in part by the presence in the city of one of the most important Italian stock exchanges.[35] In that period, finance in Genoa was undergoing a complex and apparently contradictory evolution, characterized in many cases by speculation aiming for maximum capital gains rather than by investments in securities that ensure the best long-term yield (patient capital). In other words, the investors were earning money principally through agiotage on short-term stocks.[36]

The development of the stock market and municipal and regional credit systems attracted capital, mainly from commerce and shipping, which mobilized and directed savings into various sectors: companies operating in other manufacturing and industrial sectors, real estate companies, and, as we have said, government bonds.

In spite of the expansion of the national territory, the first post-unification decade did not witness significant industrial development in Genoa, growing at less than 1.7% of the national average and concentrated in specific zones. The investors remained rooted in the traditional practices of putting their money primarily into real estate, *Rendita* securities, and banks.[37] Lastly, Genoese investments in the decade in question went to large banks or construction companies specialized in infrastructure, Banca Nazionale and Credito Mobiliare, and the Società per le Strade Ferrate Meridionali, respectively.

The percentage of joint-stock corporations remained low in industrial sectors during the following decade as well, especially in manufacturing. This municipal (Genoese) and regional (Liguria) particularity took the form of a long-term approach or mindset, favoring well-known, consolidated avenues of investment. In this sense, the city lagged behind the national average, especially at the beginning of the 1870s, which was characterized by quite dynamic trends in the establishment of industrial joint-stock companies. A link began to take form between the iron

[35] Doria (1969). Regarding finance in Genoa in the modern era: Felloni, *Gli investimenti*.

[36] Doria (1969, 160–163). Regarding these banks, see also Da Pozzo and Felloni (1964, 259–279, 281–301). Regarding the credit system in Liguria: Podestà (2004).

[37] Regarding the Genoa economic context in the years in question, see also Doria (2007) and Garibbo (2000).

and steel industry and the ship-building industry, one that would grow stronger in the following decades.

In the 1870s, the sector drawing in the most investment was the banks, perhaps because their long experience with international credit and finance made investments in this sector safer than in other, more innovative ones, such as infrastructure, steam shipping, and public services (energy, water, urban transportation). It was a veritable bank fever that witnessed Genoa as a leader in Italy.

The city's private bankers played an important role in the proliferation of banking, both as investors and as founders of joint-stock companies, as was happening in other Italian cities as well.[38]

5.3 Private Bankers and Financial Operators in the Ligurian Area: Two Emblematic Cases

Banking and finance in Liguria and Piedmont featured the presence of families whose propensity to create supranational economic networks was partially a question of lifestyle, ranging from their professional practices to their nuptial policies, both pre- and post-unification. One such international network revolved around the Rothschild family, not just in Genoa with Parodi and Spigno Gastaldi, or in Turin with Bolmida and Nigra, but also in other cities with representatives of dynasties of private bankers. Relations with the Rothschilds opened possibilities for connections with Europe's preeminent stock exchanges—London and Paris—as well as for an expansion of operational capacity on the local stock market. Notable among these dynasties are two of the most important Jewish families of financial operators in the Kingdom of Sardinia: the Avigdors and the Leoninos.

The Avigdors of Nice were important merchant bankers, working with bank acceptances and other operations typical of nineteenth-century private banks. Their counterparts were members of the European banking elite, such as the Rothschilds, the Fould Oppenheims, the Bischoffsheims and Goldschmidts, the Barings, and the Hambros. They were also active

[38] Doria (1969, 342–343) and Da Pozzo and Felloni (1964, 81–151). For the case of Milan, please refer to: Maifreda (1997, 2000a). Regarding banking and finance systems in the decades post-unification, see Pecorari (2008), De Cecco (1990), Schisani (2008), Conti (1993, 2007, 2012), Brambilla (2010), Cafaro (1999), and Confalonieri (1982).

in commodity trading (oil, wheat, tobacco, sugar, etc.).[39] continuing also after France annexed Nice in 1860.

The Avigdors continued to practice their profession in the city of Nice and, unlike other Jewish bankers, did not venture into the lucrative area of financing and trading in the government debt of certain European countries, nor did they establish primary institutes of credit or invest in railroads. Indeed, they did not embrace substantial diversification. That notwithstanding, the path of the Avigdors is significant both for the insight it provides into the internal dynamics of the city of Nice and for the family's various relationships over the course of the nineteenth century, not only on the national level, with Camillo Benso conte di Cavour and their involvement in the Risorgimento process, but also on the supranational level.

These relations are evidenced by the public profile of some members of the family. The banker Jules (d. 1855) was a member of parliament in Turin and one of the founders of the newspaper *Il futuro di Nizza*. His brother Henry (d. 1871), a banker, journalist, politician, and businessman elected to parliament in 1851, had a more international profile as partner in the Bischoffsheim, Goldschmidt, and Avigdor bank of London and ambassador of San Marino to Paris starting in the late 1860s. Henry was involved in the financial networks at the center of international finance and a member of the nucleus of elites who, for several decades, constituted the framework of the European ruling class. The Avigdor bank, directed after Jules's death by his brother Septime Nephtali (d. 1874), survived the 1860 annexation to France but went bankrupt in 1875.

Here as well, we are able to obtain precise information on the banking and finance activities of the Avigdor family through their correspondence with the Rothschilds in London and Paris. The foreign correspondents (agents) of this powerful family of European bankers were not chosen at random: the family carefully selected the best for each marketplace on the basis of their specific expertise and reputation. This was the case in Liguria and generally in the entire Kingdom of Sardinia, where the Rothschilds did not have an agency of their own but worked through correspondents or agents.[40] In the case of Nice, in particular, they found a relatively

[39] There is a great deal of literature on merchant bankers. Here we mention only: Maffi and Romani (2019), Chapman (1984), Cassis (1984), and Berta (2013).

[40] Maffi (2020).

well-developed banking and finance system with centuries of established tradition[41] and it was thus advantageous for them to rely on the principal operators in the city, the Avigdors.

These bankers developed a complementary relationship, with the Avigdors helping the Rothschilds to gain a foothold in the territorialized financial system of Nice, finding space for their financial and commercial operations. Conversely, through their relations with Rothschild banks located in the principal European finance centers, the Avigdors gained access to markets whence they would otherwise have been excluded. It was thus a mutually beneficial relationship leveraging the distinct strengths of each: the leadership role in international finance of the Rothschilds and the role of principal local mediator with deep roots in the local market of the Avigdors.

A look at the development of the Avigdor dynasty, as far as records permit, reveals that commercial initiative, relations with policymakers and financial institutions, and family bonds were all interweaving factors underpinning the success of the family's banking operations. The Avigdors settled in Nice in the early seventeenth century with the help of the banker Suson Lunello. Lunello's grandson left two banks and a business volume of 335 contracts when he died in 1691. In 1768, the brothers Moise and Abramo Avigdor established a bank. Although it failed two years later, Moise would continue on a successful banking career that would establish him as one of the most important merchant bankers in the city of Nice.[42] The Avigdors engaged in large-scale commerce, manufacturing of such products as wine barrels and casks, and money-lending, thus establishing international relations.

Moise's son, Isaac-Samuel (1773–1849), was a notable in Napoleon-era Nice and in the decades that followed as owner of the Banque Avigdor, L'Aîné et Fils, and consul general of Prussia in the city. He was also the elder secretary of the Assembly of Israelite Notaries, created by Napoleon in 1806, and later member of the Great Sanhedrin. The importance of his business dealings with the Rothschilds is documented by the presence of Baron James Rothschild in Nice in 1838 as a guest of his local correspondent, Isaac-Samuel.

[41] Regarding the banking and financial system in Genoa in the modern age and in the nineteenth century, see: Doria (1969), Felloni (1971, 475; 1997), and Zanini (2017).

[42] Tombaccini (2017, 231–233) and Foà (1955).

Inheriting his father's business sense, Isaac-Samuel's activity as a merchant banker and shipowner combined money-lending with commerce. An emblematic example of one of his mercantile operations was his trade in Apulian olive oil. Felice Garibaldi (d. 1855), the brother of Giuseppe Garibaldi and agent of the bank, was assigned the task, together with Federico Avigdor and Rubino Cohen, of "purchasing olive oil in the Province of Bari from the company Avigdor, L'Aîné et Fils of Nice". Indeed, as early as the 1830s, the Avigdors grasped the economic potential of trade in olive oil, boosted by growing demand, and decided to send Garibaldi to Apulia in 1835 as their local representative.[43]

As regards relations with the Rothschilds, the Avigdors were the correspondents from 1835 to 1874 of NM Rothschild & Sons bank of London, founded in 1811 by Nathan Mayer Rothschild. Both families carried out money-lending and financial operations as well as trade and manufacturing.[44] The Avigdors maintained an equally intense and constant correspondence with the De Rothschild Frères bank of Paris, a relationship initiated by James de Rothschild in 1838 and continuing until 1874.[45]

Isaac-Samuel's oldest son, Moise Jules (1812–1855), continued the banking and commercial business under the same company name while also personally leading efforts to defend Jewish rights. In 1839, Jules married Emily Eve Goldsmid (1820–1862), daughter of the wealthy English landowner Aaron Asher Goldsmid (1785–1860) and his wife Sophia Salomons, who was a relative of the famous Moses Montefiore. Jules took over his father's position as consul general of Prussia to Nice and in the early 1850s was the protagonist of a protest against the increase of duties in the port of Nice proposed by Cavour.[46]

When Jules died, his younger brother Septime Nephtali (1825–1874) took over the family business together with Jules's son Benjamin Arthur

[43] Riccardi (2007, 33–35) and Cotugno (1915, 103–112).

[44] RAL, XI/38/9a, Avigdor l'Aine et fils (1835–1843), XI/38/9b, Avigdor l'Aine et fils (1844–1849), XI/38/10a, Avigdor l'Aine et fils (1850–1856) and XI/38/10b, Avigdor l'Aine et fils (1857–1860).

[45] ANMT, BR, 132 AQ 1 P 0078-86, Avigdor (1838–1867), 132 AQ 1 P 0336-7, Avigdor (1868–1875) and 132 AQ non coté 7 (1851–1852).

[46] Ravara Montebelli (2019, 305–306).

James Avigdor.[47] The bank kept the name Avigdor, L'Aîné et Fils, and continued its commercial activities, trading particularly in olive oil and silk. In addition to his activity as a banker, Septime also continued the diplomatic capacities typical of his family, assuming the role of consul to the Kingdom of Württemberg, the Grand-duchy of Frankfurt, and later of Austria and Hungary.[48] In 1854, he married Ilda von Kaulla, daughter of the baron Joseph von Kaulla, a banker in Stuttgart and Munich, and Sara Hirsch. His best man was Joseph de Hirsch, husband of Clara Bischoffsheim, daughter of the important banker Raphael Bischoffsheim of the Bischoffsheim and Goldschmidt bank. A prominent network of bankers was created across Europe, stretching from France to the United Kingdom to a number of states in German territory.[49]

The Avigdors thus employed nuptial strategies to seal their membership in a European network of important private banking families, representing another example of private bankers based in a Ligurian port city with operations extending to the international level, analogous to the Parodi family of Genoa. While the latter circumscribed their matrimonial policies to the most prominent banking families in their city, they were nevertheless projected into the supranational spheres thanks to their specialized expertise.

Henry Avigdor (1823–1871) was a prime example of an international diplomat and businessman. He was the fourth son of the Niçois banker, journalist, politician, and businessman Isaac-Samuel. A member of the Sub-Alpine parliament since 1851, he became ambassador of San Marino to Paris in the late 1860s. A partner in the London bank of Bischoffsheim, Goldschmidt, and Avigdor, in 1840 he married Rachel Goldsmid, cousin of his sister-in-law (Giulio's wife). Rachel's father, Isaac, an investment banker, was one of the founders of the London Docks and a relative of the Montefiores, another example of the strategy of marital bonds among prominent European families. Henry and Rachel had a house in London but moved to Nice in 1841, maintaining nevertheless strong ties to London. The following year, Henry wrote a letter dated April 21, 1842, from Nice to Baron Rothschild in London requesting his

[47] In addition to being a partner in the family bank, Benjamin was also consul to Nice for the Kingdom of Bavaria.

[48] Ravara Montebelli (2019, 341).

[49] Ravara Montebelli (2019, 342).

protection and asking him to avail himself of Henry's services rather than those of others, exhibiting a strong desire to leverage his family ties and professional relationships in the London financial market.[50]

In February 1850, Henry was elected member of the Sub-Alpine parliament for Gavi.[51] At this point, he left the London company[52] and opened a newspaper in Turin titled *La Voix de l'Italie*, taking a position against Cavour and thus opposing the editorial line of the newspaper *Il Risorgimento*, especially on matters of economics.

His interest in finance did not wane in this period, and in 1852, he joined the Board of Directors of Compagnia Transatlantica with Carlo Bombrini, Raffaele Rubattino, Orazio Serra, Luigi Nicolay, Francesco Agnese, Francesco Viti, Giuliano Cataldi, and Stefano Giustiniani.[53] The company was officially founded on October 4, 1852, in Genoa with the purpose of providing steamship transport between Genoa and La Plata, Argentina, with passengers and cargo disembarking in Rio de Janeiro and boarding another ship belonging to the same company, and between Genoa and New York. The share capital was ten million lire in two thousand shares selling for five thousand lire each.

He was not re-elected to parliament in 1853 and decided to abandon politics and focus on the construction of transalpine railways. He joined the banker Charles Lafitte at the helm of the Compagnia Ferroviaria Vittorio Emanuele, the Frejus tunnel being one of the company's projects.

[50] RAL, XI/38/9a, Avigdor l'Aine et fils (1835–1843).

[51] Luzzatto Voghera (1998, 2003) and Levi (1952).

[52] *Atti del parlamento* (1853, 612). Cavour spoke in favor of the election of Enrico Avigdor to the council of Gavi: "Signor Avigdor's father, whom Signor Bunico would have had the opportunity to meet in person in Nice, was consul of Prussia for many years, a position that was then conferred, if I am not mistaken, on his son Giulio Avigdor; but the electee Enrico Avigdor has no diplomatic role as a foreign agent. As regards the title of count, I believe it was bestowed by a power to whom he had rendered some service, as a banker, and who, not having many means to compensate him others [*sustained laughter*] granted him that title. Signor Avigdor has always been a citizen of Sardinia. Although he established a commercial enterprise in London, Article 34 of the Civil Code expressly states that "Commercial establishments will be considered as having been created with the will never to return". Signor attorney Avigdor gave up this establishment to come to Turin; I thus do not believe that there is any motive to expel him from this Chamber".

[53] Concerning the history of this company: Doria (1990).

In July of the same year, he was one of fourteen founders of the Compagnie Générale des Eaux of Paris. He then assumed the role of director of the Compagnia Ferroviaria Pio Latina Roma-Frascati e Roma-Confine Napoletano, which was authorized by Papal decrees on November 8, 1854, and March 31, 1858. In 1854, he became involved in the Societé Universelle pour l'Encouragement des Arts et de l'Industrie. In 1856, he was named president of the Compagnie des Chemins de Fer Départementaux. In 1858, he was appointed to the Board of Directors of the Compagnie Universelle du Canal Maritime de Suez, chaired by Ferdinand de Lesseps.[54]

In 1859, at the apex of his career, he was named Chargé d'Affaires of the Republic of San Marino at the Imperial Court of Paris. From that moment until his death in 1871, he appears to have fully dedicated himself to diplomacy, becoming an able weaver of international relations. Henry Avigdor was a typical representative of the nineteenth-century European merchant class, which shifted from "regional" commercial capitalism to a system of political-financial transnational networks. He was clearly a cosmopolitan spirit, enterprising, and open to the new world of capitalism.

Henry and the Avigdor name in general are thus a further expression of a dynamism in the banking and investment sector in those decades that risks being poorly understood if considered exclusively from a national macroeconomic perspective. Its relevance risks being overshadowed by a historiographic interpretation that has at times emphasized the inadequacy of the private operators in the sector at that time. Such analysis may not adequately or accurately represent a market populated by players such as the private bankers we have described, in spite of their relatively minor role if compared to the powerful Rothschilds, Hambros, or Barings.

Another nationally and internationally successful family of bankers and financiers were the Leoninos, whose role varied depending on the contexts in which the family operated over the years. The development of their network of contacts was principally attributable to the process of Jewish emancipation taking place in the mid-nineteenth century.[55] On

[54] Hivert-Messeca (2014).

[55] Luzzatto Voghera (1998) and Levi (1952, 417–437). Regarding the support from Jews for the Risorgimento and their ties with the Italian political class, see Beer and Foa (2013). Regarding the economic value of the merit earned during the Risorgimento, see Maifreda (2000b).

March 29, 1848, Carlo Alberto di Savoia signed the decree that gave Jews equal rights with respect to other subjects of the Kingdom of Sardinia, the homeland of the Leonino family, who hailed from Casale Monferrato. A document of great importance, the decree strengthened the Kingdom's leadership role in the Italian liberal and unification movement. This integration took the form of the active, patriotic involvement of the Jews in the process of development and unification of Italy. This participation was also evidenced by the many Jewish advisors to Cavour in his political and economic programs.[56]

The members of the Leonino family engaged in money-lending, investment, and trade in Italy and Europe: Casale Monferrato, Genoa, Milan, Venice, Paris, London.[57] Sabino Leonino, a merchant in Casale in the first half of the nineteenth century, had three sons who were also money lenders and investment bankers: Abram Davide (1804–1875), a banker who lived in Genoa and Milan, decorated with the title of baron with royal decree in 1864; Ippolito (d. 1877), a banker and financier who lived in London; and Emanuele, a banker and financier in Genoa and Milan.[58]

A brief reconstruction of Abram Davide's and Ippolito's public careers will illustrate the Leoninos' approach and their national and international connections.[59]

In addition to sitting on the Genoa city council for a number of years, focusing mainly on the city's finances, Baron Abram Davide played an active role in the economy and the implementation of significant banking initiatives. He was auditor at Banca de Genova in 1849. The following year he was appointed to the Board of Directors of Banca Nazionale. Germano Maifreda writes that in the second half of the nineteenth century the baron invested 3,338,509 Italian lire, nearly his entire fortune, in the real estate market and became Milan's fourth-largest landholder.[60]

[56] Milano (1992, 364).

[57] Sandri Giachino (2016).

[58] Maifreda (2000a, 85–86). Emanuele Leonino settled in Milan in 1840, purchasing a house and a great deal of land around the city; he also rapidly acquired Austrian citizenship.

[59] Sandri Giachino (2016, 30–31).

[60] Maifreda (2000a, 222, 246–55).

His son, Baron Sabino Leonino (d. 1888) lived in London in the period 1843–1846 and then in Genoa. In addition to working as a banker and broker in the Ligurian capital, he was appointed councilor at the Chamber of Commerce in 1857 and member of the Board of Directors of the Regia Compagnia delle Ferrovie di Sardegna in 1863.[61] In 1857, shares of the Société Anonyme des Chemins de Fer de Nassau[62] could be purchased through his bank, and in 1866, he was named auditor of the Società Italiana per le Strade Ferrate Meridionali. In 1884, he joined the Board of Directors of Banca di Credito Italiana, which was founded in 1863 in Milan, with Domenico Balduino as president.[63] His acumen as an entrepreneur in the finance sector allowed him to amass a fortune of 2,581,242 Italian lire in the 1880s.[64]

The Leonino family's nuptial strategies reflected their international business network and relations with the high spheres of finance. Sabino's son Abram David (1867–1911) married Jeanne de Rothschild, the daughter of Baron Nathan.[65] Emanuel David (1864–1936), son of Giuseppe Samuel (1830–1894), married Berthe Juliette de Rothschild, daughter of Baron Gustave.[66]

Relations between the Leonino and Rothschild families date back to the first half of the nineteenth century, at which time they had already initiated a banking and finance relationship, as evidenced by their commercial correspondence.[67]

In any case, the first family member to have a clearly international profile was Ippolito (d. 1877), who carried out his work as banker and merchant in London with the company name Ippolito Leonino & Co. Merchants, in which his brothers also participated. The company was

[61] Sandri Giachino (2016, 32–33).

[62] "Société Anonyme des Chemins de Fer de Nassau" (1880, 80).

[63] Sachs (1885, 1145).

[64] Maifreda (2000a, 246–55).

[65] Maifreda (2000a, 271). He left enormous investments both in Italy and in the United Kingdom in his will. Maifreda writes in this regard: "The will [...] provides an eloquent example of the cosmopolitan culture and entrepreneurship of the Milanese Israelite component".

[66] Sandri Giachino (2016, 36).

[67] ANMT, BR, 132 AQ non coté 112, Leonino (1846–1866) and RAL, Letter copy books, 148/109 (20 March–31 July 1849).

dissolved on December 31, 1854.[68] Ippolito was already active in the London financial world in the 1840s, and in 1846 he was appointed to the Provisional Committee of the Regent's Canal Railway, a company with capital of 3 million pounds sterling.[69] His relations with Italian politics are evidenced by a coded dispatch from Cavour to the ambassador Emanuele d'Azeglio in London on August 18, 1856, in which the Piedmontese statesman asks him to contact Hambro, Heath, or Leonino for contributions to the funding of 100 cannons to protect the Alessandria fortress in Piedmont.[70] Very active in commerce, Ippolito was director of the Universal Marine Insurance Company, established in 1860.

The Banca Anglo-Italiana was founded in London in 1864 with capital of one million pounds sterling to fulfill and strengthen the credit relations between the two countries, especially after Italian unification. Trade between the two nations had already grown since the 1850s, particularly Italian exports to the United Kingdom. The Italians Ippolito Leonino and Giulio Bordier helped set up the bank together with the English bankers Thompson, Bonar & Co. and John Lubbock.[71]

These two cases we have briefly examined show that, in a context of a rapidly developing banking and finance systems, bankers from Liguria and Piedmont were able, at least in certain groupings, to integrate into international spheres, promoting and exploiting skills and expertise that allowed them to conduct business with the highest echelons of European finance. The role of these private banker and financier dynasties took form within a constantly and progressively developing political and social framework. Then, generally, the development of infrastructure and the beginning of the industrialization process in certain areas of northwestern Italy provided them with new business opportunities that helped determine their success or failure.

[68] Sandri Giachino (2016, 27).

[69] *Bradshaw's Railway Gazette* (1846, 527).

[70] Commissione Reale Editrice (1933, 50) and Pacifici (1984).

[71] Cottrell (1991, 42–43).

5.4 Private Bankers: Expert Advisors to the Chamber of Deputies

At the end of the 1870s, private bankers had gained renown as prominent, expert advisors on matters of banking and finance to politicians and legislators. Their position as authorities on national economic issues was boosted by the work in 1868 of the Parliamentary Commission of Inquiry on Fiat Money [Commissione parlamentare d'inchiesta sul corso forzoso dei biglietti di banca].

On May 1, 1866, Banca Nazionale fiat money was instituted with compulsory circulation throughout the Kingdom of Italy. This strategy led to paper money representing 36% of total circulating currency, outstripping coins in just a few years.[72] The fiat money was introduced as an extraordinary measure at the outbreak of the Third Italian War of Independence (June–August 1866) and remained in force until 1883, promoting the spread of banknotes among broad swaths of the population.

Following the implementation of this provision, some members of the Chamber of Deputies felt—given the extraordinary nature of the measure—that its causes and effects should be assessed to determine whether it should be abrogated, believing the negative effects outweighed the benefits.

After approval of the agenda presented by the deputies Tommaso Corsi and Alessandro Rossi during the March 10, 1868, session, the Parliamentary Commission of Inquiry was instituted. It was composed of the deputies Filippo Cordova, president and speaker, Fedele Lampertico, who assumed the duties of president and speaker when Cordova died, Ercole Lualdi, Angelo Messedaglia, Alessandro Rossi, Federico Seismit-Doda, and Quintino Sella. The Commission was tasked with collecting information on the status of the paper currency and the activities of the issuing banks and their relations with the government and public administrations.[73] They presented an initial report on July 25, accompanied by Bill

[72] Regarding the status as legal tender of the banknotes and their non-convertibility into gold, see: Barbiellini Amidei et al. (2016), Gigliobianco (2006), Pittaluga (1994), Barbiellini Amidei et al. (2011), Toniolo (1990), and Cardarelli (1990).

[73] The objectives and work of the Commission are illustrated in Sensales (2012, 2016, 41–64). Further information, including the materials produced by the Commission, is found on the website of the Archive of the Chamber of

no. 215, which would cap the banknotes issued by Banca Nazionale at 700 million lire and authorize the issue of six million one-lira banknotes as compulsory currency to meet the needs of retail sales. The bill was passed by the Chamber and the Senate and became Law no. 4579 of September 3, 1868. On November 28 of the same year, the Commission submitted its final report.[74]

The work of the members of the Commission was very meticulous and thorough. The president immediately ordered that the secretary, Giuseppe Fiorio, collect meeting minutes, documents, depositions, and testimony. A portion of these materials are kept in the Archive of the Chamber of Deputies and currently available in digital format. In its efforts to obtain the most detailed information possible, the Commission prepared seven different types of questionnaires, one of which was composed of thirty "special questions" for the Banca Nazionale.[75] Commission members sought to understand the effects of fiat money in the major Italian cities by querying the principal regional public authorities: from prefects, subprefects, and mayors to representatives of the chambers of commerce and a number of private citizens of recognized expertise in matters of economy and finance on the local, national, or supranational levels. Thirty-six notables were interviewed in the period from March 28 to May 9, 1868, including Scialoja, Cambray Digny, and Bombrini.[76] The interviewers obtained information from the managers of the issuing banks—excepting Banca Nazionale, which was given a tailored questionnaire—on the effects of the fiat money and, more importantly, on their assets and bank operations in recent years. The same process was conducted for the main national banks, which included in 1868: Cassa Generale di Genova, Credito Mobiliare Italiano, Cassa di Risparmio di Milano, Cassa di Risparmio di Bologna, Monte de' Paschi di Siena, Opere Pie di San Paolo di Torino, Banco di Sconto Sete di Torino, Cassa di Sconto di Genova, Cassa Nazionale di Sconto di Toscana di Firenze, Banca Anglo-Italiana, Banca di Credito Italiano, Cassa Centrale

Deputies: https://archivio.camera.it/inventari/commissione-d-inchiesta-sul-corso-forzoso-biglietti-banca-1868-marzo-10-1868-novembre-28 (visited on July 1, 2019).

[74] *Relazione della Commissione parlamentare* (1868).

[75] Sensales (2016, 49–50).

[76] Of the many depositions, the following transcription remains: *Atti della Commissione parlamentare d'inchiesta sul corso forzoso. Deposizioni* (1868). See also: *Relazione della Commissione* (1868).

di Depositi e Prestiti di Firenze, Stabilimento Mercantile di Venezia, Banca del Popolo di Firenze, and Banca Popolare di Milano.[77]

An analysis of the registry including the names of the private "interviewees receiving Volume 1" of the Commission Records has made it possible to reassemble to some extent the contents of the inquiry, which were fragmentary because some had been lost and there was no complete list of interviewees. Examining the registries of Turin, Genoa, and Milan, we observe that the recipients of these records were prevalently private bankers, commercial entrepreneurs, industrialists, economists, and university and high school teachers (see Table 5.1).[78]

The Commission prepared its reports on the basis of interviews and also collected documents, most of which were letters from police commissioners, prefects, subprefects, and mayors to the ministry of the economy, revealing much of the direct effects of the fiat money in different regions. For example, its application met with immediate obstacles and caused complications in Genoa, one of the main Italian financial marketplaces. In his letter of May 12, 1866, the local police commissioner, Felice Verga, pointed out that bankers and money changers in the city were effectively becoming monopolists in "cash" (gold coin), with effects that threatened public safety. He writes: "The exchange of 20-[lire] banknotes for gold carried a commission of 1.90 or even 2.00 [lire]. [...] while exchanging banknotes of greater value for those of smaller denomination carried a commission of 10 lire per 1000 lire".[79] The commissioner attributed this to the propensity of Genoese bankers to deal in *Rendita* bonds. At that time, the bonds were selling on the Paris Stock Exchange for 7–8% less than they did on the Genoa Stock Exchange; hence, speculators purchased them in France and sold them in Genoa. Thus, "since the securities are bought in France in exchange for cash, the speculators gather as much cash as they can [here in Genoa] and send it to France; at this rate, without there being any protection, the cash in this marketplace

[77] *Atti della Commissione parlamentare d'inchiesta sul corso forzoso. Documenti* (1868).

[78] Archivio della Camera Regia, Commissioni Parlamentari d'Inchiesta, *Commissione d'inchiesta sul corso forzoso dei biglietti di banca (10.03.1868–28.11.1868), Carte di segreteria. Carteggio relativo alla spedizione dei volumi della relazione*, busta 5, cc. 1-237. (web: archivio.camera.it, Archivio della camera regia 1848–1943, documento CD1800000270).

[79] *Atti della Commissione parlamentare d'inchiesta sul corso forzoso. Documenti* (1868, 397–398).

Table 5.1 List of interviewees in Genoa, Turin, and Milan

Genoa	*Milan*	*Turin*
Croce Giuseppe	Brot Carlo, banker	Carpi Leone, economist, journalist
De Ferrari Gaetano, entrepreneur, industrialist	Luzzati Luigi, Banca Popolare di Milano	Bernardo Gastaldi, entrepreneur, merchant
Gruber Federico, entrepreneur, merchant	Griffini Achille, Cassa di Risparmio di Milano	Rolle Pio, chamber of commerce vice-president
Mylius Federico, banker, merchant	Wonviller & C., banker, merchant	Forneris Angelo, merchant
Paganelli Alessandro, entrepreneur, merchant	Cantoni Carlo, chamber of commerce vice-president	Tasca Giovanni Battista, chamber of commerce president
Scerno Enrico, entrepreneur, industrialist	Brambilla Ernesto, board of governors, Milan branch of Banca Nazionale	Piaggio fratelli, banker
Serra brothers, entrepreneurs, merchants	Mylius & C., banker	Guadagnini Giovanni Battista, entrepreneur, merchant
Parodi Giacomo, private banker	Ponti Andrea, banker, industrialist	Casana Alessandro, banker
Cataldi Giacomo, private banker	Krumm Luigi, industrialist	Laclaire Giovanni Paolo, textile entrepreneur
Boccardo Gerolamo, economist, teacher	Pisani Giovanni, chamber of commerce secretary	Mazzucchetti Antonio, exchange agent
Piaggio Erasmo, ship owner, entrepreneur	Fumagalli and Sessa, industrialists	Fiore Ferdinando Maria, economics professor and scholar
Cabella Gaetano, entrepreneur, merchant	Noerbel M. J., merchant	D'Aurora Luigi, Istituto Tecnico Torino
Currò Antonio, entrepreneur, merchant	Belinzaghi Giulio, banker and mayor of Milan	Govi Gilberto, University of Turin professor
Montanari Antonio, entrepreneur, merchant	Servolini Carlo, Cusani & C.	Cantoni Gaetano, instructor at the Istituto Tecnico Torino
Millo Giacomo, entrepreneur, merchant, chamber of commerce president	Jacini Jacopo	Ottolenghi Leone, banker
De La Rue Emilio, private banker	Ferrari, Istituto Tecnico Santa Marta, Milan	Coppino Michele, politician and professor at the University of Turin

(continued)

Table 5.1 (continued)

Genoa	*Milan*	*Turin*
Pallavicino Camillo, banker		Lessona Michele, politician, writer, professor at the University of Turin
Queirolo G. L., merchant		Garelli Alessandro Stefano, scholar (author of *Le banche di emissione nel 1869*)
Cataldi Giuliano, banker		Lamberti Giuseppe, merchant
		Levi Felice, author of *Della riforma delle Banche*, Turin 1864

Source Archivio della Camera Regia, Commissioni Parlamentari d'Inchiesta, *Commissione d'inchiesta sul corso forzoso dei biglietti di banca (10.03.1868–28.11.1868), Carte di segreteria. Carteggio relativo alla spedizione dei volumi della relazione*, busta 5, cc. 1-237 web: archivio.camera.it, Archivio della camera regia 1848–1943, documento CD1800000270

will diminish in equal measure to the enrichment of the speculators and then totally disappear". The commissioner urged that a greater number of banknotes be introduced into circulation, especially in denominations of 10, 20, 50, and 100 lire, so that payments could be made for the most urgent transactions and neither workers nor trade, more generally, would be penalized.

This statement indirectly confirms the fact that Genoese bankers were notoriously involved in the buying and selling of government bonds, distinguishing themselves in this activity since the years around the First Italian War of Independence (March 1848–August 1849). There was at that time, as there would be later, a clear preferential relationship with the Paris Stock Exchange.

The economic situation in Genoa at the time was also described by the mayor Andrea Podestà in a letter dated June 2, 1866, discussing the problem of money circulating in the city. He underscored that not only were coins rare, but so were banknotes in small denominations—20, 50, and 100 lire—and that this had an immediate negative impact on commerce. The critical nature of the situation was made immediately evident in his letter: "One very serious symptom of the state of things is that said denominations, 20, 50, and 100 lire, carry a much higher commission than larger-denomination banknotes, a truly exceptional and extraordinary commission, whether we assess it according to the theoretical norms of science or compare it to historical and practical standards".[80] However, the mayor did not agree with the opinion then making its rounds that the source of the problem was the monopoly held by banks and bankers. Instead, he attributed it to intrinsic defects in the system of circulation that had come into force, requiring greater issue of small-denomination banknotes.

As mentioned above, the Commission was able to assemble and organize all the information collected in the interviews and draft and print a report. The expertise of private bankers is revealed in key passages in the report, especially when discussing fiat money and its impact on the farming and commercial sectors, monetary policy, unit of money, and the *Rendita* bond.[81] In the report, we learn that Giacomo Parodi, along with the banker Cataldi and Felice Levi, believed that the fiat money had no adverse effect on the primary sector for the following reasons: agricultural products were partially destined for export and thus earned the difference of the commission; land rentals were generally paid with paper money, as was previous mortgage debt.[82]

As regards currency circulation, Parodi's opinion was similar to that of most interviewees, according to whom, in the period before 1866, there was between 1.0 and 1.2 billion lire in circulation. This opinion was shared by the bankers David Levi, Carlo Brot, and Achille Griffini. Carlo Bombrini and Horace Landau[83] stated a figure of 1.2 billion, while Cataldi believed it to be 900 million.[84] As for the "[c]auses that diminish monetary imbalance in Italy", some recognized that "the exportation of

[80] Camera dei deputati (1868), *Atti della Commissione parlamentare d'inchiesta sul corso forzoso. Documenti* (1868, 405–406).

[81] *Relazione della Commissione parlamentare* (1868).

[82] *Relazione della Commissione parlamentare.* 1 (1868, 319–320).

[83] Horace Landau (1824–1903), a Jew born in Odessa, was an agent for the Rothschilds in newly unified Italy and particularly during the period when Florence was the capital. He negotiated loans, their placement, and trading on behalf of the Rothschilds of Paris. Landau's fundamental role in negotiating loans to the Italian State from the Rothschilds is described in the eight folders of correspondence in the Rothschild Archive: ANMT, BR, 132 AQ 6283-90, Lettres d'Horace Landau (1851–1871).

[84] *Relazione della Commissione parlamentare.* 1 (1868, 330).

rice, silk, wheat, sulfur, hemp, fodder, fruit, seed, livestock, etc., especially during the past year, has brought metal specie into the Kingdom". Along with Serra and Podestà, Parodi believed that the benefits should be included from the overseas "colonies", who sent from 30 to 40 million per year to Genoa from foreign markets.[85]

According to the interviewed bankers, the fiat currency generally had a negative effect on money-lending and especially on relations with foreign credit systems. In this regard, "according to Mr. Parodi, foreign countries do not accept Italian credit but insist that Italy accepts foreign credit". Along with the chambers of commerce, the bankers Bombrini and Belinzaghi and the industrialist Krumm reported the near total cease of extranational credit operations[86]; Belinzaghi and Brot of Milan also underscored difficulties in the domestic credit system and the flight of capital abroad. As regards the question of abolishing the fiat currency, Parodi, along with many other bankers, businessmen, and economists (Levi, Mortera, Kaiser, Montezemolo, Gastaldi, Meuricoffre, De La Rüe, Giuliano Cataldi, Forneris, Tasca, Boccardo, Laclaire, Piaggio, Guadagnini, and Casana), was convinced that the fiat currency was principally a consequence of financial instability and that it was not possible to eliminate the effect without first eliminating the causes; first and foremost, according to some, the government had to balance the budget and only then could fiat money be issued.[87]

The opinions of the bankers become more pertinent when they provide explanations of the "movement of the Italian *Rendita* bond abroad". Most importantly, their reviews clearly outline certain underlying critical points. First of all, it is very difficult to determine the amount of *Rendita* bonds purchased abroad and brought back to Italy after 1866 and indeed, it was expressly stated that "in this the individual criterion has no solid base on which to rest, it not being enough to know how many bonds were paid for abroad, due to the very well known problem [...] of speculators who export bonds in order to exchange them for gold abroad". Although the government took steps to prevent such practices, the interviewees were not all in agreement as regards the outcome. Carlo Brot of Milan "tells of a packet of bonds, presented and re-presented three times,

[85] *Relazione della Commissione parlamentare*. 1 (1868, 348).

[86] *Relazione della Commissione parlamentare*. 1 (1868, 379–381).

[87] *Relazione della Commissione parlamentare*. 1 (1868, 384). See also: Berselli (1957).

with different coupons, in Paris and purchased there, and recounts that, in the judgment of some, the agents of a major banker who earns a fee on this were speculating on them". Conversely, Horace Landau stated that oversight on operations in Paris was effective "since many coupons return to Italy after three or four months, it not having been possible to obtain payment for them," and opines that the *Rendita*, which is sent to Paris for payment, "cannot exceed two million lire, and is so fragmented that it is not worth running the risks of misplacing it".[88]

As regards the overall value of the *Rendita* returning to Italy, there are discrepancies among the interviewees because it is difficult to determine with any certainty the importation of the *Rendita* after 1866 and the subsequent exportation of metal specie necessary to pay for the *Rendita* in foreign marketplaces. The account of a political leader in the early post-unification period, the congressman Urbano Rattazzi, suggests an amount between 50 and 60 million, "arguing that in Genoa, since 1866, a value of a million and a half was imported per month on average, and a million in Turin". Emile de la Rüe was of the same opinion. This declaration reaffirms once again the role of the Turin and Genoa Stock Exchanges in the trade and placement of these financial products. Giacomo Parodi and Carlo Bombrini, on the other hand, agreed on the amount of 30 million.

As regards the amount of *Rendita* that came back to Italy after the application of the fiat currency, Landau's thinking differs from other statements not only in amount but most importantly in justification, shedding light on the somewhat aleatory nature of the financial mechanisms: "Mr. Landau does not believe that more than 15 million lire worth of *Rendita* in private hands has been imported back into Italy: [while others give a higher figure] according to him, we cannot say that the *Rendita* exists in Italy rather than outside of it, rather, it is suspended in the telegraph, it is the object of arbitrage, like a ball it is bounced back and forth, depending on the winds of speculation".[89] In general, the opinions on the quantity of *Rendita* still remaining abroad diverged greatly, but all agreed on underscoring its diminishment on the French market when the fiat currency was implemented. On the other hand, the beginning of its placement on new markets after 1866 included, as Landau states, "new

[88] *Relazione della Commissione parlamentare*. 1 (1868, 336–337).

[89] *Relazione della Commissione parlamentare*. 1 (1868, 336–337).

outlets in Trieste and Berlin", a trend that was destined to grow, as historiography has correctly emphasized, in the following decades.[90] As regards the names of those interviewed on questions associated with the *Rendita*, it is telling that a number of private bankers are among them, bankers who were already trading it in the late 1840s and 1850s: first and foremost, the current Rothschilds agent for Italy—at that time Horace Landau—their correspondents in Genoa, the Parodis, and in Milan, Ulrich and Brot, plus two bankers who were still active years later, Cataldi and De La Rüe.

Beyond the individual statements recorded, exemplifying the viewpoints and reasoning of the interviewees and providing interesting details outlining the situation in Italy in those years, the documentation as a whole is a clear demonstration of the extent to which the members of parliament valued the consulting services of private operators in the money-lending and finance sector. This consideration would seem to diverge from the analysis advanced by Boccardo, according to whom the figure of the private bankers had already begun to lose relevance precisely in this period.[91] The documentation would seem to validate the interpretation advanced in recent studies which, based on an analysis of the interaction between private bankers and industry, focuses on how the post-unification period provided terrain rich in opportunities and investments precisely for this category of operators and how only some of them, in close dialogue with a favorable political realm, succeeded in reaping the benefits.[92]

Bibliography

Archives

Archivio Storico della Camera dei Deputati (ASCD).

Archivio della Camera Regia, Commissioni Parlamentari d'Inchiesta, *Commissione d'inchiesta sul corso forzoso dei biglietti di banca (10.03.1868–28.11.1868), Carte di segreteria. Carteggio relativo alla spedizione dei volumi della relazione*, busta 5, cc. 1-237. (web: archivio.camera.it, Archivio della camera regia 1848–1943, documento CD1800000273).

Rothschild Archive London (RAL).

[90] *Relazione della Commissione parlamentare*. 1 (1868, 337).

[91] Boccardo (1875, 281–290).

[92] Segreto (2001, 273–306).

XI/38/9a, Avigdor l'Aine et fils (1835–1843).
XI/38/9b, Avigdor l'Aine et fils (1844–1849).
XI/38/10a, Avigdor l'Aine et fils (1850–1856).
XI/38/10b, Avigdor l'Aine et fils (1857–1860).
Letter Copy Books 148/109 (20 March–31 July 1849).
Archives Nationales du Monde du Travail – Banque Rothschild (ANMT, BR).
BR, 132 AQ 6283-90, Lettres d'Horace Landau (1851–1871).
BR, 132 AQ 1 P 0078-86, Avigdor (1838–1867).
BR, 132 AQ 1 P 0336-7, Avigdor (1868–1875).
BR, 132 AQ non coté 7, Avigdor L'Aîné et Fils (1851–1852).
BR, 132 AQ non coté 112, Leonino (1846–1866).

Printed Contemporary and Near Contemporary Sources

"Société Anonyme des Chemins de Fer de Nassau". 1857. *Gazette des Tribuneaux*, January 22.

Amici, Federico. 1867. *Le banche di circolazione, il credito fondiario e il credito agrario.* Bologna: Fava e Garagnani.

Atti del parlamento subalpino sessione del 1850 (4. legislatura), dal 20 dicembre 1849 al 19 novembre 1850. (vol. 1 dal 20 dicembre 1849 al 12 marzo 1850). 1853. Torino: Tipografia Eredi Botta.

Atti della Commissione parlamentare d'inchiesta sul corso forzoso. Documenti. 1868. Firenze: Tipografia Eredi Botta (web: archivio.camera.it, Archivio della camera regia 1848-1943, documento CD1800000272, vol. II: 1–1264).

Atti della Commissione parlamentare d'inchiesta sul corso forzoso. Deposizioni. 1868. Firenze: Tipografia Eredi Botta (web: archivio.camera.it, Archivio della camera regia 1848–1943, documento CD1800000273, vol. III: 1–707).

Benvenuti, Bartolomeo. 1856. *Delle banche di circolazione.* Torino: Tipografia Economica.

Bertolotto, Sebastiano. 1863. *Sul progetto della Banca d'Italia. Osservazioni pratiche.* Genova: Tipografia del giornale il Commercio di Genova.

Bertolotto, Sebastiano. 1867. *Banchi di sconto e di deposito e della necessità e del modo d'istituirli in Italia.* Genova: Tipografia del Commercio.

Boccardo, Gerolamo. 1863. *La Banca d'Italia. Considerazioni. Genova: Tipografia Fratelli Pellas.*

Boccardo, Gerolamo. 1875. *Dizionario universale di economia politica di commercio.* Milano: Treves.

Boccardo, Gerolamo. 1879. *Le banche e il corso forzoso. Sul riordinamento degli istituti di emissione.* Roma: Tipografia del Senato.

Bradshaw's Railway Gazette, 2. 1846. London and Manchester: William James Adams, 59, Fleet Street.

Busacca, Raffaele. 1870. *Studi sul corso forzoso dei biglietti di banca in Italia.* Firenze: Tipografia della Gazzetta d'Italia.

De Cesare, Carlo. 1867–1869. *Il sindacato governativo, le società commerciali e gli istituti di credito nel Regno d'Italia*, 1–2. Firenze: Tip. Pellas.

De Cesare, Carlo. 1874. *Le banche di emissione.* Roma: Tip. Barbera.

Ferraris, Carlo F. 1879. *Moneta e corso forzoso.* Milano: Hoepli.

Garelli, Alessandro S. 1869. *Le banche d'emissione.* Torino: Tip. C. Favale e C.

Giulio, Carlo I. 1853. *La Banca e il Tesoro.* Torino: Stamperia Reale.

Martello, Tullio, and Augusto Montanari. 1874. *Sullo stato del credito in Italia.* Padova: Fratelli Salmin.

Musso, Giacomo Andrea. 1864. "La libertà delle banche." *Rivista contemporanea* 12: 14–41.

Pallavicino, Camillo. 1863. "Come si possa conciliare l'unità e la pluralità delle banche in Italia." *Rivista contemporanea* 11: 321–26.

Pallavicino, Camillo. 1864. "Come si possa conciliare l'unità e la pluralità delle banche in Italia." *Rivista contemporanea* 12: 20–26.

Papa, Giovanni A. 1866. *Unità di emissione. Libero credito. Cenni sulla questione delle banche.* Genova: Fratelli Pellas.

Relazione della Commissione parlamentare d'inchiesta sul corso forzoso dei biglietti di banca, Vol. I, Relazione (presentata alla Camera il 28 novembre 1868). 1868. Firenze: Tipografia Eredi Botta.

Sachs, Isidore. 1885. *L'Italie, ses finances et son développement èconomique depuis l'unification du royame, 1859–1884.* Paris: Guillaumin.

Secondary Sources

Alberti, Mario, and Vittorio Cornaro. 1929. *Banche di emissione in Italia. Moneta e politica monetaria in Italia dal 1849 al 1929.* Milano: G.U.F.

Are, Giuseppe. 1974. *Alle origini dell'Italia industriale.* Napoli: Guida.

Artoni, Roberto, and Sara Biancini. 2003. "Il debito pubblico dall'Unità a oggi." In *Storia economica d'Italia*, edited by P. Ciocca and G. Toniolo, 269–380. Roma-Bari: Laterza.

Austin, Peter. F. 2007. *Baring Brothers and the Birth of Modern Finance.* London: Pickering & Chatto.

Baffigi, Alberto. 2011. *Italian National Accounts, 1861–2010.* Roma: Banca d'Italia.

Balbo, Ivan. 2000. "Banche e banchieri a Torino: identità e strategie (1883–1896)." *Impresa e storia* 21, no. 1: 61–101.

Barbiellini Amidei, Federico, Giordano Claire, and Giuseppe Luci. 2011. "Cronologia monetaria (1796–1894)." In *La moneta dell'Italia unita: dalla lira all'euro.* Roma: Banca d'Italia.

Barbiellini Amidei, Federico, De Bonis Riccardo, Rocchelli Miriam, Salvio Alessandra, and Massimiliano Stacchini. 2016. "Che cosa sappiamo sulla moneta in Italia dal 1861 a oggi? Risultati da nuove serie storiche." *Moneta e Credito* 69, no. 275: 269–315.

Bartoletto, Silvana, and Antonio Garofalo. 2014. *Il ruolo del credito nell'economia italiana 1861–2013*. Milano: Mondadori.

Battilossi, Stefano, Gigliobianco Alfredo, and Giuseppe Marinelli. 2013. "Resource Allocation by the Banking System." In *The Oxford Handbook of the Italian Economy Since Unification*, edited by G. Toniolo, 485–515. Oxford-New York: Oxford University Press.

Beer, Marina, and Anna Foa, eds. 2013. *Ebrei, minoranze, Risorgimento: storia, cultura, letteratura*. Roma: Viella.

Belli, Franco. 2008. "Gli sviluppi della legislazione bancaria italiana, una sintesi." In *Storia d'Italia*, *Annali 23*, *La Banca*, edited by C. Bermond, A. Cova, A. Moioli and S. La Francesca, 893–915. Torino: Einaudi.

Berselli, Aldo. 1957. "Accordi e disaccordi fra Quintino Sella e Marco Minghetti sui mezzi per il raggiungimento del pareggio (1861–1876)." *Rassegna Storica del Risorgimento* 44, nos. 2–3: 299–311.

Berta, Giuseppe. 2013. *L'ascesa della finanza internazionale*. Milano: Giacomo Feltrinelli Editore.

Biscaini Cotula, Anna Maria, and Pierluigi Ciocca. 1979. "Le strutture finanziarie: aspetti quantitativi di lungo periodo (1870–1970)." In *Capitale industriale e capitale finanziario: il caso italiano*, edited by F. Vicarelli, 61–138. Bologna: Il Mulino.

Bonelli, Franco. 1978. "Il capitalismo italiano." In *Storia d'Italia. Annali, I. Dal feudalesimo al capitalismo*, edited by R. Romano and C. Vivanti, 1193–255. Torino: Einaudi.

Bonelli, Franco, ed. 1991. *La Banca d'Italia dal 1894 al 1913. Momenti della formazione di una Banca Centrale*. Bari: Laterza.

Bouvier, Jean. 1968. *I Rothschild*. Bari: Laterza.

Brambilla, Carlo. 2010. *Affari di banche. Banche universali in Italia in prospettiva comparata (1860–1914)*. Pisa: Pisa University Press.

Brambilla, Carlo. 2011. "Banche ed economia nazionale (1861–1914)." In *Le Banche e l'Italia. Crescita economica e società civile (1861–2011)*, edited by L. Conte, 63–100. Roma: Bancaria Editrice.

Cafagna, Luciano. 1962. "Industrialismo e politica economica dopo l'Unità d'Italia." *Annali Feltrinelli* 5: 150–82.

Cafaro, Pietro. 1999. "Banche popolari e casse rurali tra '800 e '900: radici e ragioni di un successo." In *Le Banche popolari nella storia d'Italia*, edited by P. Pecorari, 21–78. Venezia: Istituto Veneto di Scienze.

Cafaro, Pietro. 2000. "Alle origini del sistema bancario lombardo: casse di risparmio e banchieri privati (1860–1880)." In *Banche e reti di banche nell'Italia postunitaria, 2*, edited by G. Conti and S. La Francesca, 437–502. Bologna: il Mulino.

Cameron, Rondo. 1985. *Le banche e lo sviluppo del sistema industriale*. Bologna: Il Mulino.

Canovai, Tito. 1912. *Le Banche di emissione in Italia*. Roma: Casa Editrice Italiana.

Cardarelli, Sergio. 1990. "La questione bancaria in Italia dal 1860 al 1892." In *Ricerche per la storia della Banca d'Italia. 1*, 105–80. Roma-Bari: Laterza.

Carocci, Giampiero. 1956. *Agostino Depretis e la politica interna italiana dal 1876 al 1887*. Torino: Einaudi.

Cassis, Youssef. 1984. *Les banquiers de la City à l'époque édouardienne*. Genève: Droz.

Cassis, Youssef, and Philip Cottrell, eds. 2009. *The world of private banking*. Farnham-Burlington: Ashgate.

Castronovo, Vittorio. 1969. *Economia e dall'Unità società in Piemonte al 1914*. Milano: Banca Commerciale Italiana.

Cerrito, Elio. 1999. "Cambio, ciclo, efficienza, istituzioni: problemi di politica monetaria dell'Italia di fine Ottocento. Appunti su alcune evidenze empiriche." *Rivista Storica Italiana* 111, nos. 3–4: 480–526.

Chapman, Stanley D. 1984. *The Rise of Merchant Banking*. London: Allen & Unwin.

Ciccarelli, Carlo, and Stefano Fenoaltea. 2007. "Business Fluctuations in Italy, 1861–1913: The New Evidence." *Explorations in Economic History* 44, no. 3: 432–51.

Ciocca, Pierluigi, and Anna Maria, Biscaini Cotula. 1994. "Italian Financial Structure: Long-Term Quantitative Aspects (1870–1970)." In *The Economic Development of Italy Since 1870*, edited by G. Federico, 512–64. Aldershot: Elgar.

Clementi, Fabio, Gallegati, Mauro, and Marco Gallegati. 2015. "Growth and Cycles of the Italian Economy Since 1861: The New Evidence." *Italian Economic Journal* 1, no. 1: 25–59.

Commissione Reale Editrice, ed. 1933. *Cavour e l'Inghilterra, Carteggio con V.E. d'Azeglio, I conflitti diplomatici del 1856–61*, 2. Bologna: Zanichelli.

Confalonieri, Antonio. 1979–1980. *Banca e industria in Italia (1894–1906)*. 3 vols. Bologna: Il Mulino.

Confalonieri, Antonio. 1982. *Banca e industria in Italia dalla crisi del 1907 all'agosto 1914*. Milano: Banca Commerciale Italiana.

Cohen, Jon, and Giovanni Federico. 2001. *The Growth of the Italian Economy, 1820–1960*. Cambridge: Cambridge University Press.

Conte, Leandro. 1990. *La Banca Nazionale. Formazione e attività di una banca di emissione (1843–1861)*. Napoli: Edizioni Scientifiche Italiane.

Conti, Giuseppe. 1993. "Finanza di impresa e capitale di rischio in Italia (1870–1939)." *Rivista di Storia Economica* 10, no. 3: 307–32.

Conti, Giuseppe. 1999. "Le banche e il finanziamento industriale." In *Storia d'Italia, Annali 15, L'Industria*, edited by F. Amatori, D. Bigazzi, R. Giannetti and L. Segreto, 441–504. Torino: Einaudi.

Conti, Giuseppe. 2007. *Creare il credito e arginare i rischi. L'organizzazione del sistema finanziario tra nobiltà e miserie del capitalismo italiano tra XIX e XX secolo*. Bologna: Il Mulino.

Conti, Giuseppe. 2012. "Le dimensioni nazionali della finanza. Vincoli e opportunità nei 150 anni di storia italiana." *Rivista di Storia Economica* 28, no. 1: 111–34.

Conti, Giuseppe, and Maria Carmela Schisani. 2011. "I banchieri italiani e la *haute banque* nel Risorgimento e dopo l'Unità." *Società e storia* 131, no. 1: 133–70.

Corbino, Epicarmo. 1934. *Annali dell'economia italiana. 4. (1891–1900)*. Napoli: Istituto Editoriale del Mezzogiorno.

Cottrell, Philip L. 1991. "The Coalescence of a Cluster of Corporate International Banks, 1855–75." In *Bank and Money: International and Comparative Finance History*, edited by Geoffrey G. Jones and Frank Cass, 31–52. London: Frank Cass.

Cotugno, Raffaele. 1915. "Un fratello di Garibaldi a Bari (1835–1852)." *Archivio Pugliese del Risorgimento Italiano* 2: 103–12.

Da Pozzo, Mario, and Giuseppe Felloni. 1964. *La borsa valori di Genova nel secolo XIX*. Torino: ILTE.

De Bernardi, Alberto, and Luigi Ganapini. 1996. *Storia d'Italia (1860–1995)*. Milano: Bruno Mondadori.

De Cecco, Marcello, ed. 1990. *L'Italia e il sistema finanziario internazionale 1861–1914*. Bari: Laterza.

Delli Gatti, Domenico, Gallegati, Marco, and Mauro Gallegati. 2005. "On the Nature and Causes of Business Fluctuations in Italy, 1861–2000." *Explorations in Economic History* 42, no. 1: 81–100.

De Mattia, Renato, ed. 1990a. *Gli istituti di emissione in Italia. I tentativi di unificazione 1843–1892*. Bari: Laterza.

De Mattia, Renato. 1990b. *Moneta, credito e finanze nel processo di formazione dello stato italiano (1845–1939). Sintesi storica*. Roma: Edibank.

De Mattia, Renato. 1990c. *Storia delle operazioni degli istituti di emissione italiani dal 1845 al 1936 attraversi i dati dei loro bilanci*, 3 vols. Roma: Edibank.

De Rosa, Luigi. 1964. *Il Banco di Napoli nella vita economica nazionale (1863–1883)*. Napoli: L'arte tipografica.

De Rosa, Luigi. 1989. *Storia del Banco di Napoli istituto di emissione nell'Italia unita, 1863–1926*, II. *La crisi: 1883–1896*. Napoli: Arte Tipografica.

Demarco, Domenico 1956. "Una pagina di storia bancaria italiana: la espansione territoriale della Banca Nazionale Sarda e i tentativi di soppressione del Banco di Napoli (settembre 1860–aprile 1863)." In *Archivi storici delle aziende di credito*, 1, 137–203. Roma: Associazione Bancaria Italiana.

Di Nardi, Giuseppe. 1953. *Le banche di emissione in Italia nel XIX secolo*. Torino: Unione tipografico-editrice torinese.

Doria, Giorgio. 1969. *Investimenti e sviluppo economico a Genova alla vigilia della Prima Guerra Mondiale (1815–1882)*. Milano: A. Giuffrè Editore.

Doria, Giorgio. 1973. *Investimenti e sviluppo economico a Genova alla vigilia della Prima Guerra Mondiale (1883–1914)*. Milano: A. Giuffrè Editore.

Doria, Giorgio. 1990. *Debiti e navi. La compagnia del Rubattino 1839–1881*. Genova: Marietti.

Doria, Marco. 2007. "Da un'economia di antico regime all'industrializzazione." In *Storia della Liguria*, edited by G. Assereto and M. Doria, 211–28. Roma-Bari: Laterza.

Federico, Giovanni. 1986. "Mercantilizzazione e sviluppo economico in Italia (1860–1940)." *Rivista di storia economica* 3, no. 2: 149–86.

Felloni, Giuseppe. 1971. *Gli investimenti finanziari genovesi in Europa tra il 1600 e la Restaurazione*. Milano: A. Giuffrè.

Felloni, Giuseppe, ed. 1997. *Moneta, credito e banche in Europa: un millennio di storia*. Genova: Brigati.

Fenoaltea, Stefano. 1982. "The Growth of the Utilities Industry in Italy, 1861–1913." *The Journal of Economic History* 42, no. 3: 601–27.

Fenoaltea, Stefano. 2011. *The Reinterpretation of Italian Economic History: From Unification to the Great War*. Cambridge: Cambridge University Press.

Foà, Salvatore. 1955. *Banchi e banchieri ebrei nel Piemonte dei secoli scorsi*. Città di Castello: Tipografia Unione Arti Grafiche.

Frascani, Paolo. 1988. *Finanza, economia ed intervento pubblico dall'Unificazione agli anni trenta*. Milano: Guerini e associati.

Frascani, Paolo. 2012. *Le crisi economiche in Italia. Dall'Ottocento a oggi*. Roma-Bari: Laterza.

Fratianni, Michele, and Franco Spinelli. 1997. *A Monetary History of Italy*. Cambridge: Cambridge University Press.

Fumi, Giampiero. 1993. "L'integrazione economica e i suoi limiti nei decenni dell'unificazione politica (1848–1878)." In *L'Ottocento economico italiano*, edited by S. Zaninelli, 211–352. Bologna: Monduzzi.

Gallegati, Mauro, and Luca M. Stanca. 1998. *Le fluttuazioni economiche in Italia, 1861–1995. Ovvero, il camaleonte e il virus dell'influenza*. Torino: Giappichelli.

Galli, Anna Maria. 1997. "Sviluppo e crisi della Banca Generale." In *Antonio Allievi: dalle 'Scienze civili' alla pratica del credito*, edited by E. Decleva, 561–651. Milano-Roma-Bari: Cariplo-Laterza.

Garibbo, Luciana. 2000. *Politica, amministrazione e interessi a Genova (1815–1940)*. Milano: FrancoAngeli.

Giannini, Curzio. 2004. *L'età delle banche centrali*. Bologna: Il Mulino.

Gigliobianco Alfredo. 1990. "Tra concorrenza e collaborazione: considerazioni sulla natura dei rapporti fra 'Banca Centrale' e sistema bancario nell'esperienza italiana (1844–1918)." In *Ricerche per la Storia della Banca d'Italia*, 1, 295–338. Roma-Bari: Laterza.

Gigliobianco Alfredo. 2006. *Via Nazionale. Banca d'Italia e classe dirigente. Cento anni di storia*. Roma: Donzelli.

Gigliobianco, Alfredo, and Claire Giordano. 2010. *Economic Theory and Banking Regulation: The Italian Case (1861–1930s)*. Roma: Banca d'Italia.

Gille, Bertrand. 1965. *Histoire de la Maison Rothschild, 1, Des origines a 1848*. Genève: Droz.

Gregorini, Giovanni, and Pietro Cafaro. 2018. "L'unificazione monetaria." In *L'Italia europea. Dall'Unificazione all'Unione*, edited by F. Bonini, T. Di Maio and G. Tognon, 77–91. Roma: Edizioni Studium.

Hautcoeur, Pierre-Cyrille. 2003. "Cash or Account? A Plea for a European Comparative History of Financial Systems." *Contemporary european history* 12, no. 3: 1–14.

Hertner, Peter. 1984. *Il capitale tedesco in Italia dall'unità alla prima guerra mondiale*. Bologna: Il Mulino.

Hertner, Peter. 1990. "Banche tedesche e sviluppo economico italiano (1883–1914)." In *Ricerche per la storia della Banca d'Italia*, 70–101. Roma-Bari: Laterza.

Hivert-Messeca, Yves. 2014. "La très mirifique vie de Samuel Henri Avigdor, bourgeois gentilhomme, entrepreneur et diplomate." https://yveshivertmesseca.wordpress.com/2014/05/17/la-tres-mirifique-vie-de-samuel-henri-avigdor-bourgeois-gentilhomme-entrepreneur-et-diplomate/#_ftnref16. Accessed on 14 August 2020.

Hoffman, Philip T., Postel-Vinay, Gilles and Rosenthal Jean-Laurent. 2000. *Priceless Markets. The Political Economy of Credit in Paris, 1660–1870*. Chicago-London: University of Chicago Press.

James, Harold, and Kevin H. O'Rourke. 2013. "Italy and the First Age of Globalization, 1861–1940." In *The Oxford Handbook of the Italian Economy Since Unification*, edited by G. Toniolo, 37–68. Oxford-New York: Oxford University Press.

Kindleberger, Charles P. 1984. *A Financial History of Western Europe*. London: Allen & Unwin.

Körnert, Jan. 2003. "The Barings Crises of 1890 and 1995: Causes, Courses, Consequences and the Danger of Domino Effects." *Journal of International Financial Markets, Institutions and Money* 13, no. 3: 187–209.

La Francesca, Salvatore. 2004. *Storia del sistema bancario italiano*. Bologna: Il Mulino.

Landes, David S. 1990. *Banchieri e pascià. Finanza internazionale e imperialismo economico*. Torino: Bollati Boringhieri.

Levi, Giorgina. 1952. "Sulle premesse social-economiche dell'emancipazione degli ebrei nel Regno di Sardegna (in base a documenti del periodo 1814–1840)." *La Rassegna mensile di Israel* 18, no. 10: 417–37.

Levy-Leboyer, Maurice. 1964. *Les banques européennes et l'industrialisation internationale dans la première moitié du XIXe siècle*. Paris: Presses Universitaires de France.

Luzzatto, Gino. 1957. "L'economia italiana nel primo decennio unitario." *Rassegna Storica del Risorgimento* 44, nos. 2–3: 259–300.

Luzzatto, Gino. 1963. *L'economia italiana dal 1861 al 1894*. Torino: Einaudi Editore.

Luzzatto Voghera, Gadi. 1998. *Il prezzo dell'eguaglianza. Il dibattito sull'emancipazione degli ebrei in Italia (1871–1848)*. Milano: FrancoAngeli.

Luzzatto Voghera, Gadi. 2003. "Per uno studio sulla presenza e attività di parlamentari ebrei in Italia e in Europa." *La Rassegna Mensile di Israel* 69, no. 1: 73–92.

Maffi, Luciano 2020. "Banchieri privati nel XIX secolo. Network creditizi e finanziari nello spazio ligure." In *Frontiera Judaica. Gli ebrei nello spazio ligure-provenzale dal medioevo alla Shoah*, edited by A. Carassale and C. Littardi. Saluzzo: Fusta Editore.

Maffi, Luciano, and Marina Romani. 2019. "Banche private in Italia nel XIX secolo. Il network 'ebraico' dei Parodi di Genova." *Materia giudaica* 24: 91–100.

Maifreda, Germano. 1997. "La formazione di un rapporto fiduciario: Francesco Crispi e la Banca Weill-Schott." *Archivi e imprese* 16: 283–331.

Maifreda, Germano. 2000a. *Gli ebrei e l'economia milanese. L'Ottocento*. Milano: FrancoAngeli.

Maifreda, Germano. 2000b. "Banchieri e Risorgimento. I carteggi come fonte per la storia della banca".' In *Dolce dono graditissimo. La lettera privata dal Settecento al Novecento*, edited by M. L. Betri and D. Maldini Chiarito, 369–95. Milano: FrancoAngeli.

Marongiu, Gianni. 1995. *Storia del fisco in Italia, I. La politica fiscale della Destra storica*. Torino: Einaudi.

Masi, Paola. 1989. "L'influenza del debito pubblico sulla formazione dei sistemi finanziari: il caso italiano 1860–1893." *Rivista di Storia Economica* 6, no. 1: 60–86.

Milano, Attilio. 1992. *Storia degli ebrei in Italia*. Torino: Einaudi.

Miles, William. 2002. "The Barings Crisis in Argentina: The Role of Exogenous European Money Market Factors." *Review of Political Economy* 14, no. 1: 5–29.

Nardozzi, Giangiacomo, and Giandomenico Piluso. 2010. *Il sistema finanziario e la borsa*. Roma-Bari: Laterza.

Natoli, Sandra, Paolo Piselli, Ivan Triglia, and Francesco Vercelli. 2016. *L'Archivio Storico del Credito in Italia*. Roma: Banca d'Italia 2016.

Ottolino, Maria. 2005. *L'agricoltura in Italia negli anni del corso forzoso*. Bari: Cacucci.

Pacifici, Vincenzo G. 1984. "La sottoscrizione per i cento cannoni di Alessandria: motivazioni, polemiche e svolgimento." *Rassegna Storica del Risorgimento* 71, n. 2: 173–96.

Palumbo, Pietro. 1921. *I banchieri privati*. Torino: Unione Tipografico Editrice Torinese.

Pani, Marco. 2017. *Crisis and Reform: The 1893 Demise of Banca Romana*. IMF Working Papers.

Pantaleoni, Maffeo. 1936. "La caduta della Società Generale di Credito Mobiliare Italiano." In *Scritti Storici di economia*, 217–469. Bologna: Zanichelli.

Parravicini, Giannino. 1958. *La politica fiscale e le entrate effettive del Regno d'Italia. 1860–1890*. Torino: ILTE.

Pecorari, Paolo. 1994. *La fabbrica dei soldi. Istituti di emissione e questione bancaria in Italia (1861–1913)*. Bologna: Pàtron.

Pecorari, Paolo, ed. 1995. *Finanza e debito pubblico in Italia tra Ottocento e Novecento*. Venezia: Istituto Veneto di Scienze Lettere ed Arti.

Pecorari, Paolo. 2008. "Il sistema bancario in Italia dopo l'Unità (1861–1900)." In *Storia d'Italia*, *Annali 23*, *La Banca*, edited by C. Bermond, A. Cova, A. Moioli and S. La Francesca, 299–340. Torino: Einaudi.

Piluso, Giandomenico. 1995. "Sulla struttura dell'offerta di credito in Italia: mercati e squilibri regionali (1860–1936)." *Storia e problemi contemporanei* 8, no. 16: 9–46.

Pittaluga, Giovanni Battista. 1994. "La monetizzazione del Regno d'Italia." In *Il progresso economico dell'Italia. Permanenze, discontinuità, limiti*, edited by P. Ciocca, 177–206. Bologna: Il Mulino.

Podestà, Gian Luca. 2004. "L'evoluzione del sistema creditizio dalla Restaurazione alla legge bancaria del 1936." In *Attori e strumenti del credito in Liguria. Dal mercante banchiere alla banca universale*, edited by P. Massa, 143–73. Genova: Fondazione Carige.

Ravara Montebelli, Cristina. 2019. *Diplomatici e personalità ebraiche a San Marino (XIX - prima metà XX sec.)*. Rimini: Bookstones.

Realfonzo Riccardo, and Claudio Ricci. 2000. "The Italian Debate on Free Banking (1860–1893)." *History of Economic Ideas* 8, no. 3: 25-–60.

Riccardi, Riccardo. 2007. *L'impresa di Felice Garibaldi, fratello dell'eroe dei due mondi*. Martina Franca: Congedo.

Roccas, Massimo. 1990. "L'Italia e il sistema monetario internazionale dagli anni Sessanta agli anni Novanta del secolo scorso." In *Ricerche per la storia della Banca d'Italia*, 3–67. Roma-Bari: Laterza.

Romani, Marina. 2011. *Costruire la fiducia. Istituzioni, élite locali e mercato del credito in tre province lombarde (1861–1936)*. Milano: FrancoAngeli.

Sandri Giachino, Roberto. 2016. "Collezionisti dimenticati: i Baroni Leonino." *Rivista del Collegio Araldico* 113: 15–38.

Sannucci, Valeria. 1990. "Molteplicità delle banche di emissione: ragioni economiche ed effetti sull'efficacia del controllo monetario (1860–1890)." In *Ricerche per la storia della Banca d'Italia*, 181–218. Roma-Bari: Laterza.

Scatamacchia, Rosanna. 2008. *Azioni e azionisti. Il lungo Ottocento della Banca d'Italia*. Roma-Bari: Laterza.

Scatamacchia, Rosanna. 2013. "I banchieri questi sconosciuti. Appunti di ricerca (XIX-XX secolo)." In *Studi in ricordo di Tommaso Fanfani*, edited by M. Berti, A. Bianchi, G. Conti, D. Manetti, M. Merger, and V. Pinchera, 793–800. Pisa: Pacini.

Schisani, Maria C. 2008. "I caratteri originali del mercato finanziario italiano (1861–1914)." In *Storia d'Italia, Annali 23, La Banca*, edited by C. Bermond, A. Cova, A. Moioli and S. La Francesca, 341–72. Torino: Einaudi.

Schisani, Maria C., and Francesca Caiazzo. 2018. "Relationship-Based Finance in Changing European Banking Scenarios: The Case of Parent Schaken et Compagnie (1835–66)." In *Financing in Europe. Evolution, Coexistence and Complementarity of Lending Practices from the Middle Age to Modern Time*, edited by M. Lorenzini, C. Lorandini, and D'M Coffman, 289–316. Cham: Palgrave Macmillan.

Sciarrone, Roberto. 2014. *L'Italia nella Triplice Alleanza*. Roma: Aracne.

Segreto, Luciano. 2001. "I banchieri privati e l'industrializzazione italiana." *Impresa e storia* 24, no. 2: 273–306.

Sensales, Alfredo. 2012. "Istituzioni politiche e corso forzoso nell'Italia di Vittorio Emanuele II. La Commissione parlamentare d'inchiesta del 1868." PhD diss., University of Macerata.

Sensales, Alfredo. 2016. "«...prevalse il partito dell'adozione dell'Ordine del giorno...». La Commissione parlamentare d'inchiesta del 1868 sul corso forzoso." *Itinerari di ricerca storica* 30, no. 1: 41–64.

Tombaccini, Simonetta. 2017. *La Nazione ebrea di Nizza. Popolazioni, istituzioni, usi e costumi (1814–1860)*. Torino: Centro Studi Piemontesi.

Toniolo, Gianni. 1990. *An Economic History of Liberal Italy*. London: Routledge.

Toniolo, Gianni. 2013. "An Overview of Italy's Economic Growth." In *The Oxford Handbook of the Italian Economy Since Unification*, edited by G. Toniolo, 13–16, Oxford-New York: Oxford University Press.

Toniolo, Gianni, Conte, Leandro, and Giovanni Vecchi. 2003. "Monetary Union, Institutions and Financial Market Integration: Italy, 1862–1905." *Exploration in Economic History* 40, no. 4: 443–61.

Tuccimei, Ercole. 1990. "L'ordinamento e le operazioni della Banca Nazionale nel Regno d'Italia."'In *Gli istituti di emissione in Italia: i tentativi di unificazione, 1843–1892*, edited by R. De Mattia. Roma-Bari: Laterza.

Ugolini, Stefano. 2018. "The Origins of Swiss Wealth Management? Genevan Private Banking, 1800–1840." *Financial History Review* 25, no. 2: 161–82.

Zamagni, Vera. 1998. "Il debito pubblico italiano, 1861–1946: ricostruzione della serie storica." *Rivista di storia economica* 14, no. 3: 207–43.

Zamagni, Vera. 2007. *Introduzione alla storia economica d'Italia*. Bologna: Il Mulino.

Zanini, Andrea. 2017. *Impresa e finanza a Genova. I Crosa (secoli XVII-XVIII)*. Genova: Sagep.

CHAPTER 6

The Parodis After Italian Unification

6.1 Banca Parodi in the Post-unification Decades

In 1862, the staff of the Parodi bank consisted of the bankers Bartolomeo and Giacomo (father and son, respectively), Giacomo's son Giacomo (1842–1921) and stepson and nephew Bartolomeo (1838–1912. Giacomo married Bartolomeo's mother, Anna Pavese, widow of Giacomo's brother Giambattista, thus the dual relation), and seven employees.[1] The bank was robbed that year, and the newsworthiness of the unfortunate event testifies to the stature of the bank. A total of 730,000 lire in bonds and Banca Nazionale banknotes along with over 80,000 lire in gold were stolen. Some of it was recovered by the police.[2] To get an idea of how much money that was at the time, farmworkers in northern Italy, who represented the vast majority of the workforce, earned

[1] *L'eco dei tribunali. Giornale di giurisprudenza penale*. 1863. February 23, 548–552.

[2] The theft and trial are described in: *L'eco dei tribunali. Giornale di giurisprudenza penale*. 1863. February 23: 548–552, *L'eco dei tribunali. Giornale di giurisprudenza penale*. 1863. March 15: 587–590. A brief summary of damages is found in a letter from Banca Parodi to the Rothschild bank dated May 7, 1862: ANMT, BR, 132 AQ 9 P 099, Parodi (1860–1863).

L. Maffi, *Private Bankers in the Italian 19th Century*, Palgrave Studies in Economic History,
https://doi.org/10.1007/978-3-030-63361-5_6

from 0.80 to 1.50 lire per day.[3] Other occupations earned similar daily wages: teachers earned between 1 and 2 lire[4]; construction workers from 0.80 to 3 lire, depending on specialization and zone[5]; textile workers from 0.90 to 3 lire[6]; those working in public administration,[7] from ushers to the mid-level functionaries in the pyramidal hierarchy, had a yearly salary ranging from 200 to 1,600 lire, while those at the top might have an annual salary in excess of 20,000 lire.[8]

The robbery report and documents from the court proceedings that followed provide details that allow us to obtain a more complete portrait of the Parodis, at least as regards how they were seen by their contemporaries. They reaffirm the family's role as influential bankers, their influence extending into the political sphere, and their international profile. From the trial testimony of Pietro Ciceri, one of the robbers, we learn that the decision to strike this Genoese bank represented a very clear choice, dictated by the certainty that the robbers would find cash and bonds and by their desire to strike a banker defined as a "*codino*" (conservative) who "gave money to the coffers of the Pope, who keeps the provinces of Romagna oppressed, who was an enemy of the country".[9] The clear ideological stance expressed in his testimony does not diminish the value of the prestige of the Parodi name and reveals how widely known the Parodi family's close ties to the Pope were.

Six years after the death of the elder Bartolomeo, during the Papal Jubilee of Pope Pius IX for the twenty-fifth year of his appointment, Genoa took part in the celebrations on June 16, 1871, with the ritual ringing of the bells and the illumination of many ecclesiastic and civil buildings in the evening. The lack of illumination on the Parodi building did not pass unnoticed. The author of an article in the *Giornale degli*

[3] Felloni (1960, 1963), Aleati (1961), Tucci (1960), and Vigo (1971). Essays on these topics are also published in the *Annali di Statistica* of the Ministry of Agriculture, Industry, and Commerce: Arcari (1936), Bodio (1883), and Rota (1885).

[4] Vigo (1971, 47–62).

[5] Aleati (1961, 1–16) and Felloni (1963, 16–23).

[6] Information on wages in the textile industry is found in Rota (1885, 9–19).

[7] Felloni (1960, 20–21) and Tucci (1960, 16–21).

[8] Felloni (1960).

[9] *Giornale degli studiosi di lettere* (1871, 3–4).

studiosi di lettere offered a series of justifications of the choice of the heirs of "pious Bartolomeo".[10]

Further confirmation of the excellent relations between the Genoese family and the Papal Throne is found in the correspondence of the former with Don Giovanni Bosco. In 1873, in a private letter addressed to Bartolomeo, grandson of the elder Bartolomeo, the future saint stated that during an audience with Pius IX, "there was talk about your lordship and his family".[11] The mention of the precarious health of the banker's wife pained the Pope, who made a point of mentioning her during the celebration of Mass. This anecdote extracted from an epistolary, which on its own attests to a regular dialogue between the Parodis and high-placed ecclesiastic figures, provides further proof that the consolidated relations between the banker and the highest and most influential ecclesiastic hierarchs were renewed with the changing of the generations.

In light of this observation, the existence of a transactional account registered at Banca Parodi under the name of Cardinal Giacomo Antonelli, secretary of the Papal State, with a balance that was never less than one million lire prior to the death of the account owner in 1876, only provides further proof of the solid and continuing relationship of trust and professional esteem enjoyed by the Parodis.[12]

Looking again at the post-unification development of the Parodi bank, Bartolomeo and Giacomo supported the economic policies of the Risorgimento period. They died just a few years apart, the father in 1865 and the son in 1868. Giacomo left two adult heirs, Giacomo and Giovanni Battista, and two minor heirs, Carlo and Luigi, in the care of their maternal uncle, Baron Giuseppe Cataldi, banker and senator, who shared custody with the boys' cousin and half-brother, Bartolomeo Parodi.

In his last will and testament, dated August 22, 1868, Giacomo explicitly asked that the family business be continued. His wishes were fulfilled on November 30 of the same year by the establishment of the

[10] *Giornale degli studiosi di lettere* (1871, 3–4).

[11] Bosco (2003, 76–77).

[12] A correspondence ensued after the Cardinal's death between the Secretary of State and the bank during 1877 for the final liquidation of the account: ADG, FP, 5/43, Lettere relative al conto corrente del cardinale Giacomo Antonelli; the balance sheets recording Cardinal Antonelli's account are found in: ADG, FP, 1/6, Bilanci Banca Parodi (1868–1928). Regarding the Cardinal and his political and economic role, see: Coppa (1990).

bank "Bartolomeo Parodi e Figlio", a limited partnership with five-year, renewable deed among the elder Bartolomeo's grandsons and Giacomo's heirs: Bartolomeo, Giacomo, Giovanni Battista, Carlo, and Luigi.[13] Total bank capital was 2,200,000 lire divided as follows: 1,100,000 from Bartolomeo; 350,000 from Giacomo; 250,000 from Giovanni Battista; 250,000 from Carlo; and 250,000 from Luigi. Bartolomeo and Giacomo governed and administrated the bank and held power of signature.[14]

After the initial five-year period, Carlo, who had reached the age of majority, requested that the bank be dissolved. On August 14, 1874, a new bank was constituted with the name "Ditta bancaria Bartolomeo Parodi e Fratelli" with capital of 3,200,000 lire divided as follows: 1,400,000 from Bartolomeo, 800,000 from Giacomo, 500,000 from Giovanni Battista, and 500,000 from Luigi.[15] With this structure, the Parodi family continued its banking and finance activities up to the crisis of 1893.

The intermixing of family wealth and bank wealth continued for years, making analysis ambiguous.[16] At his death in 1865, Bartolomeo left a personal estate estimated at 5,206,806 lire, not including bank assets,[17] whereas the inheritance left by his son Giacomo in 1868 amounted to some four million lire.[18] The asset structure became more complicated in this period because Giacomo's sons and his step-son/nephew

[13] ADG, FP, 4/39, Atto costitutivo della ditta bancaria "Ditta Bartolomeo Parodi e figlio" (1868).

[14] ADG, FP, 4/39, Atto costitutivo della ditta bancaria "Ditta Bartolomeo Parodi e figlio" (1868).

[15] ADG, FP, 11/116, Atto costitutivo ditta "Ditta bancaria Bartolomeo Parodi e Fratelli" (1874). The legislative references to which banks must refer are contained in the Code of Commerce of the Kingdom of Italy: *Codice di Commercio* (1868), *Codice di Commercio* (1882).

[16] Furthermore, during the first half of the century, the Parodi accumulated a great deal of real estate, applying a policy of investments in Genoa, with numerous warehouses, apartments, and the palazzo on Corso Garibaldi, in the villa in Sestri, and a large landholding in the province of Asti. Doria (1969, 96).

[17] ADG, FP, 6/51, Denuncia di successione di Bartolomeo Parodi (1865).

[18] ADG, FP, 5/44, Atti causa giudiziaria Carlo Parodi contro i suoi fratelli (1874) and FP, 6/55, Inventario dell'eredità di Giacomo Parodi (1868).

Bartolomeo, among whom the inheritance was divided, were initially partners in the banking business but then separated.[19]

Focusing our attention on the money-lending activity, at the time of the Congress of Vienna, the Parodi bank already boasted a business volume of some ten million lire.[20] Similar figures were confirmed and consolidated in the decades leading up to Italian unification, with clear recognition from the most important and influential bankers and players in international high finance. Additional and more precise information is available from the end of the 1860s, showing that early in the following decade (1870–1873) the business volume remained continuously above 16 million lire.[21] At the time, the total money deposited in Banca Parodi by family members amounted to over 2,700,000 lire. Added to the share capital of 2,200,000, this represents just under one-third of the business volume: this relatively large amount of capital as a portion of business volume of the private bank reflects the guiding principles that characterized the bank since its establishment. First of all, there was the need to be able to assure the trust of investors and customers, who thus have a relatively explicit confirmation of the solidity and good health of the bank. Furthermore, the direct involvement of capital from the partners and the entire family demonstrates the propensity of the Genoese to personally promote their money-lending and financial operations. Nevertheless, in the 1870s, the era of private bankers began to deteriorate as a result of the proliferation of public banks and more general changes in the economic system.[22] Indeed, during that period, the bank became increasingly specialized in financial investments and the weight of "securities and assets" on the bank balance sheet grew steadily to beyond four million lire, and continued to rise in the following years to over seven million (1873–1877).

[19] Regarding Giacomo's successors, see his will and testament: ADG, FP, 4/39, Testamento di Giacomo Parodi fu Bartolomeo (1868).

[20] Rollandi (2014, 404). Regarding the fortunes of the Parodi in the early decades of the nineteenth century, see also: Doria (1969, 95–96).

[21] ADG, FP, 1/6, Bilanci Banca Parodi (1868–1928).

[22] This aspect was already noted by the Genoese economist Gerolamo Boccardo in the second edition of his dictionary: *Banchieri*, in Boccardo (1875, 281–290). Regarding Genoese economic culture in the second half of the nineteenth century: Zanini (2003) and Rollandi (2003). See also: Boccardo (1858, 1863).

The transformation of the Parodi, like that of other private bankers, into an investment bank led to an asset class in their portfolio consisting mainly of bank stocks and bonds. In the 1860s and 1870s, over 70% of the stocks held by the bank were in this category, the proportion diminishing in the 1880s to 40–50%, paralleled by an increase in investments in the railroads.[23]

6.2 The Development of the Italian Financial Market in the 1880s

In the 1880s, the economy of Genoa witnessed a surge in development that also boosted the industrial sector, thanks to the investment of both local and foreign capital. The most attractive sectors for investors were agrifoods (sugar refining above all), chemicals, and mining, continuing the trend that had begun in the previous decade.

Speculation in banking and construction also continued, giving the city a new face, with urban development expanding up onto the hillsides and the refurbishment of the central areas.[24] Relatively little investment, for the moment, was directed to urban services and infrastructure, such as lighting and transportation.

In the decades in question, there was a steadily growing trend among joint-stock banks, themselves a target of investment for capitalist families, toward putting money in the financial system. Capital flows extended both locally and nationally in a system of relations that combined entrepreneurship and banking in various regions of Italy. Ligurians made up a large portion of the shareholders in Credito Mobiliare and Banca Generale, banks headquartered in Rome that invested in major operations in industry, ship-building, and construction and held large stock portfolios in numerous businesses. Cassa Generale, the Banca di Sconto, and the Banca Provinciale, on the other hand, were headquartered in Genoa. The development of the large stock portfolios of numerous enterprises in various sectors, including banking, was the work of Genoese private bankers, among whom the Parodi played a leading role. Other Genoese banks operating in this direction include: the Casereto brothers,

[23] The data derive from documents in ADG, FP, 1/6, Bilanci Banca Parodi (1868–1928).

[24] Doria (1973, 3–6, 71–73). Concerning the economical context: Rugafiori (1994) and Paola Massa (2004, 57–62).

Giuliano Cataldi and sons, Henry Dapples, Graziani and Romanengo, Rodolfo Hofer and Co., Penchienati and Gatti, the Quartara brothers, and Adolfo Bingen.[25] There was also a continuing attachment to the railroad sector, with investments mainly in the Società Italiana per le Strade Ferrate Meridionali and in the Società Italiana per le Strade Ferrate del Mediterraneo.

The crisis in the banking sector that began in the late 1880s continued into the early 1890s, leading to the failure of numerous banks. However, despite the clear signs of instability of many banks and of the entire system generally, Genoese investors continued to support certain large banks, such as Credito Mobiliare and Banca Generale, which were specialized in providing support to industrial and real estate enterprises. The collapse of the two banks in 1893–1894 was a tremendous shock to the system. Certain investors created the Commandite Cooperative Association (Associazione cooperativa in accomandita semplice) among the shareholders of the Società Generale di Credito Mobililare Italiano in order to assert their rights during liquidation of the bank. Based on Pantaleoni's study, Doria has calculated that the Genoese owners of some 40,000 shares purchased in 1892 had lost some 15–16 million lire by 1895 due to depreciation.[26]

The economic situation in 1894 was inauspicious if not highly critical also for some Genoese private bankers, such as Isaia Tedeschi e C., the Rodolfo Hofer group, and Banca Parodi. At the same time, the most important banks of the city—Banca di Genova, Cassa di Sconto, Cassa Generale, and Banco Cooperativo Unione Ligure—witnessed a loss in capital. The duration of the crisis caused the failure of Banca Bingen in 1895,[27] one of the biggest in Genoa, with financial interests spread throughout the entire local banking system, as well as the Genoa branch of Banque Dreyfus Frères et C.

The repercussions of the banking debacle rippled out to local industry, especially the metallurgy, metalworking and mechanical engineering, and textile sectors. The shifting prospects translated—as had happened before and would happen again—into the flight of capital from the stock market

[25] Doria (1973, 83).

[26] Doria (1973, 101). Regarding Credito Mobiliare: Pantaleoni (1936, 303–325).

[27] Corbino (1934, 379). According to Corbino, the failure of Bingen was caused partly by downward speculation on the *Rendita* and by an increase in exchange rates.

and into government bonds (*Rendita*). We can get an idea of the size of this capital migration by noting that in a single five-year period, from 1889 to 1894, the total nominal value of the *Rendita* bond held by Ligurian investors climbed from 420 million to 685 million.[28]

The financial context in which the Parodis were operating, as well as certain market trends, is better delineated by crucial information regarding the stock market in the decade prior to the crisis, particularly the Genoa Stock Exchange, one of the most important together with Turin and Milan.[29] In 1885, as a result of international events and sell-offs in the main European Stock Exchanges, the Genoa Stock Exchange witnessed a slump both in the price of *Rendita* bonds and in stock prices generally, with a slight decrease in circulation of securities. The stability of the following years was not echoed on the European level until 1888 with signals of growth in the markets and a rise in commercial discounts, stock market speculation, and an increase in stocks and bonds. However, recovery on the international level was not reflected in the assets traded on the Genoa exchange, mainly because of local economic difficulties induced by a decrease in port traffic and construction, among other things.[30] Compounding this was the bankruptcy of the Panama Canal Society and the instability of the Comptoir d'Escompte de Paris, which had negative repercussions on Italian markets, with the result that prices of bank stock began to fall. This trend continued in 1889, with the divergence between bank shares and other stocks actually increasing. Banca Provinciale di Genova was liquidated that year and the Tiberina and Banco Sconto e Sete both went into crisis.

At the beginning of the 1890s, financial markets were in clear upheaval and—as observed by Giuseppe Felloni—the depression continued internationally until 1894, while in Italy the domestic difficulties were only compounded by global problems. Felloni also notes that from the first quarter of 1888 to the fourth quarter of 1896, the price of securities fell by 54% on average, but varying greatly by category, with bank stock dropping by 70.3% and railway stock by only 12.3%, and other types by

[28] Da Pozzo and Felloni (1964, 70).

[29] For the origins and history of the Genoa Stock Exchange, see: Da Pozzo and Felloni (1964, 1–12). For the Milan Stock Exchange: Baia Curioni (1995) and De Luca (2002).

[30] Da Pozzo and Felloni (1964, 133–137).

8.2%. Yearly dividends reflected this trend; bank dividends in particular fell quickly to their minimum level in 1894–1895.[31]

6.3 The Crisis of the 1890s and Its Consequences

The case study of the Banca Parodi provides insight into the behavior of private bankers in the post-unification period, thanks partially to the availability of year-end balance sheets from 1868 to 1928, an archival source that allows us to analyze the structure and size of the portfolio of these Genoese bankers and, more generally, to get an overview of the progress of their money-lending and financial activity over a broad time span.[32]

For the purposes of this study, we have chosen the period from the first decade after Italian unification to the first decade of the twentieth century. Although the bank went through a number of changes in bylaws and management structure, the available balance summaries show, albeit with some variations, relative stability in composition and content. They are gathered in pamphlets, most of which, in addition to the items credits ("*avere*") and debits ("*dare*"), also contain sheets providing a detailed description of profits and losses.

The principle items under "credits" are: loans, accounts receivable, and assets and securities.[33] These three items accounted for more than 80% of the total balance in the years from 1868 to 1892 (Fig. 6.1 and Table 6.1).

The item "other" was significant briefly in the early 1870s: in 1871, for example, there was a large amount of cash on hand, and in 1874, the item "liquidation of assets and securities" was rather high. The business volume of Banca Parodi was consistently above 10 million lire from 1868 to 1892, with a minimum of approximately 10.3 million in 1880 and a maximum of 18.3 million in 1874. The volume never dipped below

[31] Maffi (2019).

[32] ADG, FP, 1/6, Bilanci Banca Parodi (1868–1928). The choice was made to limit study within this period to the years from 1868 to 1901.

[33] The item "assets and securities" ("*titoli e valori*") normally includes the quantities held and their value in lire. As a snapshot of the financial status of the bank at a given moment, the balance sheet does not allow us to derive a detailed chronology of trade in a given security, which is why the number of shares in the annual balance sheets contains a comparison with the previous balance sheet, suggesting a trend, but not telling us how many shares were actually bought or sold during the year.

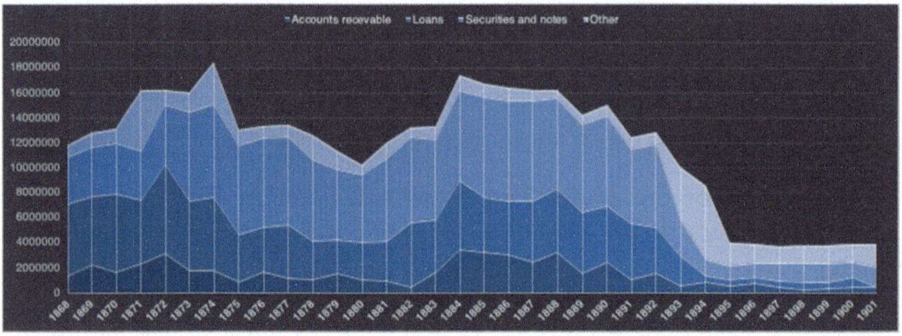

Fig. 6.1 Banca Parodi credits, balance sheets from 1868 to 1901 (Lire) (*Source Fondo Parodi*, 6 [1])

13 million during two periods: 1870–1874 and 1882–1890. The years with the highest business volume (over 16 million) fell between 1871 and 1874 and between 1884 and 1888. However, the composition of the balance sheet differed during these two periods of greatest success. In the 1870s, the item "loans" was particularly significant, while in the 1880s, it was the stock portfolio that increased significantly.

The increase in the financial portfolio and assets in the 1880s and 1890s is mainly the work of Giacomo Parodi (1842–1921), who was particularly interested in finance, also holding important positions in joint-stock companies. He served for a number of periods as a member of the High Council of the Banca Nazionale in the Kingdom of Italy, the Board of Directors of the Società Generale di Credito Mobiliare Italiano,[34] the Società Ligure Lombarda per la Raffineria degli Zuccheri, the Società di Assicurazione Italia, and the Società Italiana delle Strade Ferrate Meridionali.[35]

The most significant items under "dare" (debits) are the following: the family's transactional accounts, customer transactional accounts, creditors (customer transactional accounts plus money owed to other banks), notes payable, bank capital, and profits (Fig. 6.2 and Table 6.2).

It is interesting to observe, given the financial system of the period, the composition and trend of the bank's stock portfolio. The Parodi family

[34] Sachs (1885, 1137–1138, 1140–1141).

[35] ADG, FP, 9/95q-95r, Atti del Consiglio di famiglia "Il provvedimento di inabilitazione di Giacomo Parodi" (1904).

Table 6.1 Banca Parodi credits, balance sheets from 1868 to 1907 (Lire)

Year	*Accounts receivable*	*Loans*	*Securities and notes*	*Other*
1868	1,412,537.40	5,736,723.02	3,785,088.50	962,525.80
1869	2,283,116.98	5,468,586.73	4,042,676.45	1,086,815.38
1870	1,705,857.75	6,261,280.76	4,059,871.70	1,070,036.05
1871	2,364,877.28	5,089,665.22	4,028,012.20	4,751,851.12
1872	3,170,095.64	7,144,636.21	4,821,233.54	1,119,918.76
1873	1,786,140.84	5,550,172.04	7,174,222.80	1,498,302.19
1874	1,775,768.09	5,857,364.93	7,515,263.99	3,210,366.69
1875	929,142.25	3,787,618.86	7,156,939.27	1,173,141.62
1876	1,722,435.90	3,605,526.20	7,126,287.63	850,585.33
1877	1,218,786.68	4,298,162.28	7,026,846.15	910,673.51
1878	1,142,152.40	3,101,611.83	6,482,954.29	1,876,886.92
1879	1,591,681.73	2,689,290.44	5,632,821.83	1,407,906.07
1880	1,093,303.20	3,017,617.07	5,452,165.90	718,214.98
1881	1,017,190.60	3,181,089.72	6,608,559.44	1,190,589.66
1882	560,574.30	5,083,446.00	6,857,498.98	778,566.03
1883	1,742,651.31	4,162,934.01	6,454,852.99	942,904.87
1884	3,493,115.39	5,529,253.17	7,208,474.75	1,135,413.46
1885	3,289,750.95	4,418,522.58	7,995,693.70	984,790.14
1886	3,077,358.50	4,336,842.43	8,016,313.67	969,087.07
1887	2,543,279.40	4,839,656.70	8,028,603.67	761,762.55
1888	3,351,657.95	5,002,118.62	7,300,240.13	612,259.19
1889	1,644,401.05	4,875,683.54	6,975,974.60	724,667.30
1890	2,485,016.75	4,483,549.32	7,245,534.50	811,645.01
1891	1,153,572.75	4,425,252.49	6,004,102.07	891,410.27
1892	1,653,440.50	3,682,254.28	6,570,072.81	928,789.00
1893	612,939.55	2,424,610.60	2,818,454.60	4,243,500.86
1894	957,788.24	503,355.83	1,234,934.40	5,857,455.67
1895	620,557.43	544,192.76	1,022,176.50	1,859,448.47
1896	825,658.30	516,976.14	1,111,690.45	1,422,560.23
1897	519,114.90	554,222.01	1,311,307.92	1,330,641.89
1898	313,646.45	574,701.43	1,526,489.01	1,385,219.84
1899	418,922.80	521,001.53	1,494,973.48	1,389,875.38
1900	559,541.55	765,639.28	1,166,958.70	1,406,588.32
1901	512,132.90		1,572,523.92	1,858,573.37

Source Fondo Parodi, 6 (1)

appears to behave according to the guidelines typical of the international financial elite.

The balance item "assets and securities" ("*titoli e valori*") exhibits the following trend in the period under consideration. It begins at 3,785,088 lire in 1868 and trends upward in the following years, remaining above

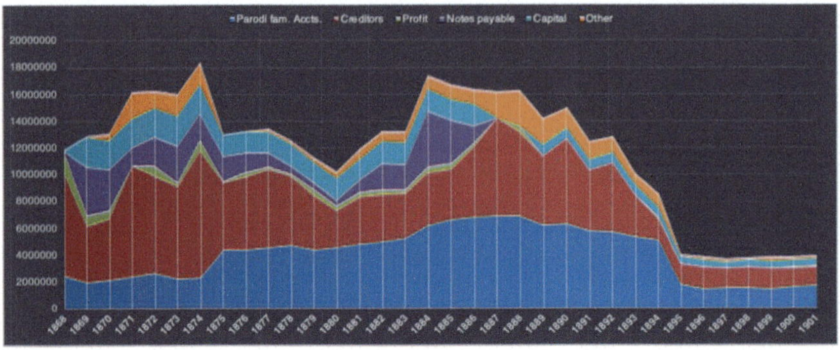

Fig. 6.2 Banca Parodi debits, balance sheets from 1868 to 1901 (Lire) (*Source* Fondo Parodi, 6 [1])

4 million lire between 1869 and 1871. Its value in 1872 is 4,821,234 lire, an increase of approximately 800,000 over the previous year. The Parodis' stock portfolio witnessed a turning point in 1873, growing to 7,174,223 and remaining consistently above 7 million until 1877. From 1878 to 1883, there is a decrease in value, ranging between a minimum of 5,452,166 in 1880 and a maximum of 6,857,499 in 1882. The five-year period 1884–1888 shows the highest values, never dipping below 7 million, and in the two-year period 1886–1887, it exceeds 8 million. In 1888, it falls back to 7,300,240 and in 1889 to 6,975,975, losing approximately 1.2 million in two years. The item "assets and securities" climbs back to 7,245,534 in 1890 before beginning an inexorable slide: 6,004,102 in 1891; 6,570,073 in 1892, and then collapsing in 1893 to 2,818,455 and to 1,234,934 in 1894. Thus, in two years, the portfolio loses 5,335,138 lire, partially because of a loss in value of the stocks (especially those of Credito Mobiliare Italiano and Cassa Generale) and partly because of sales (Ferrovie Meridionali).

Looking at the Parodi portfolio in detail, we note the presence of stocks in 74 different companies during the period in question, bonds from 38 different companies and public corporations, especially the *Rendita* bond and government bonds. However, these numbers are the sum of assets that may only be in the portfolio for a very limited amount of time or of negligible capital investments. This variety, while evidencing the Genoese bank's financial competence and detailed knowledge of the stock market, requires careful selection for the purposes of a long-term

Table 6.2 Banca Parodi debits, balance sheets from 1868 to 1901 (Lire)

Year	*Parodi fam. accts.*	*Creditors*	*Profit*	*Notes payable*	*Capital*	*Other*
1868	2,559,400.00	7,652,059.25	1,685,415.47			0
1869	2,071,752.18	4,209,929.92	735,285.74	3,664,227.70	2,200,000	0
1870	2,253,479.71	4,519,352.85	656,048.85	3,059,370.83	2,200,000	408,794.02
1871	2,514,593.61	8,253,064.71		1,334,552.29	2,200,000	1,932,195.21
1872	2,740,837.13	7,248,835.66	777,528.24	2,144,035.00	2,200,000	1,144,648.12
1873	2,317,580.52	6,852,320.43	303,958.87	2,797,801.69	2,200,000	1,537,176.36
1874	2,435,922.23	9,473,186.75	723,434.94	1,989,043.42	2,200,000	1,539,176.36
1875	4,486,367.16	5,024,634.78	5,973.28	1,929,866.78	1,600,000	0
1876	4,442,949.49	5,460,544.90	305,690.07	1,495,650.60	1,600,000	0
1877	4,617,863.54	5,850,101.82	206,566.96	1,029,480.60	1,600,000	150,455.70
1878	4,773,246.84	5,193,786.88	203,421.32	603,150.40	1,600,000	230,000
1879	4,481,692.16	4,031,244.99	400,173.72	518,589.20	1,600,000	290,000
1880	4,652,627.04	2,762,163.41	350,857.43	425,653.27	1,600,000	490,000
1881	4,857,665.60	3,597,357.77	302,689.71	962,756.34	1,600,000	676,960
1882	5,069,285.31	3,573,854.65	345,920.26	1,951,025.09	1,600,000	740,000
1883	5,294,168.82	3,379,854.56	301,569.43	1,887,750.37	1,600,000	840,000
1884	6,268,695.06	3,957,905.65	445,351.91	4,165,038.82	1,600,000	929,265.33
1885	6,732,850.48	3,807,758.93	403,223.22	3,156,007.00	1,600,000	988,917.74
1886	6,866,890.85	5,313,393.18	191,660.46	1,357,512.62	1,600,000	1,070,144.56
1887	6,926,407.75	7,347,672.19				1,899,222.38
1888	6,935,057.56	6,351,288.84	431,896.26			2,548,033.23
1889	6,296,870.67	5,122,750.27	55,149.27		800,000	1,945,956.28
1890	6,339,735.81	6,378,599.41	3,418.78		800,000	1,503,991.58
1891	5,832,933.37	4,544,099.04	121.41		800,000	1,297,189.76
1892	5,773,330.13	5,147,355.06			800,000	1,113,871.40
1893	5,429,325.59	3,054,276.47			800,000	815,903.55

(continued)

Table 6.2 (continued)

Year	*Parodi fam. accts.*	*Creditors*	*Profit*	*Notes payable*	*Capital*	*Other*
1894	5,173,971.16	1,540,269.55	178,891.84		700,000	960,401.59
1895	1,880,242.96	1,560,281.82			492,592.60	113,257.78
1896	1,510,348.19	1,633,550.93	35,394.47		492,592.60	204,998.93
1897	1,660,505.23	1,384,024.78	20,172.21		492,592.60	157,991.90
1898	1,623,763.09	1,509,872.39	30,066.72		492,592.60	143,761.93
1899	1,552,763.53	1,525,552.56	46,404.05		492,592.60	207,460.45
1900	1,695,741.11	1,424,785.33	53,523.84		492,592.60	232,084.97
1901	1,766,433.32	1,435,134.33	44,697.42		492,592.60	204,372.52

Source Fondo Parodi, 6 (1)

analysis to highlight strategies and, more generally, the operating method of the Parodis in the post-unification period.

Considering the financial portfolio of the Banca Parodi, it is most opportune to categorize the asset classes, separating them into stocks, bonds, real estate, and coupons.

As is evident from Table 6.3, the bankers apply a portfolio management strategy that strongly favors stocks and bonds. For this reason, this study focuses on well-defined stock packages, and their management, from companies that are particularly representative of their asset class.[36]

In general, from 1868 to the beginning of the twentieth century, of the 112 different products, from stocks to bonds, making up the Banca Parodi's financial portfolio, only 15 account for, by themselves and at different times, over 70% of the invested capital. The stocks were from the following companies: Credito Mobiliare Italiano, Banca Nazionale, Banca d'Italia, Cassa Generale, Istituto Italiano di Credito Fondiario, "Italia" Compagnia di Assicurazioni, Compagnia la Fondiaria Assicurazioni, Società Italiana per le Strade Ferrate del Mediterraneo, Società Italiana per le Strade Ferrate Meridionali, Compagnia Generale delle Miniere, Società Ligure Lombarda per la Raffinazione degli Zuccheri, and Società Scerno e Gismondi. The bonds are mainly government bonds, but there are also bonds from the Società Italiana per le Strade Ferrate Meridionali and the Società Ferrovie Italiane (Fig. 6.3 and Table 6.4).

The sectors preferred by the Parodis are thus banks and railroads, and these alone make up the bulk of their stock portfolio. Nevertheless, we observe some changes in behavior regarding this type of stock over time. From 1868 to 1872, the aggregate value of bank stocks never fell below 2.5 million lire. In 1873, it more than doubled, reaching 5,657,561 lire. The value of bank stocks never fell below 5 million lire in the period from 1873 to 1878, peaking in 1874 and 1876 at over 5.8 million lire. This value decreased between 1879 and 1892, remaining within the range of 3.0 and 4.5 million. The years 1879 and 1880 are interesting, with values of 4,229,898 and 3,990,128, respectively. Compared with 1878, we observe a 1.2 million drop in bank stock, the result of a large sale of shares. From 1881 to 1886, the value was consistently above 4 million. From 1887 to 1892, the value decreases progressively from roughly 3.6 to 3 million. This is the sector most strongly impacted by the crisis. In

[36] Maffi (2019).

Table 6.3 Banca Parodi assets from 1868 to 1913 (Lire)

Asset class	*1868*	*1869*	*1870*	*1871*	*1872*	*1873*	*1874*
Bonds	940,649	941,859	1,149,615	1,128,711	1,441,905	774,756	484,541
Stocks	2,844,440	2,913,420	2,801,041	2,754,400	3,252,611	6,233,474	6,812,554
Real Estate	–	–	–	–	–	–	–
Coupons	–	11,436	17,969	185,907	118,642	138,451	119,827
Total	3,785,089	3,866,715	3,968,625	4,069,018	4,813,159	7,146,680	7,416,922
	1868 (%)	1869 (%)	1870 (%)	1871 (%)	1872 (%)	1873 (%)	1874 (%)
Bonds	25	24	29	28	30	11	7
Stocks	75	75	71	68	68	87	92
Real Estate	0	0	0	0	0	0	0
Coupons	0	0%	0	5	2	2	2
Asset class	*1875*	*1876*	*1877*	*1878*	*1879*	*1880*	*1881*
Bonds	403,117	402.22	578,616	408,837	420,287	153,006	509,544
Stocks	6,684,477	6,600,281	6,263,920	5,983,917	5,120,039	5,095,195	5,975,303
Real Estate	–	–	29.44	29.44	40.44	40.44	26,001
Coupons	4,845	13,537	10.62	28.76	105	6,415	15.21
Total	7,092,439	7,016,038	6,882,596	6,450,954	5,580,871	5,295,055	6,526,058
	1875 (%)	*1876 (%)*	*1877 (%)*	*1878 (%)*	*1879 (%)*	*1880 (%)*	*1881 (%)*
Bonds	6	6	8	6	8	3	8
Stocks	94	94	91	93	92	96	92
Real Estate	0	0	0	0	1	1	0
Coupons	0	0	0	0	0	0	0
Asset class	*1882*	*1883*	*1884*	*1885*	*1886*	*1887*	*1888*
Bonds	514.13	3,951	732,275	1,679,870	1,390,784	1,259,588	1,647,296
Stocks	6,295,634	6,331,329	6,389,191	6,268,071	6,418,467	6,599,334	5,571,442
Real Estate	26,001	26,001	1	1	1	62,450	2,300
Coupons	–	4,464	–	1,017	20,327	15,355	1,079
Total	6,835,765	6,365,744	7,121,466	7,948,959	7,829,579	7,936,727	7,222,116

(continued)

Table 6.3 (continued)

	1882 (%)	*1883 (%)*	*1884 (%)*	*1885 (%)*	*1886 (%)*	*1887 (%)*	*1888 (%)*
Bonds	8	0	10	21	18	16	23
Stocks	92	99	90	79	82	83	77
Real Estate	0	0	0	0	0	1	0
Coupons	0	0	0	0	0	0	0
Asset class	*1889 (%)*	*1890 (%)*	*1891 (%)*	*1892 (%)*	*1893 (%)*	*1894 (%)*	*1895 (%)*
Bonds	1,314,262	1,543,106	901,495	1,602,177	803,786	144,986	98,921
Stocks	5,511,077	5,414,146	4,850,724	4,800,219	2,115,292	965,987	990,768
Real Estate	1	201,749	201,749	201,749	59,801	71,232	26,590
Coupons	17,385	6,229	2,584	17,227	–	42,680	14
Total	6,842,724	7,165,230	5,956,553	6,621,373	2,978,879	1,224,884	1,116,293
	1889	*1890*	*1891*	*1892*	*1893*	*1894*	*1895*
Bonds	19	22	15	24	27	12	9
Stocks	81	76	81	72	71	79	89
Real Estate	0	3	3	3	2	6	2
Coupons	0	0	0	0	0	3	0
Asset class	*1896*	*1897*	*1898*	*1901*	*1902*	*1903*	*1904*
Bonds	267,654	236,531	173,473	626,209	308,809	371,078	18,697
Stocks	808,802	1,056,673	1,322,141	926.69	611,069	1,119,375	884,222
Real Estate	24,500	12,800	5,000	5,000	4,000	4,000	4,000
Coupons	6,484	5,304	5,501	4,524	2,959	990	240
Total	1,107,440	1,311,308	1,506,114	1,562,424	926,837	1,495,442	907,158
	1896 (%)	*1897 (%)*	*1898 (%)*	*1901 (%)*	*1902 (%)*	*1903 (%)*	*1904 (%)*
Bonds	24	18	12	40	33	25	2
Stocks	73	81	88	59	66	75	97
Real Estate	2	1	0	0	0	0	0
Coupons	1	0	0	0	0	0	0

(continued)

Table 6.3 (continued)

Asset class	*1905*	*1908*	*1909*	*1910*	*1911*	*1912*	*1913*
Bonds	156,154	99,169	121,215	28,656	260,188	510,002	404.5
Stocks	994,777	1,236,585	1,068,489	390,615	1,220,346	1,139,935	945,476
Real Estate	17,600	68,359	65,549	4,000	62,124	41,978	30,405
Coupons	279	5,732	2,379	–	230	2,007	819
Total	1,168,809	1,409,846	1,257,632	423,271	1,542,888	1,693,922	1,381,200
	1905 (%)	*1908 (%)*	*1909 (%)*	*1910 (%)*	*1911 (%)*	*1912 (%)*	*1913 (%)*
Bonds	13	7	10	7	17	30	29
Stocks	85	88	85	92	79	67	68
Real Estate	2	5	5	1	4	2	2
Coupons	0	0	0	0	0	0	0

Source Fondo Parodi, 6 (1), our elaboration

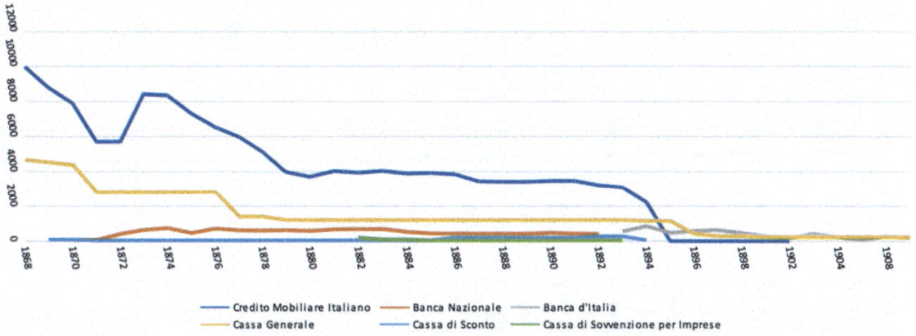

Fig. 6.3 Trend of banks shares (quantity) in the Banca Parodi portfolio from 1868 to 1909 (*Source* Fondo Parodi, 6 [1])

1893, the balance sheet shows 1,056,006, falling to 743,091 in 1894 and then continuing the downward trend in the following years (Figs. 6.4 and 6.5, Tables 6.5 and 6.6).

Between 1868 and 1900, the Parodis held stocks in the following 18 banks: Banca Nazionale (later Banca d'Italia), Credito Mobiliare Italiano, Cassa Generale, Cassa di Sconto, Cassa di Sovvenzione per Imprese, Banca Toscana di Credito, Banca Toscana, Banca Internazionale, Banca Generale di Roma, Banco Commerciale Ligure, Banca di Genova, Banco di Roma, Banca Commerciale Italiana, Banca Italiana di Costruzione, Banca Napolitana, Banca Popolare di Genova, Banco di Sconto e di Sete, and Istituto Italiano di Credito Fondiario. Investments were not evenly distributed within this group, with significantly larger portions going to certain select institutes. The Parodis invested most heavily in Credito Mobiliare Italiano, Banca Nazionale, Cassa Generale, and Istituto Italiano di Credito Fondiario, followed by Banca Internazionale, Cassa di Sconto, Banca Toscana di Credito, and Banca Italiana di Costruzione, albeit limited to certain periods.

6.4 Credito Mobiliare Italiano and Cassa Generale: Two Case Studies in the Parodi Portfolio

Credito Mobiliare Italiano is clearly the preferred investment destination for the Parodi family. From 1868 to 1870, they invested more than 2 million lire in this bank. This is clear from the first balance sheet we have

Table 6.4 Trend of banks shares (quantity) in the Banca Parodi portfolio from 1868 to 1909

	1868	*1869*	*1870*	*1871*	*1872*	*1873*	*1874*	*1875*	*1876*	*1877*	*1878*
Credito Mobiliare Italiano	9,972	8,772	7,898	5,700	5,705	8,413	8,338	7,306	6,531	5,979	5,130
Banca Nazionale	69		81	84	430	657	758	481	732	633	618
Banca d'Italia											
Cassa Generale	4,690	4,540	4,390	2,840	2,843	2,843	2,843	2,843	2,843	1,421	1,421
Cassa di Sconto		88	88	38	38	40	40	40	40	40	40
Cassa di Sovvenzione per Imprese											
	1879	*1880*	*1881*	*1882*	*1883*	*1884*	*1885*	*1886*	*1887*	*1888*	*1889*
Credito Mobiliare Italiano	3,974	3,699	4,026	3,932	4,032	3,888	3,912	3,837	3,435	3,410	3,410
Banca Nazionale	640	595	688	698	700	544	453	444	444	440	440
Banca d'Italia											
Cassa Generale	1,221	1,221	1,221	1,221	1,221	1,221	1,221	1,221	1,221	1,221	1,221
Cassa di Sconto	40	40	40	40	40	40	40	200	200	200	200
Cassa di Sovvenzione per Imprese				200	100	100	50	50	50	50	50
	1890	*1891*	*1892*	*1893*	*1894*	*1895*	*1896*	*1897*	*1898*	*1901*	*1902*
Credito Mobiliare Italiano	3,460	3,460	3,204	3,079	2,229	2	2	2	2	2	2
Banca Nazionale	485	440	420								
Banca d'Italia				552	854	466	580	637	466	292	182
Cassa Generale	1,221	1,221	1,221	1,221	1,171	1,171	431	306	306	268	268
Cassa di Sconto	200	200	273	273	53						
Cassa di Sovvenzione per Imprese	50	50	50	50							

	1903	1904	1905	1908	1909
Credito Mobiliare Italiano					
Banca Nazionale					
Banca d'Italia	420	232	76	290	220
Cassa Generale	268	268	268	268	268
Cassa di Sconto					
Cassa di Sovvenzione per Imprese					

Source ADG, FP, 1/6, Bilanci Bana Parodi (1968–1928)

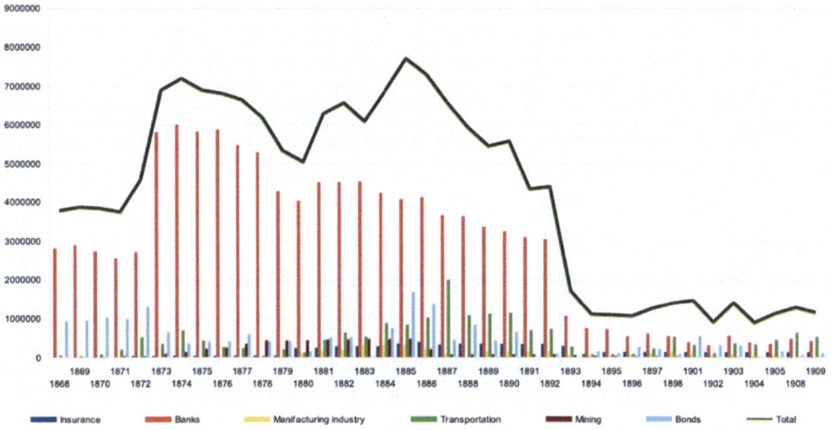

Fig. 6.4 Price shares trend in the Banca Parodi assets from 1868 to 1909 (*Source* Fondo Parodi, 6 [1])

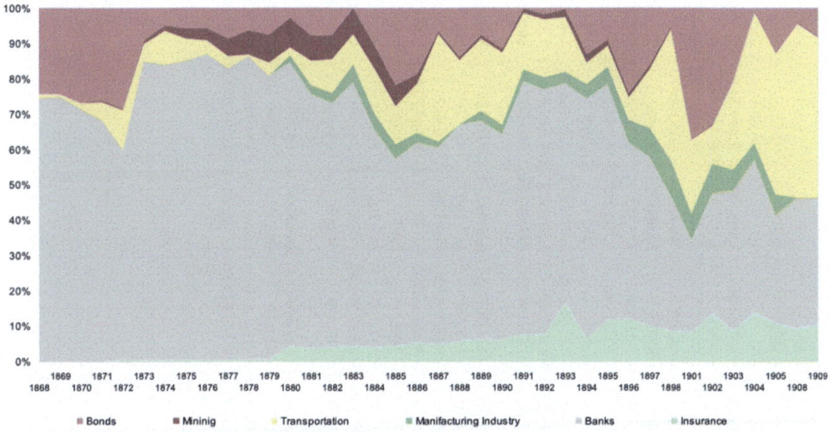

Fig. 6.5 Trend of shares percentage in the Banca Parodi asset class from 1868 to 1909 (*Source* Fondo Parodi, 6 [1])

at our disposal. Dated 1868, it shows the bank owning 9972 shares for a value of 2,193,840 lire, amounting to no less than 58% of the asset class defined above. Starting in 1869, Credito Mobiliare Italiano witnessed

Table 6.5 Price shares trend in the Banca Parodi assets from 1868 to 1909

	1868	*1869*	*1870*	*1871*	*1872*	*1873*	*1874*	*1875*	*1876*	*1877*	*1878*
Insurance	0	0	0	0	26,000	26,000	26,000	29,250	29,250	29,250	34,000
Banks	2,802,440	2,884,420	2,726,970	2,548,750	2,699,511	5,801,761.50	5,986,191.50	5,810,416.90	5,863,266.90	5,460,904.90	5,285,514.28
Manifacturing Industry	0	0	0	0	0	0	0	0	0	0	0
Transportation	42,000	25,000	66,071	185,650	507,100	335,712.50	680,362.49	420,310.55	256,264.25	221,165.25	29,562.95
Mining	0	4,000	8,000	20,000	20,000	70,000	120,000	205,000	232,000	333,100	420,340
Bonds	919,348.50	941,859	1,021,905	975,891	1,297,685.15	638,275.55	355,303	401,776.50	401,220	577,616	401,581
Total	3,763,788.50	3,855,279	3,822,946	3,730,291	4,550,296.15	6,871,749.55	7,167,856.99	6,866,753.95	6,782,001.15	6,622,036.15	6,170,998.23
	1879	*1880*	*1881*	*1882*	*1883*	*1884*	*1885*	*1886*	*1887*	*1888*	*1889*
Insurance	29,250	221,955.78	235,955.78	270,883.95	270,883.95	270,883.95	343,383.95	387,605.95	314,200	339,200	337,200
Banks	4,263,497.73	4,023,722.73	4,495,001.73	4,501,927.73	4,513,825.73	4,221,937.73	4,065,192.73	4,111,534	3,652,960	3,618,326	3,356,825
Manifacturing Industry	0	100,000	153,238.70	183,888.70	306,502.95	306,502.95	306,502.95	196,160	104,500	900	145,675
Transportation	194,051	110,276	433,267.25	625,043.25	516,226	867,776	824,701	1,010,501	1,986,168.75	1,071,511	1,105,183
Mining	418,740	424,740	443,340	447,340	457,340	453,540	459,740	192,400	60,004	60,004	62,004
Bonds	410,271.40	142,990	503,188.95	510,570	3,040.2	731,279.72	1,678,927.36	1,369,348	433,225	821,225	420,492.5
Total	5,315,810.13	5,023,684.51	6,263,992.41	6,539,653.63	6,067,818.83	6,851,920.35	7,678,447.99	7,267,548.95	6,551,057.75	5,911,166	5,427,379.50
	1890	*1891*	*1892*	*1893*	*1894*	*1895*	*1896*	*1897*	*1898*	*1901*	*1902*
Insurance	333,737	332,737	332,737	282,201	70,001	126,222.25	126,066.45	125,619	120,001	120,626	120,626
Banks	3,235,408.40	3,082,408.40	3,031,792.80	1,056,005.85	743,091	715,104	522,029	592,622	527,186	377,136.80	301,676.80
Manifacturing Industry	145,675	145,000	147,850	54,001	45,001	52,051	64,901	101,688.50	137,226	105,909.75	73,299.60
Transportation	1,130,719.50	688,874	719,334	264,560	66,000	64,000	66,950	205,855	510,294	303,666.90	96,115.50
Mining	62,104	62,003	62,003	40,465	26,892.50	18,390	13,855	15,887.50	12,432.5	4,350	4,350
Bonds	647,337	5,725.75	81,312.75	5,364	144,066	98,041	252,157	201,389.70	73,268.15	535,775.82	292,976.20
Total	5,554,980.90	4,316,748.15	4,375,029.55	1,702,596.85	1,095,051.50	1,073,808.25	1,045,958.45	1,243,061.70	1,380,407.65	1,447,465.27	889,044.10

(continued)

Table 6.5 (continued)

	1903	*1904*	*1905*	*1908*	*1909*
Insurance	120,626	120,626	120,625	118,125	118,125
Banks	552,274	378,428.25	339,934.10	468,516.80	408,649.30
Manifacturing Industry	79,386.25	42,205.35	62,886.15	0	0
Transportation	347,738.60	323,612.25	446,181.35	621,993.60	513,764.45
Mining	4,350	4,350	4,350	4,350	4,350
Bonds	286,548.94	7,134.69	139,515.14	54,704.14	91,853.96
Total	1,390,923.79	876,356.54	1,113,491.74	1,267,689.54	1,136,742.71

Source Fondo Parodi, 6 (1), our elaboration

Table 6.6 Trend of shares percentage in the Banca Parodi asset class from 1868 to 1909

	1868	*1869*	*1870*	*1871*	*1872*	*1873*	*1874*	*1875*	*1876*	*1877*	*1878*
Insurance	0.00	0.00	0.00	0.00	0.57	0.38	0.36	0.43	0.43	0.44	0.55
Banks	74.46	74.82	71.33	68.33	59.33	84.43	83.51	84.62	86.45	82.47	85.65
Manifacturing Industry	0.00	0.00	0.00	0.00	0.00	0.00	0.00	0.00	0.00	0.00	0.00
Transportation	1.12	0.65	1.73	4.98	11.14	4.89	9.49	6.12	3.78	3.34	0.48
Mining	0.00	0.10	0.21	0.54	0.44	1.02	1.67	2.99	3.42	5.03	6.81
Bonds	24.43	24.43	26.73	26.16	28.52	9.29	4.96	5.85	5.92	8.72	6.51
	1879	*1880*	*1881*	*1882*	*1883*	*1884*	*1885*	*1886*	*1887*	*1888*	*1889*
Insurance	0.55	4.42	3.77	4.14	4.46	3.95	4.47	5.33	4.80	5.74	6.21
Banks	80.20	80.10	71.76	68.84	74.39	61.62	52.94	56.57	55.76	61.21	61.85
Manifacturing Industry	0.00	1.99	2.45	2.81	5.05	4.47	3.39	2.70	1.60	0.02	2.68
Transportation	3.65	2.20	6.92	9.56	8.51	12.66	110.74	13.90	30.32	18.13	20.36
Mining	7.88	8.45	7.08	6.84	7.54	6.62	5.99	2.65	0.92	1.02	1.14
Bonds	7.72	2.85	8.03	7.81	0.05	10.67	21.87	18.84	6.61	13.89	7.75
	1890	*1891*	*£1,892.0*	*1893*	*1894*	*1895*	*1896*	*1897*	*1898*	*1901*	*1902*
Insurance	6.01	7.71	7.61	16.57	6.39	11.75	12.05	10.11	8.69	8.33	13.57
Banks	58.24	71.41	69.30	62.02	67.86	66.60	49.91	47.67	38.19	26.05	33.93
Manifacturing Industry	2.62	3.36	3.38	3.17	4.11	4.85	6.20	8.18	9.94	7.32	8.24
Transportation	20.36	15.96	16.44	15.54	6.03	5.96	6.40	16.56	36.97	20.98	10.81
Mining	1.12	1.44	1.42	2.38	2.46	1.71	1.32	1.28	0.90	0.30	0.49
Bonds	11.65	0.13	1.86	0.32	13.16	9.13	24.11	16.20	5.31	37.01	32.95

(continued)

Table 6.6 (continued)

	1903	*1904*	*1905*	*1908*	*1909*
Insurance	8.67	13.76	10.83	9.32	10.39
Banks	39.71	43.18	30.53	36.96	35.95
Manifacturing Industry	5.71	4.82	5.65	0.00	0.00
Transportation	25.00	36.93	40.07	49.07	45.20
Mining	0.31	0.50	0.39	0.34	0.38
Bonds	20.60	0.81	12.53	4.32	8.08

Source Fondo Parodi, 6 (1), our elaboration

continuous growth, producing good dividends for the shareholders, over 3% semi-annual interest, sharing in the booming market, raising the value of its stocks above one thousand lire, and increasing profit margins. A look at the profits on the balance sheet will suffice to give a full appreciation of the earnings produced by this investment for Banca Parodi: in 1870, for example, the total of three items—dividend, margins, and premiums—amounted to 407,821 lire, roughly 25% of the value of the invested capital (Table 6.7).

An analysis of the data reveals that in the three-year period 1869–1871 a total of 4272 securities were sold, reducing by nearly half the portfolio of stocks held by the Parodis. Reviewing the associated profits recorded on the balance sheets for 1869 and 1870, including dividends and premiums, one wonders what motivated them to sell securities producing 837,863 lire of profit on an investment of around 2 million. The most likely hypothesis, based on the interpretation of available data, is that the very wide profit margin available on the Genoa exchange from the constantly rising quotation of the securities fully justifies the sale of significant portions. Table 6.7 shows yield of 118.18 in those years, not so advantageous by itself to justify foregoing such healthy profits. However, that index is the result of a calculation based on the value of the stocks registered on the balance sheet. According to these parameters, the amount obtained from the sale of 2198 shares in 1871 would be 87,920 lire. If instead we look at the minimum and maximum quotations of the same shares on the Genoa Stock Exchange for the same year, the prospective earnings range between 450,590 and 1,560,580 lire. Applying this analysis to the three-year period, the overall profit from the sale of Credito Mobiliare Italiano stock rises from approximately 171,000 lire, calculated on the basis of available balance sheet data, to two more likely figures anchored to the current prices of the shares, from a minimum of approximately 680,000 to a maximum of approximately 2,150,000 lire. Sums such as these make the decision to sell the stock much more comprehensible.

The absence of archival documentation providing more precise data on the amount of these earnings prevents us from a more in-depth investigation of the Banca Parodi's financial operating methods and thus from better identifying the motivations behind its operations. Nevertheless, the unpublished data from the archive, which reveal details of great value in delineating the profile of bankers of such stature, must be analyzed in conjunction with published sources that make it possible to reconstruct

Table 6.7 Credito Mobiliare Italiano stock in the Banca Parodi portfolio from 1868 to 1895

	1868	*1869*	*1870*	*1871*	*1872*	*1873*	*1874*
Value in lire	2,193,840	2,280,720	2,053,480	1,482,000	1,486,300	3,690,612	3,625,762
Number of shares	9,972	8,772	7,898	5,700	5,705	8,413	8,338
Variation in number of shares		−1.200	−874	−2.198	5	2,708	−75
Percentage of asset class (%)	58.0	59.0	51.7	36.4	30.9	51.6	48.9
Price per share in lire	220.00	260.00	260.00	260.00	260.53	438.68	434.85
Min. quotation on Genoa stock exchange, in lire	255	354	300	425	865	765	635
Max. quotation on Genoa stock exchange, in lire	388	483	539	930	1.320	1.271	925
Calculated yield	100.00	118.18	118.18	118.18	118.42	199.40	197.66
Profits on shares recorded on balance sheets		430.042	407.821				534,250.4
	1875	*1876*	*1877*	*1878*	*1879*	*1880*	*1881*
Value in lire	4,208,256	3,761,856	3,443,904	2,954,880	2,289,024	2,130,624	2,392,224
Number of shares	7,306	6,531	5,979	5,130	3,974	3,699	4,026
Variation in number of shares	−1.032	−775	−552	−849	−1.156	−275	327
Percentage of asset class (%)	59.3	53.6	50.0	45.8	41.0	40.2	36.7
Price per share in lire	576.00	576.00	576.00	576.00	576.00	576.00	594.19

(continued)

Table 6.7 (continued)

Min. quotation on Genoa stock exchange, in lire	615	604	548	640	698	780	848
Max. quotation on Genoa stock exchange, in lire	820	701	702	711	988	1.045	951
Calculated yield	261.82	261.82	261.82	261.82	261.82	261.82	270.09
Profits on shares recorded on balance sheets		274,721.3	227,115.7	218.499	357.762	273,945.2	163,991.55
	1882	*1883*	*1884*	*1885*	*1886*	*1887*	*1888*
Value in lire	2,359,200	2,419,200	2,402,750	2,420,455	2,455,680	2,084,625	2,046,000
Number of shares	3,932	4,032	3,888	3,912	3,837	3,435	3,410
Variation in number of shares	–94	100	–144	24	–75	–402	–25
Percentage of asset class (%)	34.5	38.0	33.7	30.4	31.4	26.3	28.3
Price per share in lire	600.00	600.00	617.99	618.73	640.00	606.88	600.00
Min. quotation on Genoa stock exchange, in lire	738	694	801	823	912	940	860
Max. quotation on Genoa stock exchange, in lire	935	826	978	1,020	1,090.50	1,052	1,030
Calculated yield	272.73	272.73	280.91	281.24	290.91	275.85	272.73
Profits on shares recorded on balance sheets		165,814.5	220,117.45	197,117.9	199,699.1		181,861.15
	1889	*1890*	*1891*	*1892*	*1893*	*1894*	*1895*
Value in lire	1,875,500	1,685,925	1,607,175	1,501,309.4	172.424	8.916	1
Number of shares	3,410	3,460	3,460	3,204	3,079	2,229	2

(continued)

Table 6.7 (continued)

Variation in number of shares	0	50	0	−256	−125	−850	−2,227
Percentage of asset class (%)	27.4	23.5	27.0	22.7	5.8	0.8	0.0
Price per share in lire	550.00	487.26	464.50	468.57	56.00	4.00	0.50
Min. quotation on Genoa stock exchange, in lire	552	517.5	321	361	147	100	106
Max. quotation on Genoa stock exchange, in lire	883	654	532	609	487	183	111
Calculated yield	250.00	221.48	211.14	212.99	25.45	1.82	0.23
Profits on shares recorded on balance sheets	151,057.55	99,443.10	78,158.40	64.74	−1,203,400.65		

Source Fondo Parodi, 6 (1), our elaboration

the financial events, incorporating a larger context and keeping bank data from being analyzed in isolation.

The analysis of the year 1873 reveals another example of the keen ability of Banca Parodi to seize securities-trading opportunities and leverage its expertise in the dynamics of the stock market, and also provides a further opportunity to compare the newly available accounting information with what we already know from the studies by Giuseppe Felloni.

The constant upward trend in value of the Credito Mobiliare Italiano shares ended in late spring of 1873, caused by a bearish movement counteracting the bullish speculation at the beginning of the year and the repercussions of the financial crisis that had spread from Vienna to the major international stock exchanges. This caused the progressive loss in value of the security, culminating in the liquidation of September, forcing the auctioning off of several thousand shares, dragging the quotation down to 765 lire at the end of October.

What could be the reasons justifying the acquisition that year of no fewer than 2708 shares of a security that continues to bring in excellent profits and that maintains a quotation much higher than the acquisition price recorded on the balance sheet? Why interrupt an advantageous sales trend? We may hypothesize two scenarios. One is an improbable participation in the bullish speculative strategies seen in the early months of 1873, a supposition that raises questions if we consider the amount of capital necessary to purchase such a large block of shares and the generally prudent nature of the Genoese bank. The alternative is that Banca Parodi successfully took part in the autumn auction mentioned by Felloni. This would explain the increase in number of shares still in their possession at year end and the subsequent price adjustment in later balance sheets, as well as a return to management of the stock package trending toward sales for the rest of the decade. According to the balance sheets, the 4639 shares sold between 1875 and 1880 earned the bank approximately 1.65 million lire. Actually, applying the minimum and maximum quotations of the stock in those years, we obtain minimum potential earnings just under 2 million lire and a maximum of approximately 2.8 million lire. These figures do not account for yearly dividends and interest on the stock package, which are well above 200,000 lire on average.

Our examination of the five-year period in question once again highlights the expertise of the Parodi in financial markets: thanks to the opportune trading in Credito Mobiliare shares, probably with some amount of speculation (although the archives do not provide clear support for this) and the complementary business associated with the stock package, the Parodis earned millions. The 1880s, while the trend toward selling shares continued, were less effervescent and dynamic: the rising yield from stocks and their prices recorded on the balance sheets, however, show that, in terms of strategic investment planning, Credito Mobiliare remained an excellent long-term choice, with an index of yield consistently above 270. In general, from 1878 to 1888, the value of capital invested in this security was never less than 2 million lire, with a maximum of 2,954,880 in 1878 and a minimum of 2,046,000 in 1888. In 1889, the investment decreased to 1,875,000 and was still above 1.6 million in the two-year period 1890–1891, with the stock package always containing more than 3400 shares.

In the three years from 1889 to the end of 1891, the quotation of the stock progressively diminished: this was common among shares in joint-stock companies quoted on the stock exchange in that period. However, in the specific case of Credito Mobiliare, the general slump in the market caused significant damage to the value of its stock portfolio, causing large losses in capital reserves. Nevertheless, Banca Parodi kept its package of Credito Mobiliare stocks unvaried until 1893, when the collapse of their quotation decreased the value of their investment from 1,501,309 to 172,424 lire, with a yield index plummeting from 212.99 to 25.45. The well-known conclusion to the affair is also reflected in the Parodi balance sheets, recording a total of 2229 shares valued at 8916 lire, with yield falling to 1.82.

Observing the overall weight of the Credito Mobiliare stock package in the asset classes held by Banca Parodi, it is interesting to observe the change in percentage over the course of the decades considered. At the end of the 1860s, it represented an impressive 59%; during the following decade, it ranged from 30 to 50%, excluding 1875 when it peaked at 59.3%; in the 1880s to the collapse of 1893, the percentage continued its slow decline from an initial 40% to just over 22%.

This trend supports the thesis whereby, starting in the 1880s, the Parodis begin to diversify their investment strategies, distributing portions of their capital previously concentrated in bank stock to other sectors, favoring railroad companies. The investment in Credito Mobiliare amounted to some 1.4 million lire in 1871–1872 and more than 3.6 million in the years 1873 and 1874. The peak came in 1875 with 4,208,256 invested. The investment remained at levels well over 3 million lire in the two-year period 1876–1877. From 1878 through 1888, it remained above 2 million lire, hitting a maximum of 2,954,880 for the period in 1878 and the minimum of 2,046,000 in 1888. In 1889, it decreased to 1,875,500. In the two years 1890–1891 (some 3400 shares), it was still above 1.6 million. In 1892 (3204 shares), it was 1,501,310. The fate of Credito Mobiliare after that is well known and reflected in the Parodi portfolio. In 1893, their 3079 shares were worth 172,424 and the following year 2229 shares are recorded with a value of 8916 lire.[37]

A second case for analysis, exemplifying the value of the documentary material, is that of Cassa Generale, a bank which the Parodi helped establish in 1856 with six other founders: the initial share capital of the bank was to be 8 million lire composed of 32,000 shares with a nominal value of 250 lire. However, the founders paid 100 lire in August 1856 and an additional 50 the following month for total paid-up capital of 4.8 million lire. In 1868, the Parodi owned a package of 4690 shares, just under 15% of the total of 32,000, with a recorded value of 469,000 lire. This figure leads us to suppose that they were still holding a significant portion of the share they purchased when the bank was established, for which they paid the initial 100 lire per share (Table 6.8).

The progressively rising quotation of Cassa Generale shares starting in 1869, coupled with the strategies of the new management at Banca Parodi, explains the three years of sales of the stock culminating in 1871 with 1550 shares, sold on the market at a time when the calculated gain ranged from a minimum of 186,000 lire—not very plausible—to a maximum of 596,750 lire in the case where the transaction was carried out during a spike in prices during the second half of the year.

The year 1877 is an interesting one for reconstructing the strategies and dynamics reflected in the balance sheets and bookkeeping data under examination: with invested capital remaining unvaried with respect to 1876, the total number of shares owned dropped by half while per-share prices doubled from 160 to 320 lire, in line with the average quotation for the year. This snapshot suggests a sell-off aiming to take speculative advantage of an auspicious moment in the trend for the stock. However, here again, a comparison with information from published sources allows us to interpret the data in a more precise and historically accurate manner. In 1875, the Cassa Generale shareholder assembly deliberated to reduce

[37] Regarding Credito Mobiliare stock quotations in the years in question, see Da Pozzo and Felloni (1964, 303–325).

Table 6.8 Cassa Generale stock in the Banca Parodi portfolio from 1868 to 1905

	1868	*1869*	*1870*	*1871*	*1872*	*1873*	*1874*	*1875*	*1876*
Value in lire	469,000	454,000	439,000	284,000	284,936	284,936	284,936	454,880	454,880
Number of shares	4,690	4,540	4,390	2,840	2,843	2,843	2,843	2,843	2,843
Variation in number of shares		−150	−150	−1,550	3	0	0	0	0
Percentage of asset class (%)	124	11.7	11.1	7.0	5.9	4.0	3.8	6.4	6.5
Price per share in lire	100.00	100.00	100.00	100.00	100.22	100.22	100.22	160.00	160.00
Min. quotation on Genoa stock exchange, in lire	195	195	190	220	390	295	150	220	252
Max. quotation on Genoa stock exchange, in lire	203	240	243	485	485	448	313	279	277
Calculated yield	100.00	100.00	100.00	100.00	100.22	100.22	100.22	160.00	160.00
Profits on shares recorded on balance sheets		45,230.00	39,657.5				29,851.51	19,851	28.48
	1877	*1878*	*1879*	*1880*	*1881*	*1882*	*1883*	*1884*	*1885*
Value in lire	454,720	326,710.55	390.720	390,720	390,720	390,720	390,720	390,720	390,720
Number of shares	1,421	1,421	1,221	1,221	1,221	1,221	1,221	1,221	1,221
Variation in number of shares	−1,422	0	−200	0	0	0	0	0	0
Percentage of asset class (%)	6.6	5.1	7.0	7.4	6.0	5.7	6.1	5.5	4.9
Price per share in lire	320.00	229.92	320.00	320.00	320.00	320.00	320.00	320.00	320.00

(continued)

Table 6.8 (continued)

Min. quotation on Genoa stock exchange, in lire	285	314	345	485	505	395	360	390	405
Max. quotation on Genoa stock exchange, in lire	343	355	516	595	565	505	420	445	445
Calculated yield	320.00	229.92	320.00	320.00	320.00	320.00	320.00	320.00	320.00
Profits on shares recorded on balance sheets	35,650.50	29,130.50	61,944	41,964	41,514		25,946.25	30,525.00	30,525.00
	1886	*1887*	*1888*	*1889*	*1890*	*1891*	*1892*	*1893*	*1894*
Value in lire	488,400	518,925	518,925	518,925	518,925	518,925	518,925	341,880	275,185
Number of shares	1,221	1,221	1,221	1,221	1,221	1,221	1,221	1,221	1,171
Variation in number of shares	0	0	0	0	0	0	0	0	−50
Percentage of asset class (%)	6.2	6.5	7.2	7.6	7.2	8.7	7.9	11.5	23.3
Price per share in lire	400.00	425.00	425.00	425.00	425.00	425.00	425.00	280.00	235.00
Min. quotation on Genoa stock exchange, in lire	430	495	450	350	325	260	270	280	148.5
Max. quotation on Genoa stock exchange, in lire	550	536	518	465	380	330	348	330	270
Calculated yield	400.00	425.00	425.00	425.00	425.00	425.00	425.00	280.00	235.00
Profits on shares recorded on balance sheets	32,967		30,525	31,746	21,978	18,315	18,315	−158.73	0

(continued)

Table 6.8 (continued)

	1895	*1896*	*1897*	*1898*	*1901*	*1902*	*1903*	*1904*	*1905*
Value in lire	265,877	128,007	104,040	104,040	93,800	93,800	93,800	93,800	93,800
Number of shares	1,171	431	306	306	268	268	268	268	268
Variation in number of shares	0	−740	−125	0	−38	0	0	0	0
Percentage of asset class (%)	23.8	11.6	7.9	6.9	6.0	10.1	6.3	10.3	8.0
Price per share in lire	227.05	297.00	340.00	340.00	350.00				
Min. quotation on Genoa stock exchange, in lire	197	200							
Max. quotation on Genoa stock exchange, in lire	242	240							
Calculated yield	227.05	297.00	340.00	340.00	350.00				
Profits on shares recorded on balance sheets	8,803.50	8,817.50	5,902.50	5,339.80		5,360.00		5,420.20	5,446.85

Source Fondo Parodi, 6 (1), our elaboration

share capital from 8 million to 4.8 million lire, consisting of 16,000 shares with nominal value of 300 lire—this time all paid up. In effect, every two shares from 1856 (2 × 150 lire paid up) were replaced by one with a nominal value of 300 lire, paid up. This change took place in 1877 and thus explains the significant variation in the figures recorded that year, obviating interpretations that are reasonable but incorrect. During the following years, the share witnessed a rise in quoted value and the stock package owned by the Parodis comprised approximately 8% of the 16,000 shares issued by the bank, remaining at that level until 1893 in spite of the fact that the quotation began to diminish starting in 1888. If we compare this time period with the clearly more dynamic and complex performance of the Credito Mobiliare shares, we note a clear difference in management. While both are joint-stock companies operating prevalently in investments in moveable assets, Cassa Generale and Credito Mobiliare are very different in terms of share capital, business volume, and, most importantly, the profiles of their founders. While the Parodis are actively involved in the lively market performance of Credito Mobiliare shares, bringing in impressive profits considering the amount of capital invested and its weight as a proportion of the asset class, thus demonstrating bold speculative acumen, in the case of Cassa Generale, we observe the cautious behavior more typical of these Genoese bankers. The reasons for such behavior may be ascribed to the role played by the family in this bank, from its initial establishment to the portion of share capital owned, correlated to the close relations with other founding members, all fellow Genoese. Furthermore, an institute such as Cassa Generale represents an excellent opportunity for the Parodis to exert an influence on the decision-making processes of an investment bank specialized in moveable assets with more available resources than their own private bank, which was no longer in the condition to make investments on a par with the demands of the industrial transformation underway.

The year 1893 was particularly critical for Cassa Generale, which had to cope with a significant drop in the quotation of its shares as well as the risk of a bank run. The bank devalued its stock portfolio, zeroed its reserves, and sold other stocks it owned and managed to avoid failure. In 1895, it witnessed a slight increase in its quotations and deposits. The crisis was also clearly reflected in the Parodi balance sheet, which still contained its stock package, which was useful in 1896–1897 for sales of a security that, although devalued, still had a sufficiently high quotation to allow them to generate liquidity.

A final important observation on this thirty years of shareholding derives from an analysis of the weight percentage of Cassa Generale stocks in the Parodi portfolio: excluding the first three years for which the balance sheet is available, it never exceeds 10% through 1892. After that, it rises to nearly 24% in 1894–1895. This evidences that Banca Parodi and the capital invested in this particular asset class suffered significant losses, making a stock package that had represented a relatively small portion of assets up to a few years earlier suddenly outsized by comparison.[38]

Since its establishment in 1844, the Banca di Genova, the first bank of issue in the Kingdom of Sardinia, later becoming Banca Nazionale and finally Banca d'Italia in 1894, is quite notably associated with the Parodi family. Among its founding partners, the Parodis are also protagonists of its governance: Bartolomeo Parodi served as its president for the first three-year term.[39] It is thus not surprising that the family held a notable stock package in the second half of the nineteenth century, albeit with variations over the time period in question.[40]

In the years 1873 to 1880, the number of shares recorded on the balance sheet fell to a minimum of 481 in 1875, with a value of 841,750 lire and hit a maximum of 758 in 1873 for a value of 1,310,290 lire. In the second half of the 1870s, the value of the stock remained consistently above one million lire, with a maximum of 1,331,000 lire in 1876 and 732 shares. From 1881 to 1884, it again remained above one million

[38] Regarding the history of the bank and Cassa Generale stock quotations in the years in question, see Da Pozzo and Felloni (1964, 269–279).

[39] Regarding the role of Banca Parodi in the socioeconomic context of Genoa and in the Banca di Genova (later Banca Nazionale) see Rossi and Nitti (1968, 7–8): "Among the promoters of Banca di Genova we also find Bartolomeo Parodi, owner of one of the largest private banks in the city. According to a report from the French consul dated February 21, 1850, he was the head of '*one of the most important and best established banks, doing business of some ten million lire in this marketplace. It is party, one says, to a quarter of all financial operations taking place in Genoa*' (Archives Ministère des Affaires Etrangères, Correspondance consulaire, série commerciale, Gênes, vol. 111, pp. 301–308). Appointed vice president [errata corrige: he was president], Parodi provided a large sum of initial capital to the bank. Based on the minutes of the Consiglio di Reggenza of July 4, 1845, we learn that when the bank found itself unable to meet the demand for conversion of its banknotes by the banker Barbaroux, owner of an agency in Turin, Parodi ceded large Turinese assets and offered a significant contribution to the bank".

[40] Regarding the role of the Genoese in the Banca Nazionale and stock distribution, see Scatamacchia (2008).

lire, ranging from a minimum of 1002, 864 in 1884 (544 shares) to a maximum of 1,300,904 in 1882 (698 shares).[41]

From 1885 to 1892, the number of shares in the portfolio was less than 500, ranging from a minimum of 420 in 1892 (recorded value of 685,800 lire) to a maximum of 485 lire in 1890 (value of 793,050 lire). The Parodis' investment continued during the following years with ownership of shares in Banca d'Italia, although the value was lower. From 1893 to 1899, it ranged from a minimum of 466 shares in the years 1895 and 1898 (with a value of 255,240 and 341,135 lire, respectively) to a maximum of 854 in 1894 (recorded value of 439,810).

The Parodi balance sheets always include the item "Rendita Italiana e prestito nazionale", which contains, without specific detail, various types of government debt, such as the *Rendita* bond, treasury bonds, and consolidated loans, characterized by differing interest rates.[42] In trading on the Genoa Stock Exchange in the nineteenth century, government bonds held a prominent position among quoted public securities. Trading on the Italian financial market in the second half of the nineteenth century involved a much higher proportion of government bonds than company stock.

The value of the government bonds recorded on the Parodi balance sheets during the first decade in question ranged from a minimum of 218,056 lire in 1870 to a maximum of 791,004 lire in 1872. In the 1880s, it went from 135,150 in 1880 to 1,677,910 in 1885. In 1886, the value remained above 1.2 million lire.

Investments in this type of security dropped significantly in the 1890s, starting at a value of 237,900 lire in 1890 and diminishing drastically in the following years: 5726 in 1891, 81,313 in 1892, and 5364 in 1893. It then began to climb in 1894 (144,066 lire), 1895 (98,041 lire), and especially in 1896–1897 (over 200,000 lire).

[41] Regarding the quotation of stock in Banca Nazionale and later Banca d'Italia during the years in question, see Da Pozzo and Felloni (1964, 215–242).

[42] Da Pozzo and Felloni (1964, 133–137).

6.5 Other Investment Sectors: Transportation, Insurance, Mining, Chemicals

Another typical sector of investment is the railroads, but with a different pattern. Interest in the railroad industry began in the 1870s and grew significantly in the following decade. In 1871, the Parodi family owned railroad stock with a value of 185,650 lire, which surged to 507,100 lire the following year, falling off in the second half of the decade to 110,275 lire in 1880.

Railroad investments in 1881 amounted to 433,266 lire, rising to a million in 1886. The peak came the following year, with 2,742,168 invested in railway stock. From 1888 to 1892, the value of the stock in the portfolio diminished but remained within the range of 1.5 million to 1,956,719. In 1893, it fell to 979,410 before dropping to 66,000 lire in 1894. The largest investment was in the Società Italiana delle Ferrovie Meridionali: in the second half of the 1880s, the stocks owned by the Parodis ranged in value from 700,000 to a peak of over 1.7 million in 1887.[43] From that year until 1893, the balance sheets record 826,000 lire in bonds from the Società Ferrovie Italiane. In 1887–1888, the family also held 120,000 lire in shares of the Società Italiana per le Ferrovie del Mediterraneo. This investment in railways in the late 1880s can be attributed to the renowned prudence of the Genoese bankers or perhaps to an awareness of the complex situation in the banking system, from which they began to divest, albeit slowly. Moreover, these were the years of a change in the government's industrial policy, which then focused on the construction of secondary railways.

As evidenced by Giuseppe Felloni's analysis of the Genoa Stock Exchange, the stock quotations of the major railroad companies did not suffer the same slump experienced by bank stocks in the crisis of 1893.[44] The Parodis' caution in this circumstance allowed their bank, although losing significant amounts, to halt the fall and offset the losses from bank stocks by selling shares in the railroads.

[43] Regarding the history of the railroad company and the quotations of the stock in the Società Italiana per le Strade Ferrate Meridionali in the years in question, see Da Pozzo and Felloni (1964, 361–386). Capodaglio (1939). For listed corporations, see also: Piccinelli (1905).

[44] Da Pozzo and Felloni (1964, 361–386).

The Parodis also invested in the insurance sector, holding shares—generally a modest number—in the following joint-stock companies: "Italia" Compagnia di Assicurazioni; "Italia" Società di Assicurazioni e Coassicurazioni Generali; "Liguria" Società di Assicurazioni; Compagnia la Fondiaria Assicurazioni a Vita; and Società d'Assicurazione la France Marittime. The company absorbing the greatest amount of their capital was Fondiaria Assicurazioni a Vita. From the mid-1880s to the crisis of 1893, they held a stock package with a value constantly in excess of 200,000 lire.

As regards real estate, the family held shares in Esquilino but their principal investments in this sector were with Società Risanamento di Napoli. From 1890 to 1892, they held 800 shares with a value of approximately 198,000 lire. In 1893, the number of shares rose to 1994 but their value had fallen to a mere 39,880 lire.

Investments in the mining industry tended to be small as a rule but well diversified, especially among companies operating in Sardinia: Società Mineraria Lanusei; Società Mineraria Montelora; Miniere Correboi; and Compagnia Generale delle Miniere. In a slight quantitative exception, the family held stocks in Compagnia Generale delle Miniere with a value of 386,000 lire in the early 1880s, an investment which had already become marginal by the end of the decade.

Again looking at investments limited to the 1880s, the family held stock in the Società per la Raffinazione Zuccheri: in 1881, the 613 shares were recorded with a value of some 153,000 lire. The number of shares remained unchanged in the following years but increased in value: from 1883 to 1885, they were worth more than 300,000 lire, falling to 196,160 in 1886 and then disappearing from the books.[45]

As mentioned above, the Parodis had only a marginal presence in other sectors, such as the chemical industry. Apart from the Società per la Raffinazione Zuccheri, the only other investment recorded on the balance sheets that we have reviewed was in the Società Scerno e Gismondi of Genoa, which produced potassium and sodium nitrate. From 1875 to 1877, the bankers held 439 shares with a value of 219,500 lire. From 1878 to 1885, their number had decreased slightly to 429 for a corresponding value of 214,500 lire. After 1887, they nearly doubled to 830 with a total value of 456,500 lire (with the exception of 1891, when they

[45] For historical notes on this corporation and the quotations of its stock, see, Da Pozzo and Felloni (1964, 449–463).

were recorded with a value of 489,700 lire). In 1893, the value decreased to 415,000 lire while in 1894 only 30 shares are recorded with a value of 15,000 lire.

It is interesting, in general, to note the difference between the investment behavior of the Parodis with respect to other Genoese families of large investors, such as the Bombrini,[46] Raggio, Piaggio,[47] and Durazzo Pallavicino[48] families, who showed preferences for other sectors.[49]

6.6 The Preferred Investments of Private Bankers

The Parodi portfolio is characterized by a continuous presence of shares in other banks, some of which are specialized in credit to industry, such as Credito Mobiliare, Cassa Generale, and Cassa di Sovvenzione per Imprese. Their investment strategies clearly derive from their expertise, relations, and opportunities for earnings, but also from the possibility to shape the policies of large banks. Genoa is not an isolated case: also in Turin in the 1880s and 1890s, the most famous private banking families gravitated to Banca di Torino (such as the Ceriana, Geisser, Merlo, Casana, Nigra, Donn, Vogel, Weill Weiss, and Sacerdote families) and the Banco di Sconto e Sete (Defernex, Mylius, Montù, Cassinis, Beltramo, and Maspero).[50] In many cases, moreover, there is a correlation between the participation of a medium- and long-term credit institute in the establishment of a corporation and the presence of figures (often private bankers) having both vested interests in the institute and directorial functions (generally as members of the BoD) in the corporation.[51] As we have seen with the Parodi, transportation is a preferred sector of investment also in Piedmont (Turin): thus, Fratelli Nigra invested in the Società anonima ferrovia da Fossano a Mondovì; Ulrico Geisser e C. in the Società anonima ferrovie economiche e tramvie di Pisa;

[46] Doria (1989, 22–52) and Daneo (1889).

[47] Giulianelli (2012) and Canella and Maifreda (2012).

[48] Tolaini (2019, 160–249).

[49] In general, investors tend to prefer sectors where they play the most significant role as entrepreneurs or professionals. In this regard, see the portfolio analyses in Doria (1973, 653–666).

[50] Balbo (2000, 75–87), on p. 76 there is a detailed analysis of the problems with interpreting the investment policies of private bankers. Balbo (2007), Polsi, *Alle origini*.

[51] For other exemples, Balbo (2000, 77–79).

Antonio Kuster in the Società anonima delle ferrovie centrali e tramvie del Canavese; and Francesco Ceriana in the Settimo-Rivarolo rail line, the Turin-Pinerolo-Torre Pellice line, and the Turin-Acqui line. Along with banks and transportation/infrastructure, the Turinese bankers also purchased stock in food companies, mining companies, metalworking and mechanical engineering firms, and construction companies. Another similarity between Genoese and Turinese bankers is that "far from being pawns moved by the credit institute to control the boards of directors of satellite corporations",[52] they have their own strategies, adapting to the shifting economic context and seizing opportunities as they arise.

A study of the political relations of the Weill-Schott bank of Milan highlights its role in major financial operations in the post-unity decades, especially in railroad companies and banks.[53] In his analysis of the holdings and investment strategies of the most important Milanese Jewish families of bankers and investors, Germano Maifreda shows that, along with the strong focus on real estate that made them one of the largest property owners in Milan, some members of the Leonino Sacerdoti family held stock in banks, where they also sat on the boards of directors, such as Banca Nazionale and Banca di Credito Italiano, and railroad companies, particularly the Ferrovie Meridionali.[54] In general, however, their portfolios are dominated by prudent investments, steering clear of industrial sectors, as we have also seen to some extent with the Parodis. Private bankers cultivate relations with and greatly prefer investing in banks, where they often hold some sort of directorial position. Next in line are railroad companies, often the outcome of intricate interests involving networks of relations in the political and financial spheres, which generate good results in terms of profits. In the background are investments in industry involving smaller amounts of capital.

6.7 Decline and New Strategies for Banca Parodi

The effects of the crisis on Banca Parodi are manifested both in the losses recorded on the balance sheet, especially in the stock portfolio, and in the organization of the private bank itself. On August 30, 1894, Giacomo

[52] Balbo (2000, 88).

[53] Maifreda (1997, 283–331; 2019).

[54] Maifreda (2000, 261–267).

Parodi signed a writ of rescission from the bank.[55] Living between Genoa and Florence, Giacomo had been the family member most involved in the bank's financial affairs in the previous years. He was also an active member of the boards of directors of important corporations, including the Società Ligure Lombarda per la Raffineria degli Zuccheri, the Società di Assicurazione Italia, and the Società Italiana delle Strade Ferrate Meridionali, positions that provided him with "lavish" yearly compensation.[56] His personal involvement in the instability obliged him to inject a part of his personal wealth and borrow money from the other family members. He was the principal player behind the bank's excellent financial performance in the 1870s and 1880s, as recorded on the Banca Parodi balance sheets, and the one who guided its investments. Most of the earlier successes and the millions lost during the year of the crisis are mainly to be attributed to him.

Giacomo was succeeded by Giambattista and Barolomeo[57]: reference is made in the bulletin of the prefecture of Genoa[58] on September 12, 1894, to Giacomo's rescission from the bank and to the appointment of the lawyers V. Capellini, M. Caveri, and G. B. Boraggini as "amicable compounders" with a mandate to "ascertain the status of the account of the rescinding partner from said company and determine both the amount and the effective payment of the respective debt, which may be resolved also via the transfer of either mobile or immobile assets owed to said two parties".

Giacomo Parodi's outstanding debt to Banca Parodi was resolved via an arbitration panel ruling on December 27, 1895. However, ten years later, Giacomo still figured as being indebted to his family and to the bank. The banker's downward trajectory is described in a document from 1904, where we read that, in addition to owing money to his family, he was also indebted to other banks (Banca Commerciale Italiana, Ditta

[55] ADG, FP, 8/90, Atto di recesso dalla società di Giacomo Parodi (1894).

[56] ADG, FP, 9/95q-95r, Atti del Consiglio di famiglia "Il provvedimento di inabilitazione di Giacomo Parodi" (1904). Regarding the financial situation in Florence in that period, see: Coppini (1976), Conti (Conti 1989), and Armani (2006). Regarding the political and economic context in that period: Romanelli (1978) and Conti and Scatamacchia (2009).

[57] The power of signature, which until then had been in the hands of Bartolomeo and Giacomo, was then extended to Giambattista.

[58] ADG, FP, 8/90.

Bancaria Fratelli Rossi di Genova) and a number of individuals. Marked by the collapse of his wealth, the banker and financier's reputation suffered and he was forced to resign from any remaining positions he still held on the various boards of directors.[59]

Additional information about the repercussions of the crisis on the bank is found in the repeated requests for an audit of the income tax on moveable assets advanced by the Parodis in those years. As early as 1894, the bank had declared that it had suffered large losses due to the general business trend and more specifically to the depreciation of many of the securities in its portfolio.[60] A clear example is the reference "to the 3,000 Credito Mobiliare shares still held", a notable stock package whose value plummeted in a short amount of time to just a few lire.

In 1895, the bank reported the cessation of profits and the negative impact of the enormous depreciation of its shares in banks and construction companies.[61] The document also mentions a conversion in its banking activities and a partial abandonment of financial operations. This is also reflected in the balance sheets from the last years of the nineteenth and first decade of the twentieth century. "The bank has decided to remain for the time being in a prudent pause, and to limit itself almost exclusively to banking activities with America, which will certainly not generate enough income to cover the cost of its personnel". The new strategy for Banca Parodi was to develop relations with South America, where numerous Italians had moved or were in the process of moving. The situation did not improve in the following years. In 1898, contesting the assessment of income on capital, business, and wages, the Parodis stated that the bank had reduced its business to the point where it was merely sufficient to pay employee salaries,[62] going so far as to declare that: "if it has not completely withdrawn from doing business, it was out of a desire to retain its old clerks who have worked for it for so many years, and if it remains open with its meagre commercial earnings it is only in tribute to its honorable and historic name".

[59] ADG, FP, 9/95q-95r, Atti del Consiglio di famiglia "Il provvedimento di inabilitazione di Giacomo Parodi" (1904).

[60] ADG, FP, 12/127, Tasse e riscossioni (1894).

[61] ADG, FP, 12/127, Avviso di accertamento di rettiti di ricchezza mobile del 29 settembre 1894.

[62] ADG, FP, 12/127, Tasse e riscossioni (1898).

The crisis exposed all the structural weaknesses of the Italian financial and political system and especially the lack of adequate investment banks. This gap in the credit system induced issuing banks and large commercial banks to fill it, taking positions that were often risky.[63] The issuing banks supported industrial and real estate development, financing their exposure in part with an increase in the circulation of paper money. This strategy was tolerated by the government, which interpreted the approach as an attempt to support the economy via the expansion of credit.

The objective of this study is to highlight the role of private bankers, working in conjunction with issuing banks and commercial banks to support the development of industry, real estate, and joint-stock banks. Emblematic representatives of the category, albeit with their own particular characteristics, the Parodi family are emblematic of this trend during the post-unification period. They made diversified investments in banks, insurance companies, mining, railroads, real estate, and the sugar industry. They thus assembled a significant stock portfolio while helping finance entrepreneurs and establish commercial banks, such as Cassa Generale and Cassa Sovvenzione Imprese.

However, the expansion of credit ended up inflating asset prices, generating a speculative bubble in an economy where opportunities for productive investments—those that promote real growth—were still rather modest.

Our analysis of this period reveals a complex set of imbalances that was difficult to untangle, especially in the absence of detailed and readily implementable strategies, for those, like the bankers of the time, who might have discerned the intrinsic risk.[64] An analogous viewpoint might be applied to the case of the Parodi family. However, their renowned prudence in long-term banking and finance operations, their membership in an elite financial network with international reach, and their recognized expertise in different areas would tempt us to suppose that this Genoese family was not completely unaware of what was happening, as is suggested by the strategies they adopted to manage their portfolio and, more generally, the assets held by their bank.

The crisis of 1893 had the positive effect of forcing rationalization in the banking sector that might otherwise have been delayed for years. The

[63] Pani (2017) and Vitale (1972).

[64] Pani (2017).

snags in the system finally convinced money lenders and financial operators, and also the general public, of the need for a well-managed and regulated banking sector. The negative economic situation clarified the roles of issuing banks and the responsibilities of government, providing a stimulus for renewal and growth. The capacity to quickly resolve the situation derived in part from the fact that a reform of the banking system had been in the works for some time and had thus already been discussed in parliament, although not yet been approved. The guidelines for reorganizing the sector had already been analyzed, shared, and were awaiting enactment.[65]

As the century came to an end, the downward slide of Banca Parodi leveled off with business volume stabilizing at around 3.5–4.0 million lire until World War I. The crisis of 1907 was another upheaval with which the bank was forced to cope, setting the stage for subsequent industrial growth in Italy while also representing a setback in the Genoese capitalists' investments in the banking and industrial sectors.[66] The year was characterized globally by a liquidity crisis and a serious depression in the securities industry. The situation was difficult for the mixed banks established after the crisis of the 1890s, which had immobilized deposits in stock portfolios, stock market operations, and credit to industry. The most important ones were Banca Commerciale Italiana, Credito Italiano, and Società Bancaria Italiana, which found themselves unable to meet the demand for withdrawal of funds by depositors, both due to their exposure to losses and due to the degree to which they had immobilized their resources.[67] The fact that the stock market crisis did not lead to another banking debacle was only thanks to the intervention of Banca d'Italia, which bailed out the ailing institutes. Nevertheless, in a critical juncture featuring business failures and the relocation of the headquarters of many corporations, new equilibria were established among investors. In general terms, Milan gained an increasingly relevant role, especially as regards the capacity for investment of its own capital in the banking sector

[65] Maifreda (2011), Brambilla (2011), and Negri (1989).

[66] Regarding the conduct of Genoese capitalists during the crisis of 1907, see Doria (1973, 329–342, 516–522).

[67] Bonelli (1971, 7–10, 13–38) and Confalonieri (1982).

and industry, rising as a viable alternative to the role hitherto played by Genoa.[68]

Some Genoese private bankers, whose role in the development of the principal credit institutes proved to be fundamental in the post-unification decades,[69] suffered such a serious setback from the crisis of the early 1890s that they were unable to invest in shares of the mixed banks set up in the second half of that decade. The Parodis belonged to that category and thus did not invest in any of the credit unions stricken during the crisis of 1907.[70] More generally, no significant changes were made to the portfolio of the Genoese banking family in the years 1905 to 1911,[71] with the predominant capital flows being in the railroad sector, with shares in the Società Italiana Strade Ferrate del Mediterraneo, and Ferrovie Meridionali, and bonds from the Società Ferrovie Italiane, in the banking sector, particularly with shares of Banca d'Italia, and in insurance. They thus continued an investment strategy characteristic of their customary approach, albeit at a greatly diminished business volume. They thus shunned the industrial sector, even though this was precisely where the mixed banks and private bankers were making direct investments via stock purchase, or indirect investments by extending credit to the businesses themselves.

Looking at the national context in Italy, in 1912, per capita GDP had grown by nearly 60% in nominal terms and 25% in real terms with respect to 1893. However, not all credit and finance operators were able to return to the levels of business in the pre-crisis period, as we have seen in the case of the Parodi family. Having suffered a serious blow to their stock portfolio and bank assets, and in spite of the fact that they implemented new conversion strategies, for example, with regard to South America, the Genoese bankers never again achieved the levels they had seen in previous years.

[68] Vasta and Baccini (1997) and Toniolo (1990).

[69] The role of the financial investments of the principal private Genoese banks in the Italian credit sector is also underscored in Doria (1973, 82–90).

[70] The analysis of the Parodi portfolio shows Banca Commerciale Italiana stock recorded only in 1905: 100 shares with a value of 94,723 lire. ADG, FP, 1/6, Bilanci Banca Parodi (1868–1928).

[71] ADG, FP, 1/6, Bilanci Banca Parodi (1868–1928).

Bibliography

Archives

Archivio Doria di Genova (ADG).
FP, 1/6, Bilanci Banca Parodi (1868–1928).
FP, 4/39, Atto costitutivo della ditta bancaria "Ditta Bartolomeo Parodi e figlio" (1868).
FP, 4/39, Testamento di Giacomo Parodi fu Bartolomeo (1868).
FP, 5/43, Lettere relative al conto corrente del cardinale Giacomo Antonelli.
FP, 5/44 Atti causa giudiziaria Carlo Parodi contro i suoi fratelli (1874).
FP, 6/51, Denuncia di successione di Bartolomeo Parodi (1865).
FP, 6/55 Inventario dell'eredità di Giacomo Parodi (1868).
FP, 8/90, Atto di recesso dalla società di Giacomo Parodi (1894).
FP, 9/95q-95r, Atti del Consiglio di famiglia "Il provvedimento di inabilitazione di Giacomo Parodi" (1904).
FP, 11/116, Atto costitutivo ditta "Ditta bancaria Bartolomeo Parodi e Fratelli" (1874).
FP, 12/127, Avviso di accertamento di rettiti di ricchezza mobile (1895).
FP, 12/127, Tasse e riscossioni (1898).
FP, 12/127, Tasse e riscossioni (1894).
Archives Nationales du Monde du Travail – Banque Rothschild (ANMT, BR).
BR, 132 AQ 9 P 099, Parodi (1860–1863).

Printed Contemporary and Near Contemporary Sources

Boccardo, Gerolamo. 1858. *Manuale di storia del commercio delle industrie e dell'economia politica*. Torino: Tipografia Scolastica di Sebastiano Franco e Figli.

Boccardo, Gerolamo. 1863. *Il Negoziante italiano. Manuale degli uomini d'affari*. Genova: Tipografia Fratelli Pellas.

Boccardo, Gerolamo. 1875. *Dizionario universale di economia politica di commercio*. Milano: Treves.

Bodio, Luigi. 1883. "Sulla statistica dei salari. Risultati sommari di una indagine iniziata sulla alimentazione delle classi operaie." *Annali di Statistica* 7.

Codice di Commercio del Regno d'Italia annotato dal cavaliere Luigi Borsari. 2 vols. 1868. Torino: Società L'Unione tipografico-Editrice.

Codice di Commercio del Regno d'Italia. 1882. Roma: Regia Tipografia.

Daneo, Gian C. 1889. *Les usines Ansaldo des frères Bombrini et les industries mécaniques en Italie*. Rome: Impresa Editrice Romana.

Giornale degli studiosi di lettere, scienze, arti e mestieri dedicato alla Società Ligure di Storia Patria. 1871. 3, no. 30: 3–4.

L'eco dei tribunali. Giornale di giurisprudenza penale. 1863. February 23.

L'eco dei tribunali. Giornale di giurisprudenza penale, 1863. March 15.
Piccinelli, Ferdinando. 1905. *Il capitalista nelle Borse e nel commercio dei valori pubblici*. Milano: Hoepli.
Rota, Pietro. 1885. "Salari degli operai addetti ad alcune delle principali industrie della Lombardia negli anni 1847, 1859, 1866, 1874." Annali di Statistica 14.
Sachs, Isidore. 1885. *L'Italie, ses finances et son développement èconomique depuis l'unification du royame, 1859–1884*. Paris: Guillaumin.

Secondary Sources

Aleati, Giuseppe, ed. 1961. "Le retribuzioni dei lavoratori edili in Milano, Pavia e nei rispettivi territori dal 1819 al 1890." *Archivio economico dell'unificazione italiana* 11, no. 1.
Arcari, Paola Maria. 1936. "La variazione dei salari agricoli in Italia dalla fondazione del Regno al 1933." *Annali di Statistica* 36.
Armani, Barbara. 2006. *Il confine invisibile. L'élite ebraica di Firenze (1840–1914)*. Milano: FrancoAngeli.
Baia Curioni, Stefano. 1995. *Regolazione e competizione. Storia del mercato azionario in Italia (1808–1938)*. Bologna: Il Mulino.
Balbo, Ivan. 2000. "Banche e banchieri a Torino: identità e strategie (1883–1896)." *Impresa e storia* 21, no. 1: 61–101.
Balbo, Ivan. 2007. *Torino oltre la crisi. Una "business community" tra Otto e Novecento*. Bologna: Il Mulino.
Bonelli, Franco. 1971. *La crisi del 1907. Una tappa dello sviluppo industriale italiano*. Torino: Fondazione Luigi Einaudi.
Bosco, Giovanni. 2003. *Epistolario, 4 (1873–1875)*, edited by Francesco Motto. Roma: LAS.
Brambilla, Carlo. 2011. "Banche ed economia nazionale (1861–1914)." In *Le Banche e l'Italia. Crescita economica e società civile (1861–2011)*, edited by L. Conte, 63–100. Roma: Bancaria Editrice.
Canella, Maria, and Germano Maifreda, eds. 2012. *L'Italia dei Piaggio. Uomini e imprese a Genova dall'Unità*. Milano: Editrice Nexo.
Capodaglio, Giulio. 1939. *Storia di un investimento di capitale. La Società Italiana per le Strade Ferrate Meridionali (1862–1937)*. Milano: Bietti.
Confalonieri, Antonio. 1982. *Banca e industria in Italia dalla crisi del 1907 all'agosto 1914*. Milano: Banca Commerciale Italiana.
Conti, Giuseppe. 1989. *Terra, commercio e credito nella Toscana del XIX secolo. Crescita e decadenza di un sistema di arricchimento*. Pisa: Studi e ricerche del Dipartimento di Scienze economiche dell'Università di Pisa.
Conti, Giuseppe, and Rosanna Scatamacchia. 2009. "Stato di fiducia, crisi finanziarie e crisi politiche nell'Italia liberale prima del 1914." *Discussion paper del Dipartimento di Scienze Economiche dell'Università di Pisa* 87: 1–34.

Coppa, Frank J. 1990. *Cardinal Giacomo Antonelli and Papal Politics in European AFFAIRS*. Albany: State University of New York Press.
Coppini, Romano P. 1976. "Banche e speculazione a Firenze nel primo ventennio unitario." *Quaderni Storici* 32, no. 2: 582–612.
Corbino, Epicarmo. 1934. *Annali dell'economia italiana. 4. (1891–1900)*. Napoli: Istituto Editoriale del Mezzogiorno.
Da Pozzo, Mario, and Giuseppe Felloni. 1964. *La borsa valori di Genova nel secolo XIX*. Torino: ILTE.
De Luca, Giuseppe, ed. 2002. *Le società quotate alla borsa valori di Milano dal 1861 al 2000. Profili storici e titoli azionari*. Milano: Libri Scheiwiller.
Doria, Giorgio. 1969. *Investimenti e sviluppo economico a Genova alla vigilia della Prima Guerra Mondiale* (1815–1882). Milano: A. Giuffrè Editore.
Doria, Giorgio. 1973. *Investimenti e sviluppo economico a Genova alla vigilia della Prima Guerra Mondiale* (1883–1914). Milano: A. Giuffrè Editore.
Doria, Marco. 1989. *Ansaldo. L'impresa e lo Stato*. Milano: FrancoAngeli.
Felloni, Giuseppe, ed. 1960. "Stipendi e pensioni dei pubblici impiegati negli stati sabaudi dal 1825 al 1859." *Archivio economico dell'unificazione italiana* 10, no. 2.
Felloni, Giuseppe, ed. 1963. "Le retribuzioni dei lavoratori edili a Genova dal 1815 al 1890." *Archivio economico dell'unificazione italiana* 12, no. 3.
Giulianelli, Roberto. 2012. *I Piaggio. La parabola di un grande gruppo armatoriale e cantieristico italiano (1875–1972)*. Bologna: Il Mulino.
Maffi, Luciano. 2019. "Banca e finanza a Genova nel XIX secolo. La ditta Parodi dall'Unità alla crisi degli anni Novanta." *Storia Economica* 22, no. 1: 139–79.
Maifreda, Germano. 1997. "La formazione di un rapporto fiduciario: Francesco Crispi e la Banca Weill-Schott." *Archivi e imprese* 16: 283–331.
Maifreda, Germano. 2000. *Gli ebrei e l'economia milanese. L'Ottocento*. Milano: FrancoAngeli.
Maifreda, Germano. 2011. "Banche e società civile (1861–1914)." In *Le Banche e l'Italia. Crescita economica e società civile (1861–2011)*, edited by L. Conte, 27–61. Roma: Bancaria Editrice.
Maifreda, Germano. 2019. *Using the Past, Building Trust. Ethnicity, the Risorgimento, and the Relationship Lending Between the Weill-Schott Bankers and Prime Minister Francesco Crispi in Nineteenth-Century Italy*, testo della relazione tenuta il 6 febbraio 2019 a Parigi, presso la PSE, Paris School of Economics, consultabile al website http://www.pseweb.eu/ydepot/seance/512889_MaifredaPaperParis2019-0402.pdf.
Massa, Paola. 2004. "Vicende economiche e percorsi individuali nell'imprenditoria genovese tra Otto e Novecento." In *Le eredità della Liguria. Viaggio nell'Ottocento attraverso i documenti fiscali*. Genova: San Giorgio Editrice.
Negri, Guglielmo, ed. 1989. *Giolitti e la nascita della Banca d'Italia nel 1893*. Roma-Bari: Laterza.

Pani, Marco. 2017. *Crisis and Reform: The 1893 Demise of Banca Romana*. IMF Working Papers.

Pantaleoni, Maffeo. 1936. "La caduta della Società Generale di Credito Mobiliare Italiano." In *Scritti Storici di economia*, 217–469. Bologna: Zanichelli.

Rollandi, Maria S. 2003. "Agli albori dell'istruzione tecnica a Genova: le scuole professionali della Camera di Commercio (1847–1865)." In *Miscellanea di studi in onore di Giorgio Mori*, edited by A.M. Falchero, A. Giuntini, G. Nigro and L. Segreto, 631–62. Varese: Lativa.

Rollandi, Maria S. 2014. "Parodi." In *Dizionario biografico degli italiani, 81*, 401–5. Roma: Treccani.

Romanelli, Raffaele. 1978. *L'Italia liberale*. Bologna: Il Mulino.

Rossi, Ernesto, and Gian Paolo Nitti, eds. 1968. *Banche, Governo e Parlamento negli Stati Sardi, Fonti documentarie (1843–1861)*. Torino: Fondazione Luigi Einaudi.

Rugafiori, Paride 1994. "Ascesa e declino di un sistema imprenditoriale." In *Liguria. Storia d'Italia. Le regioni dall'Unità a oggi*, edited by A. Gibelli e P. Rugafiori, 255–333. Torino: Einaudi.

Scatamacchia, Rosanna. 2008. *Azioni e azionisti. Il lungo Ottocento della Banca d'Italia*. Roma-Bari: Laterza.

Tolaini, Roberto. 2019. "La formazione di un banchiere. Per una biografia di Giacomo Filippo Durazzo Pallavicini (1848–1921)." *Atti della Società Ligure di Storia Patria* 59: 160–249.

Toniolo, Gianni. 1990. *An Economic History of Liberal Italy*. London: Routledge.

Tucci, Ugo, ed. 1960. "Stipendi e pensioni dei pubblici impiegati nel Regno Lombardo-Veneto dal 1824 al 1866." *Archivio economico dell'unificazione italiana* 10, no. 4.

Vasta, Michelangelo, and Alberto. Baccini. 1997. "Banks and Industry in Italy, 1911–1936. New Evidence using the Interlocking Directorates Technique." *Financial History Review* 4, no. 2: 139–59.

Vigo, Giovanni. 1971. *Istruzione e sviluppo economico in Italia nel secolo XIX*. Torino: ILTE.

Vitale, Eligio. 1972. *La riforma degli istituti di emissione e gli "scandali bancari" in Italia, 1892–1896*. Roma: Archivio Storico.

Zanini, Andrea. 2003. "Insegnamento e diffusione della scienza economica a Genova fra Otto e Novecento." In *Economisti liguri dell'Ottocento. La dottrina economica nell'Ateneo Genovese e in Liguria*, edited by P. Massa, 14–57. Genova: Accademia Ligure di Scienze e Lettere.

Index

L. Maffi, *Private Bankers in the Italian 19th Century*, Palgrave Studies in Economic History,
https://doi.org/10.1007/978-3-030-63361-5

C

The manufacturer's authorised representative in the EU is Springer Nature Customer Service Centre GmbH, Europaplatz 3, 69115 Heidelberg, Germany. If you have any concerns regarding our products, please contact ProductSafety@springernature.com

Printed and bound by CPI Group (UK) Ltd, Croydon, CR0 4YY
30/09/2026
02225443-0005